Managing Business Analysis Services

A Framework for Sustainable Projects and Corporate Strategy Success

Barbara Davis

ISBN-13: 978-1-60427-079-2

Printed and bound in the U.S.A. Printed on acid-free paper.

10 9 8 7 6 5 4 3 2 1

Library of Congress Cataloging-in-Publication Data

Davis, Barbara, 1969–
 Managing business analysis services : a framework for sustainable projects
and corporate strategy success / by Barbara Davis.
    p. cm.
  Includes index.
  ISBN 978-1-60427-079-2 (hbk. : alk. paper)   1. Business analysts.
  2. Strategic planning.   I. Title.
  HD69.B87D38 2012
  658.4'012—dc23

                                                      2012019964

Phone: (954) 727-9333 Ext. 5
Fax: (561) 892-0700
Web: www.jrosspub.com

This book is dedicated to

My loving husband, Robert, who gave me room to grow and nurtured me along the way,

Son, Donovan,

Siblings Chopper, Tonya, and Donovan for helping to compete and collaborate through all the fun and trouble that we got into, and

Mentor, Jim, for the countless discussions.

CONTENTS

FOREWORD

The business analysis profession has been around a long time, although no one called it that. With the introduction of the International Institute of Business Analysis (IIBA®) in 2003 and the efforts of many thought leaders, the profession has finally taken form. Today, there is more clarity around what tasks and techniques are part of the profession. These efforts have given practitioners insight into commonly used practices and how to approach analysis efforts. More and more companies have begun to recognize the need for business analysis skills on their teams, especially in the software development arena. In many of these companies, there is a defined role with some form of a career path for those with the title Business Analyst (BA).

The BA role continues to evolve, but there are many challenges that exist largely throughout the profession. Two major challenges are: what does a good business analysis practice look like and how do individual BAs and teams quantify their results? Barbara Davis covers a lot of this in the following pages. When analysis is not done well it is very obvious. Development efforts take longer than anticipated, the wrong thing gets built, there are unhappy stakeholders, and the list goes on. However, when analysis is done well, the project runs smoothly, people are happy, and the team works on the right solution tightly aligned to the business need.

However, analysis is not a science, and it is not concrete, therefore it can be difficult to separate the person from the process. You often see people saying they want a specific BA on their team because they had a successful project or projects with that person. The focus is on the person and not the BA skills that person must possess in order to be successful. It is for this reason that there is no guarantee of consistency in deliverables. A component to achieving consistent success on all projects is a focus on improving business analysis practices as a whole.

To do this right, there is no single answer and no silver bullet. There are components that increase one's likelihood of success in developing a mature business analysis practice. In *Managing Business Analysis Services*, Barbara Davis gives readers a framework to help build success. The guidance given will help business analysis practitioners and those leading both large and small BA teams improve their business analysis practice.

The first piece of the puzzle that Barbara addresses is how to bring organization to the different techniques commonly used by BAs and frame the core components that need to be addressed. Barbara presents a high-level model that will help both business analysts and BA teams focus their efforts on the process of translating strategic goals into tangible solutions to meet those goals. Next, Barbara shares an approach around how to best utilize business analysis professionals, how to keep them motivated, and how to put them in the best position to be successful. All of this leads to being able to manage your business analysis performance to drive results. However, she does not stop there. You don't improve your business analysis practice just for the sake of it. Barbara gives advice on how to ensure the model that you implement is actually addressing projects issues and is positively impacting the company's top line (revenue) and bottom line (profit).

The concept of "if you build it, they will come" usually only happens in the movies. You cannot just build the framework. That is exactly why the last critical step Barbara covers is how to "sell" the framework. You have to bring the impacted parties—business analysts, management, development and test team members, and other stakeholders—into the process and make sure there is support for the new structure. If you are leading the effort to improve your business analysis practice, your job then becomes more of a marketer and salesman to ensure that all of the other teams follow through with the pieces that impact their areas. For success, you need the right level of training, the right support, and the right culture to drive improvements. *Managing Business Analysis Services* provides a compelling framework to drive improvement for your business analysis practice. I hope you enjoy the book!

Kupe Kupersmith, *BA Certified™*, CBAP®
President, B2T Training

PREFACE

The Purpose of This Book

For well over ten years, I have listened as "poor requirements" are routinely cited as a major contributing factor in the challenges and failures of technology projects, when in fact it is certainly not the only one. While some progress has been made recently by addressing the symptoms of this contributing factor as well as a few others, little has been done to effectively and consistently address the root causes of these problems in any comprehensive way that has been universally accepted as standard practice. We have seen the birth of a new association to help address these issues thanks to the volunteer efforts of a few individuals from a handful of progressive training and consulting firms in the business analysis profession. However, from a big picture perspective, very little progress has been made thus far.

The purpose of this book is to effectively help change the less-than-optimal results currently produced by business and technology projects. Within the pages that follow, the cause-and-effect relationships between project areas and the results seen by business analysts are illustrated and a comprehensive way to address the challenges and failures of technology projects is provided. I have also highlighted some of the areas within business analysis that can heavily contribute to more positive results at both the tactical and strategic level.

Managing Business Analysis Services: A Framework for Sustainable Projects and Corporate Strategy Success demonstrates an effective method for the management and delivery of business analysis services. It is intended to be a guide and desk reference for chief information officers, business analysis managers, consultants, recruiters and anyone involved in the management of projects. The three focal points of this book are:

- How business analysis can be utilized as a technique and strategy for maintaining fiscal sustainability of the business and its technology division.
- How to plan, manage, and deliver end-to-end business analysis services.
- How to build a sustainable business analysis practice.

The objective of this book is simple: to reposition business analysis and enable technology and business organizations to maximize value by more effectively managing business analysis resources and processes.

Who Will Benefit From This Book?

1. *Chief information officers* (CIOs) who are looking to accomplish at least one of the following objectives: reduce operating costs, increase alignment between technology products and business needs, and obtain peace of mind by establishing a functional framework for business analysis that effectively reduces break-and-fix cycles on projects and defect rates that cause post-implementation headaches.
2. *Business analysis managers* and leaders who have been given or are seeking the blessing of upper management to either improve the results of their existing business analysis services or to develop them as a self-sustaining group.
3. *Consulting firms* that are interested in establishing a framework for themselves or clients that will enable them to reduce operating costs, increase alignment between technology products and business needs, and obtain a higher return on investment for their business analysis services.
4. *Recruiters* who are interested in improving their assessment and selection criteria for business analysis candidates, or are interested in improving the management of business analysis resources across all engagements, as a means of improving the quality and consistency of candidates who are being placed in client organizations.
5. *Business analysts and project managers* who are interested in elevating their performance and understanding of the roles and responsibilities of the business analyst and moving toward leadership roles within the business analysis community.

How This Book Is Organized

This book is organized in a step-by-step approach to building and establishing the frameworks and models for the management of business analysis as a *service*. In effect, this book follows a simple formula as it takes the reader on the journey. The formula highlights what is wrong with business analysis that is creating inconsistent, less-than-optimal, or catastrophic project results. This book walks the reader through the existing processes upon which business analysis is founded and services are delivered, and then decomposes the entire business analysis services model utilizing a SWOT analysis.

Once the reader is exposed to what might go wrong in projects or why business analysis might generate poor results, business analysis services are discussed in terms of what should be done, and how services should be provided to technology and business organizations. The book elaborates on the potential of business analysis services as a key enabler of strategy and a crucial element to business continuity.

Next, the book takes a look at how management can be structured to achieve its potential and deliver on the value proposition that business analysis brings to both the business and to technology organizations. This in-depth discussion highlights the elements of a management model and describes how each element impacts and shapes business analysis.

Before discussing how to put the whole model into place, methods for delivering and engaging new business analysis services are discussed, enabling a realistic look at the implications of and impacts on the quality outcomes of business analysis. The model is only going to be useful if it is managed across delivery and engaged by clients in that same spirit.

Finally, how to implement a new model so that it becomes a full and accountable part of your managed organization is discussed, as well as how both business and technology organizations can realize the maximum value from the services that are managed under that new model. The model establishes the framework to assure that potency and integrity are maintained across delivery so that what is sold is delivered and utilized.

In Section 1, the reader should gain an understanding of the correlation that exists between how business analysis is currently performed and managed and the outcomes that are produced by processes and resources. Readers should also gain insights into the areas of improvement, as well as some opportunities that could be capitalized on.

This section also redefines business analysis services and proposes a new model. The new model proposes that business analysis is being underutilized by the majority of the information technology industry and should be made up of business process modeling, needs analysis, stakeholder alignment, benefits realization planning, requirements planning, definition and analysis, requirements management, verification and validation, and finally, governance. The new model effectively defines new objectives for business analysis that will create a win-win partnership between the business and technology organizations. It further discusses the expanded role that business analysis can play in the enablement of strategy as a champion for the business organization.

This section then discusses the management, care, and control of business analysis processes and techniques as a means of drastically altering the outcomes of those processes, achieving lower defect rates, and reducing the rates of failed and challenged projects across the board. These results are achieved by establishing the foundations for standardization and consistent application of the services through a system of functional governance. This functional system of governance also prescribes consistent improvement methods to ensure that business analysis is a carefully measured and monitored practice, as opposed to an ad hoc or random chain of events.

In Section 2, the discussion switches to how to manage business analysis services and resources so that the prescribed processes are applied appropriately, and the full integrity of the services provided can be optimized through continuous improvement processes. It illustrates the organizational structure that will create the framework for the management of both resources and services as a means of producing higher quality outcomes and deliverables. It also outlines the appropriate career path and describes how that career path fits into the existing infrastructure, formalizes the processes, and creates accountability, as well as how that career path positively impacts the factors that detract from the business analyst's ability to perform according to expectation.

Next, how to staff the services with qualified resources is detailed. This process includes finding, assessing, and allocating resources, as well as promoting, retaining, and replacing them. In addition, the reader will see how capacity planning is supported by the new model and the ability to pinpoint resources and skill levels as a means of creating both a capability and capacity plan for the business analysis services organization.

Business analysis competencies that support the measurement and determination of role-based and skill-appropriate key performance indicators are described next. The discussion demonstrates how to align those competencies to organizational and business analysis services goals to achieve the highest value proposition possible.

In Section 3, the details of delivery mechanisms are presented, with a look at how engagement models impact the success of business analysis services, outlining the key elements to include in each. The issues that exist in the current delivery and engagement systems that cause deterministic problems in projects and lead to challenges and outright failures are elaborated upon, and deserve study in view of the quality of resources and services that may be in place.

Finally, Section 4 describes the considerations that must be made and the corresponding offshore, on shore, and near-shore models to ensure that the integrity of the services, processes, and resources is maintained across transition points in ownership and responsibility. Section 4 also helps the reader to develop a solid understanding of strategies for rolling out the new model across the organization, as well as the project docket and resources that will carry it forward. Steps for how to successfully implement the new model across various types of projects are given, so that a plan is readily adopted and socialized across all organizations that interact with business analysis services. This implementation can be the difference between adoption or continued complacency.

The final section also clearly defines criteria for quick-win pilot projects and change management to increase the likelihood of buy-in. Done well, the model should empower the resources and market the benefits to all stakeholder and resource groups so that they can see the value proposition of the new services and leverage them to improve technology results. Overall, adoption will help make certain that the business is able to assure its own continuity, and that the technology practices become more financially sustainable.

The Key Takeaways

The strongest takeaways can be found in the answers to each of the following questions:

1. What is wrong with business analysis today? This takeaway is formed through an in-depth review of the basic model for business analysis services as they are delivered and operated today. This model is decomposed by using a SWOT analysis to uncover the fact that the majority of the issues with poor requirement quality are embedded within this model.

2. What does an optimized business analysis model look like? This new detailed model for business analysis describes each of the task sets that are required for business analysts to perform and goes beyond requirements and illustrates full end-to-end business analysis services.

3. How do you best manage resources? This takeaway is provided by a detailed discussion on managing the resources through organizational structure, defined career paths, key performance indicators, and competencies. Many organizations could benefit from this information because they simply do not have the means or metrics in place to qualitatively and quantifiably assess performance of resources and services.

4. How do you deliver services? The establishment of business analysis services does not start and end with a service definition. It takes more than defining processes and managing the resources; there are integration points across delivery models and engagement models where resource responsibility and accountability changes. These integration points can reverse any defined methods and throw resources back into *ad hoc* mode if they are not managed appropriately and assessed across all boundaries.

5. How can a CIO, business analysis manager or consultant get there from here? A step-by-step implementation strategy is defined for implementing new practices across business and technology organizations. This discussion defines criteria for staged implementations and highlights the need for marketing the new model to all groups that interact with business analysis. This is important because there are processes outside the scope of responsibility for managing busi-

ness analysis that will need to change in order to support and enforce new processes.

A Personal Message

Throughout my career, I have brought a passion into business analysis. This book serves as the culmination of my passion, knowledge, and diverse experiences in business analysis. It is my hope that, through this knowledge, others will no longer have to struggle, and that companies will see a way to end a large part of the waste and frustration that is associated with information technology. Above all else, I am hopeful for a realization that we can utilize technology as a means of establishing a truly global society.

I am convinced that we could have technologies far beyond the current means if we simply changed the way in which business analysis is performed. In order for that to happen, the real value of business analysis must be understood as the ability to translate goals and strategies into reality through the creation of tangible solutions.

—Barbara Davis

ABOUT THE AUTHOR

Barbara Davis, President of E2 Consulting LLC and Requirements Toolkit.com LLC, has over 15 years of IT, business, and change management experience. Since 2001, Barbara has worked as a solutions consultant and senior business analyst and has been a champion for business analysis standards, infrastructure, and practice. In 2003, she developed the world's first university-level, accredited business analysis diploma program and helped lead the way for a new professional association, the International Institute of Business Analysis (IIBA), to begin their Certified Business Analysis Program (CBAP). She developed a lean project methodology and pioneered requirements methodologies by creating the Comprehensive and Robust Requirements Specification Process (CRRSP), as well as methodologies for organizational change, resource management, project management, and organizational capability.

Davis has published many white papers and articles and created and delivered numerous workshops and professional skills training sessions. In addition to her writing, blogging, consulting, and training, Davis has become a sought-after speaker for corporate venues with Fortune 500 companies, and often speaks about a variety of BA topics at Project Summit and BA World conferences.

Davis has worked with Fortune 500 companies across North America to design and implement business analysis services, rescue projects, and train business analysts to be great at what they do. Some of her clients have included UST Global, Safeway, HEB, ICBC, WellPoint, and Drugstore.com. While at UST Global, Barbara worked to develop an autonomous Center of Excellence for Business Analysis and Requirements. She formalized the BA practice through standardized processes, ongoing training and networking, career planning, and performance management. She interviewed, assessed, and networked with hundreds of business analysts and developed a business analysis community.

Davis currently resides with her husband, Robert, and son, Donovan, in Prescott Valley, AZ. To learn more about her consulting services or blog, readers are welcome to visit www.e2consultinginc.com or Requirements Networking Group at www.requirementsnetwork.com.

At J. Ross Publishing we are committed to providing today's professional with practical, hands-on tools that enhance the learning experience and give readers an opportunity to apply what they have learned. That is why we offer free ancillary materials available for download on this book and all participating Web Added Value™ publications. These online resources may include interactive versions of material that appears in the book or supplemental templates, worksheets, models, plans, case studies, proposals, spreadsheets and assessment tools, among other things. Whenever you see the WAV™ symbol in any of our publications, it means bonus materials accompany the book and are available from the Web Added Value Download Resource Center at www.jrosspub .com.

Downloads for *Managing Business Analysis Services* include a business analyst interviewing guide and a change management and benefits realization implementation tool.

EXPOSING BUSINESS ANALYSIS THEORIES AND PRACTICES

This section provides a pragmatic view of business analysis services, and how those services are managed and delivered in today's marketplace. Within this view, business analysis is an *ad hoc* role that is inconsistently delivered across multiple projects, from resource to resource, and is equally inconsistent when the same resources deliver the same services multiple times.

In addition, this section discusses two primary business analysis services models (the current, as-is model and a new, proposed optimized model) and introduces the concept of Business Analysis Stewardship. The discussion is intended to expose the inherent weaknesses in the management of business analysis, and then propose an alternative solution.

The current model is inconsistent and chaotic, being highly subjective to the whims, interpretations, and applications of individuals within specific companies. It is predicated on a rudimentary understanding of business analysis, which has only a very small margin of commonality amongst practitioners and companies that employ business analysis resources.

The proposed model is an optimized one that displays the central tasks and functions of business analysis as a driving force for the translation of strategic goals into practical solutions for the business in order to ensure complete alignment between what is needed and what is actually being built. The optimized model is founded on the principles of a planned and managed approach to business analysis, as well as the idea that business analysis is a catalyst for the sustainability and continuity of the business through technology.

Finally, this section introduces the concept of Business Analysis Stewardship as a fundamental obligation on the part of business analysts to ensure the protection of the client organization's interests and assets through careful planning and management, and by employing financially sustainable methods. This is a new concept that elevates the role of the business analyst to the role of strategic partner with the business in order to help that business achieve its goals and continue to remain viable. This information can be used to empower business analysis managers and resources and to enable CIOs to quickly move beyond their current project challenges to a more streamlined and viable model for business analysis. This model presents a stronger means of achieving greater alignment between business, strategy, and information technology.

The key precept is that the objective of business analysis is to safeguard and protect the interests of the business. This objective is accomplished by creating solutions and products that enable the strategy to be realized, and by utilizing fiscally sustainable practices in the creation of those solutions. However, it also demands an approach that is carefully planned, managed, measured, monitored, and controlled, so that it may be optimized through a continuous improvement process.

Again, the most prolific model that is being applied today is fundamentally flawed, serving to exacerbate underlying problems within business and technology organizations, and ultimately leading to project challenges and failures. In some cases, where the failures mount and recovery actions are not taken, the results can be catastrophic failure of the business.

While this section effectively "kicks the tires" of business analysis in theory and in practice, it is meant to shatter the myths of business analysis, shake up technology management, and remove the complacent attitudes toward this critical function. The intent of this shake up is not only to talk about the elephant in the room, but also to provide management with a realistic alternative to leaving things as they are.

MISCONCEPTIONS, PROBLEMS AND THE AVERAGE BA MODEL

Business analysis as a discipline has been around in one form or another for over a decade. No matter what you call it, or how you prioritize it, its roles and expectations are roughly the same: Enable the development of technology products that more closely align to business and consumer needs. Business analysts do this by understanding the problems, limitations, needs, business model, and the industry, and then utilize their understanding of that information to define requirements for a solution.

COMMON MISCONCEPTIONS

Unfortunately, there are a few misconceptions about business analysis, and there are also misconceptions about the significance of the roles that analysts play in the continuity of the overall business. One misconception is that business analysis, in and of itself, is wholly the task of defining and creating requirements. In essence, the business analyst is regarded and then treated like an "order taker." This means that most analysts are not given opportunities to contribute fully towards the business goals and objectives by getting involved in the creation of a solution.

What is being missed is that the business analyst is in a unique position to be a key enabler of the long-term strategy and goals of a business simply because of the types of solutions that are needed, and the specific accumulation of knowledge and skills that they must have and be able to draw from in order to be successful within their positions. While it is appropriate to delegate and allocate specific tasks within business analysis according to levels of knowledge and experiences of the individual resources involved, the technology industry and business community at large must recognize that business analysts have the ability and unique insights to play a more critical role in the successful realization of strategic plans through the development of solutions by which the business will bring its strategic plans to life and meet their overall objectives.

It must also be recognized that, in the same way that a server at a restaurant helps to create an experience for the patron or diner and plays a critical role in the overall dining experience, the business analyst is equally involved in the creation of the experience of the business customers (both internal and external). Indeed, when the wait staff engages the customer in conversation and offers recommendations for the meal and various side dishes, the customer has a more rewarding experience and is far more likely to continue to return to the restaurant.

As a case in point, several years ago I stepped into a Fortune 500 outsourcing company as the Senior Business Analyst. My objective was simple: I was hired to set a standard for the business analysts within the company. The company was dealing with some common industry-wide issues with the placement of business analysts, and faced stiff competition from other boutique vendors with a more formalized structure in place to manage and govern business analysis. At that point in time, the customer satisfaction scores for business analysis averaged 2.5 to 3 points out of 10. The analysts themselves were struggling and feeling neglected by the executive management. Morale was quite low among the team and within individual team members.

To start my work, I began creating the processes that all business analysts would be required to utilize in order to conduct their tasks and activities. I devised training programs to roll out the new processes quickly and effectively, and authored role descriptions, a competency model, and an assessment framework for screening all business analyst candidates. I quickly found myself in high demand for interviewing prospective candidates. I also started getting calls from account managers to make recommendations for specific roles within their accounts. During one such conversation, where I was being asked by an account manager for a recommendation of an available business analyst resource, I realized that I had no idea who was available because I had not yet been made privy to that information.

Shortly after that discussion, I was asked by that same manager to prepare a resource forecast for the remainder of the year. I realized that I could not do that, either. So, I brainstormed on how I was going to accomplish both tasks and get the blessing of upper management to do it. I made a quick presentation to my manager about how I needed to "take stock" of the existing business analyst team before I could complete the forecast that was requested. I also mentioned that I had been getting requests for resource recommendations and could not make any because I did not know the majority of the analysts on the team. I argued that this assessment effort could accomplish both objectives.

Since I already had the framework for conducting assessments in place, and it was well implemented into our interviewing processes, I requested authorization to use the framework to conduct assessments of all permanent, internal business analyst resources. My point was that I could make well-informed recommendations and complete the necessary forecast with a more accurate picture of the numbers of analysts already on board, including current project allocations and domain knowledge, as well as skill levels.

Using this framework, I personally screened over 300 analysts for this company, and in doing so, discovered quite a lot about the business analyst talent pool. This effort, in turn, drew the attention of other groups that had been trying to accomplish the same standards, and so I started getting calls to support their internal framework development resource pool assessments. I was shocked to learn that groups like the project management office (PMO) had been struggling with completing this task for over two years! I initially started getting calls because they wanted to know how it was that I had managed to accomplish the task single-handedly within only seven months. Their interest peaked when they learned that it was completed in a manner that was 100% billable.

I learned a lot from this experience in terms of motivating others through structure and accountability. Successful business analysis requires the practitioner to be an *expert* in processes and requirements, and a *generalist* in every other aspect of business. I had utilized simple techniques for requirements and business analysis to create the processes and frameworks, then utilized my knowledge and experiences in inventory control, human resources management, conflict resolution, training, and leadership to support the people as part of finalizing the infrastructure. Management also caught a glimpse of how the application of this type of accumulated knowledge and skill, with a clearly defined structure or framework in place, can impact the internal and external customer experience. The BA team became highly charged, cohesive, and motivated, and the company's customer satisfaction scores for business analysis jumped to an average of 6 to 7 out of 10. We implemented the structure and organization, and they ran with it.

Homeless: A Business Analyst's Life

Without the adequate management, structure, and framework for performing the job of a business analyst, there is a resemblance to the displacement of homeless people. Business analysts move from project to project like temporary shelters that give them a sense of empowerment over their situation for a short while, but in the end, they almost always have to move on.

Whereas homeless people have little or no shelter from nature or other people, many business analysts do not have the protection and shelter that comes from having a structure within an organization where they belong, and where they could grow and thrive. The analysts go on about their work on requirements as if it is the most important work in the world. However, there often seems to be little recognition of the value of that work by the business stakeholders or their technology peers, who are looking only at the bottom line in terms of how much time it will take or how much it will restrict their ability to be creative in development.

Like the homeless, there can be little or no routine or predictability in the work of a business analyst because there are so few standard frameworks to provide that level of guidance for them. Analysts trying to change their circumstances often look like the guy on the street corner carrying an "End of the World" sign, warning of the doom and gloom of the shared situation.

However, it does not have to be this way. Business analysis managers and BA communities can make a difference and change this underappreciated situation. Many business analysts do not report into a formal operational structure. They report temporarily to project managers and recruiters, but for the most part, do not have the basic infrastructure that so many other roles within an organization take for granted. It is infrastructure that enables personal and professional growth, job satisfaction, leadership, consistent improvement, and ongoing performance. Each of these attributes of infrastructure has a direct and indisputable, deterministic impact on the end product and the quality of the work done to build that end product. This lack of infrastructure for business analysts is definitely a problem that needs to be properly addressed.

CENTERS OF EXCELLENCE

Many companies are transitioning to a Center of Excellence (COE) as a model for building a structure, a formalized process, and consistency. While I can attest to the merits of this model (having built several from the ground up for clients), this is not a permanent solution until we start really looking at building out a full-scale operational and delivery model for business analysis as a part of the organization. Until that structure exists, Centers of Excellence are only like temporary housing; they lack the stability and continuity of an operational model.

Does that mean that Centers of Excellence are not important? Absolutely not! Centers of Excellence are absolutely valuable in that they provide and foster skills within all members of the organization to readily adopt a business analysis group, and for the business analysts themselves to internalize the structure and processes advocated by that Center.

In fact, Centers of Excellence can be quite dynamic and foster a level of innovation and leadership that you may not see within a typical business model that comes with a standardized organizational structure because every member of the team contributes and adopts more accountability and responsibility for the ownership of processes, templates, and events. The Center becomes a focal point for learning and knowledge-sharing in the same way that coffee houses often spark pedagogical debates and discussions among college patrons.

COE as a Functional, Educational and Unifying Force

As a case in point, an outsourcing consulting firm was searching for someone to set the standard for all of the business analysts within their company. I was hired, in part, because of the university-accredited business analysis diploma program that I had created in 2003 for a Canadian university. I was considered a strategic hire and was able to capitalize on the experience gained in creating the BA diploma program to create better training programs and to implement the overall processes more effectively.

At the time, business analysts were considered to be a part of accounts unless they were strategic hires. In the case of strategic hires, the business analysts reported to Software Quality Requirements and Testing. With new standards and a solid business analysis framework in place, the COE was split into two independent centers: one for quality and the other for business analysis and requirements. The founding of a Center of Excellence was an overwhelming success. The business analysis portfolio within the Fortune 500 consulting firm grew from approximately $500K to more than $8 million within two years.

The trust of the account managers, customer base, and vendors that supplied us with additional business analysts increased as well. Most importantly, the impact that this assessment and shift in management had on the business analysts themselves was immensely positive. Their confidence and loyalty to the company increased exponentially because they suddenly knew where they belonged, and what was expected of them. The analysts felt as though they had a voice and a role to play in the development of the business analyst community.

Centers of Excellence can challenge the norms of the company's social fabric, and the discussions and resulting work can be both rewarding and cutting-edge. But in order to progress, a solid business model needs to be in place to ensure the continuity and health of both projects and people, and to ensure the synergy and alignment of the centers and their patrons to the overall mission and values of the company at large.

A Center of Excellence model can be a cost center much like other research and development (R&D) labs. However, normalized and acclimated business units have the potential and opportunity to be both cost and revenue generating centers, and we need both. Much like a coffee shop, the Center is where many discussions take place, and process and action can be fluid and sporadic, whereas a socialized business unit must work within the strict parameters of the company and the organizational structure. They must demonstrate return on investment (ROI) for all activities, meetings, and events in order to justify taking people off the shop floor when they could be performing revenue-generating activities for clients.

However, the biggest difference between the two models is that typically, within an organizational model, there is a standard reporting structure for the analysts up to a functional manager, project manager, or recruiting manager, and in the Center of Excellence model they have an informal reporting structure to leadership. Therefore, the head of the Center very often has no formal ability to manage the analyst resources for allocation, competency, and key performance indicators (KPIs). In fact, the competencies, unless well-defined and marketed by the Center and then socialized by the remainder of the company, can have little impact on the actual competency expectations of the line managers to whom the analysts actually report. The competencies are merely "suggestions" for performance expectations and measurement, with little or no bearing on the actual performance.

Because business analysts are well-dressed and show up on time, people do not notice that they are "homeless." Or, even how that sense of homelessness impacts their performance and attrition, and how ultimately the quality of their work could become detrimental to the entire business. (Even the smallest termites—in this case bad projects—can bring down a house when there are enough of them and they are not managed.)

It is no wonder that some business analysts jump ship and move on to become project managers, or something else. They are tired of living in the park and sleeping on benches, and want a real "home." At some point, they realize that in order to fully belong somewhere, they have to move into a house, and any house is better than no house at all.

For anyone who believes that analyst's are satisfied with the current business analysis model, and further believes that these services are well-managed and well-defined, you will be shocked to learn that there is a long way to go before we can consider the business analysis area to be optimized. Business analysis as a whole is not optimized to the point that it contributes in a major or consistent way to the overall health, effectiveness, competitiveness, or compliance of the business organization.

The forthcoming sections of this chapter present and discuss the current, most widely used application for business analysis services, exploring the application of services by applying the SWOT analysis technique to expose underlying strengths, weaknesses, opportunities, and threats that are inherent in the business analysis model. These sections elaborate on the losses in productivity, quality control, and effectiveness of the results that are created as a result of the management situation in this model. This elaboration exposes the common requirements missteps that can occur as a result of poor management, and a lack of standardized and formalized processes.

Business analysis is more than just getting users and stakeholders into a room and taking down their wish list of features, putting the wishes into a formal document, and then getting back into the room later to get everyone to agree to what has been written down.

THE AVERAGE BUSINESS ANALYSIS MODEL

First, let's be honest, there really is no "average" business analysis model *per se*, but merely a rudimentary process that is followed by many companies, including consulting firms. In this process, individual business analyst resources are expected to be project-ready and come to the table with the required skills and experiences. The problem is that there are few trusted avenues to acquire those skills and experiences outside of the emerging International Institute for Business Analysis (IIBA), and these resources have little or no support to acquire them. Companies rarely pay the kind of money for training that business analysts really need in order to formalize their skills through legitimate training organizations.

As to how the management of business analysts is conducted, and how they report into the company's organizational structure, really depends on the individual company. If anything, the management model for business analysts could be said to fall under the service delivery model or the PMO, but this, in and of itself, really only defines the basic role, costs for the service, and a limited number of success factors and expectations. Unfortunately, this means that there is a huge gap in terms of specific deliverable expectations, quality, consistency, and general outcomes.

In many companies, as illustrated in Figure 1.1, the general process for allocating resources is that business analysts typically report to either the PMO or resource management group (RMG) operationally. When a new project need arises, the analysts are allocated to the project and suddenly find themselves either reporting jointly to the PMO *and* a project manager, or to the RMG *and* a project manager. In the case of

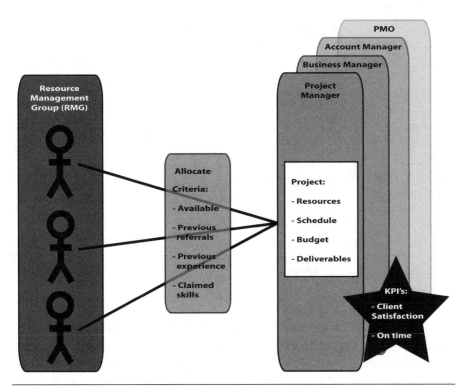

Figure 1.1 The general allocation process

consulting firms, they may also find themselves reporting to an account manager, or a stakeholder, or quite simply, once they are allocated to a project, all other management goes away and they simply report to the project manager.

Once the project wraps up, the analyst moves back into the talent pool or onto the bench, and is once again managed by the PMO or the resource management group. They remain under the control and direction of this same management until they are allocated to a new project, or they simply move on to a new role.

During a project, however, the project manager and key stakeholders manage the deliverables and activities. In this model, the basic KPIs are teamwork, stakeholder satisfaction, and on-time completion of deliverables. Unfortunately, these KPIs are open to interpretation and are subjective to the moods, personalities, likes, dislikes, and political agendas of the project manager, stakeholders, and others as they could be judging without a tangible framework to measure against. Therefore, it is not really a *management model* in the true sense of the term because there is no quantitative, qualitative, or ongoing, consistent management of the resources within the model.

DECOMPOSING THE AVERAGE BA MODEL UTILIZING SWOT ANALYSIS

One of the ways to analyze and explore an average business analysis model is to utilize a simple SWOT analysis. A SWOT analysis exposes the strengths, weaknesses, opportunities, and threats of the model in order to illustrate the current situation from all angles. Then, this illustration can be used to start building a new and improved model for business analysis.

Another benefit of conducting a SWOT analysis is that it cuts right to the chase of the glaringly obvious issues in the existing model without having to perform years of careful analysis. It also gives us an accelerated starting point that we can utilize to springboard consistent improvement activities. This means that the process of improving the business analysis model, and the situation for business analysts, can start right away, instead of later when more damage has been done.

By looking at the average management model and general allocation process using a simple SWOT analysis, as depicted in Figure 1.2, some strengths and tremendous opportunities for immense improvement can be discovered in consumer confidence and loyalty, and ultimately, business continuity. However, many of the inherent weaknesses and the overt threats to projects are also exposed, as well as weaknesses in and threats to the business itself.

Strengths of the Average Business Analysis Model

Let's start by exploring some of the strengths of the typical, existing model. When we consider the strengths and other internal factors, there are indeed attributes that make the current model good enough "as-it-is" and an argument for maintaining the

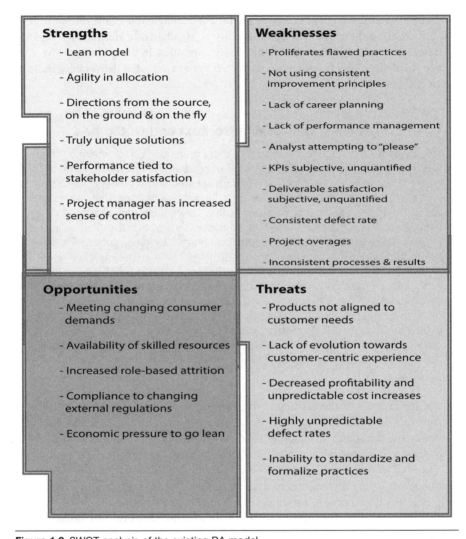

Strengths

- Lean model

- Agility in allocation

- Directions from the source, on the ground & on the fly

- Truly unique solutions

- Performance tied to stakeholder satisfaction

- Project manager has increased sense of control

Weaknesses

- Proliferates flawed practices

- Not using consistent improvement principles

- Lack of career planning

- Lack of performance management

- Analyst attempting to "please"

- KPIs subjective, unquantified

- Deliverable satisfaction subjective, unquantified

- Consistent defect rate

- Project overages

- Inconsistent processes & results

Opportunities

- Meeting changing consumer demands

- Availability of skilled resources

- Increased role-based attrition

- Compliance to changing external regulations

- Economic pressure to go lean

Threats

- Products not aligned to customer needs

- Lack of evolution towards customer-centric experience

- Decreased profitability and unpredictable cost increases

- Highly unpredictable defect rates

- Inability to standardize and formalize practices

Figure 1.2 SWOT analysis of the existing BA model

status-quo could be proposed. This argument would be based on attributes such as how lean the current model could be considered, less red tape, ability to quickly redirect resources, that all solutions (as well as the work done) are genuinely unique, and that project managers have an increased sense of control.

The argument could be made that the existing model is lean with low "baggage"; by baggage, I mean that there is really no hard and fast role definition to hold business analysts accountable. As a result, there is no real definition for success and failure here, so almost any project could be arguably considered to be successful. This argument could be advanced not only because of the lack of a solid and tangible role definition, but also because there are little or no consistent standards for deliverables, and the processes utilized to get the work done. There is nothing in place to really give context to the deliverables (in other words, to tell the analyst what deliverables must be produced, and why).

Objectives, Deliverable Context and Outcomes

There was a project at a consulting firm that I once worked for where our team was brought on by the client to assess the testability of a software solution for claims processing and to propose a testing solution for the system. The client's own team had decided that this would be the first system that they would create without use cases because they felt that cases were unnecessary. In their own words, the situation was the first "monster system" that they had built, and it was also deemed almost completely un-testable by other companies when asked to propose a testing solution. In reality, with little in the way of guidelines for the deliverables and the work that needed to be done, what they had built really was a monstrosity. With no framework and no hard and fast rules for business analysis in this situation, no one questioned the decision to move ahead on such a large project without use cases. The business analysts were not really accountable for creating the big picture of the system in order to guide the development. In the end, even the most generous estimate for testing was for only a single iteration over one full year (under the best circumstances).

In the analysis of the existing model, there is a lot more agility in that there is less red tape to go through in order to allocate resources. In this model, since there are fewer standards and virtually no solid role descriptions, almost anyone could be considered a "business analyst," become allocated to a project, and then struggle along.

Sure, allocating people might be faster, but compare that model to how much time will be spent trying to ramp them up, fix mistakes, or in scrap and rework. In the long run, it is like choosing a used car. How much are you willing to invest to make sure that you can drive it off the lot and not have to come back in a week because there are serious issues that you chose to accept for the lower cost and the ability to get the car right away?

In addition, another argument could be made in favor of the strength of this model: resources take direction directly from the source (i.e., the stakeholders and project managers), both on the ground and on the fly. This could mean that expectations could be set for the resources on a project-by-project basis for the work to be accomplished, but, in reality, the problem is that this is *not* business analysis. Instead, the situation ends up being like someone else's interpretation of business analysis, and the perception of performance is very closely tied to completing the assigned work on time, client satisfaction, and getting along with the project manager. Resources cannot be adequately assessed for actual capabilities, and their next assignment could be a real dud if they failed to meet any one of the highly subjective performance expectations. Conversely, actually meeting the highly subjective performance expectations is not indicative of true ability in business analysis.

Again, the concept of *performance* is highly subjective to the whims, opinions, and knowledge of the project manager and those around the analyst, so this means that the true capabilities, skills, and knowledge of the analyst are not measured in a meaningful or consistent manner. Unfortunately, this can lead to infighting and favoritism, and devaluation of the overall performance reviews or ratings provided by the project manager or client at the end of the project. While this may increase the project manager's sense of control, it really does not equate to realistic, consistent, sustainable, and scalable resource management or allocation.

Another aspect that could be considered a strength of this model (at face-value, anyway) is that the project manager has an increased sense of control over the project schedule (although that perception may or may not be accurate!) simply because they not only hold the fate of the analyst in their hands, but they also control what deliverables the analyst creates and how much time is allocated to each of these tasks. While this "strength" may lead to situations like the monstrous claims processing system, it really means that every solution has the opportunity to be unique and customized down to the finest details simply because there is no standard to follow, and only customers to please.

In the case of the claims processing system, all the way along the four-year project, the business stakeholders were happy. They were happy because they thought they were going to get everything that they had wanted and asked for. Every time they asked for something, no one told them "no," or that it was something better left alone until another update or enhancement. The project manager dictated that the business analysts simply give the stakeholders what they wanted, despite scope creep, rising costs, and constant change requests.

The result was that they did end up with something unique and they were all happy during the process. In fact, it was not until the end when they tried to find an outsourced testing firm that they realized what they had done, and just how bad the new system was. Any business analysts that may have left the project during the four-year build would have gotten a good recommendation because they made the client happy, and another if they made the project manager equally happy by complying with their ideas for the work to be done, or not done. In the end, they would have all been a lot happier if they had empowered and listened to their business analysts for at least a periodic sanity check.

From decomposing the model, its perceived strengths are really only superficial. When the outer layer of that perception is peeled back, the underlying threats, weaknesses, and flaws are exposed that contribute to systemic issues with projects and their products. As with any other mild blemish, the full gamut of the systemic problems that lie beneath the surface may not always be realized.

Weaknesses of the Average Business Analysis Model

On the flip side, when the weaknesses of the typical model are explored, in general, bad practices can proliferate. An improvement is neither quantifiable nor demonstrable, and the perception of improvement is highly subjective, leading to an overwhelming dissatisfaction on the part of the resources in the analyst role.

First, the model spreads flawed and unhealthy "incestuous" practices in which there is no consistent measurement of improvement in place. The improvement practices that are utilized are usually held within a single company, unrelated to external industry practices (such as those prescribed by the IIBA), and sheltered from the larger external practice community. In this way, analysts who have "their own way of doing things" can flourish and hide within the confines of a single company. Unfortunately, when they become responsible for training other business analysts as they join the ranks, the trainers' bad practices spread to others within that same company.

The biggest weakness, however, is that this model is not based on solid, consistent improvement principles, so it is hard to measure, monitor, and manage improvements because there simply is not enough tangible evidence to demonstrate that improvements are actually being made.

Another related weakness in this model is that analysts are often pulled in multiple directions by trying to "please" stakeholder groups, the project manager, development, and testing. Without adequate focus on soft skills and core competencies that include attributes like assertiveness, it can be very difficult for the analyst to say "no" and attempt to negotiate with the business.

To compound this weakness, the KPIs are light, subjective, and not quantifiable. The most common KPIs are getting sign-off and having the requirements document delivered "on time." To make matters worse, once the requirements are delivered, the final document (or deliverable) satisfaction is also subjective, not quantifiable and can actually be impacted by the project manager or stakeholder.

Recall how both the ability to direct the analyst and the project manager's sense of control over the project could be considered "strengths." Yet, the same ability to direct and sense of control would have actually been merely superficial strengths because, in the end, the analyst's performance rating was subjective to the happiness of the client and the project manager. As it turns out, this is a weakness, not a strength, because it merely appeases the project manager by giving him or her inappropriate levels of control over business analysis tasks and resources.

All of these weaknesses have a detrimental effect on project scrap and rework, as well as defect rates. This can be seen every year when The Standish Group releases its annual *Chaos Report*, because it clearly illustrates that there are project overages (time and budget) due to poor requirement quality.

In general, there are also inconsistent processes leading to inconsistent results in requirements. That which is harder to measure and quantify are the attrition rates, overall dissatisfaction rates, and lack of confidence that so many business analysts feel as a result of rework and defects. In effect, systems and foundations are being built with components and resources that are inherently flawed or incomplete. Utilization of flawed components makes it incredibly difficult to produce a quality result without also considering how to compensate for the existing flaws.

FIVE CRITICAL REQUIREMENTS STEPS THAT GET MISSED

The lack of professional formalization means that there is no single "tried and true" set of business analysis best practices. There are indeed some commonalities, but without a standardized set of best practices, there can be no real assurances that enough has been done to capture the right requirements for the right products. This is exactly how we get stats that illustrate that only 20% of features are used all the time, and 42% are never used at all![1]

Over the years, I have worked with, mentored, trained, managed, and interviewed hundreds of business analysts. What I am about to say may shock you: Approximately 99% of the analysts that I have worked with and assessed are missing some of the most critical steps in requirements.

Nevertheless, do not blame the analysts. They are missing these steps because business analysis is still a collective practice, and not a formal profession with standardized tasks, metrics, and tools. Many analysts are simply borrowing tasks, tools, and techniques from other development areas.

So, what are the crucial tasks that business analysts could be doing to change all of this? More importantly, how can you know if business analysts are doing these tasks of research, gap assessment (vs. gap analysis), ambiguity management, requirements validation (including facilitated sign-off), and quantification of the effectiveness of requirements activities? Let's examine each task in detail to understand what they are, what they look like, and what the directly quantifiable results should be.

Research

There are a lot of components that need to be understood in order to develop accurate requirements, and only one of those components is user input. Going to the users should be the last task that a business analyst does in requirements elicitation, yet, when interviewed, the single-most common answer provided when asked to determine requirements is "I go to the user."

The fact is that there is already a lot of detailed information contained within the project documentation, existing application, and documentation on the technical environment to define a substantial chunk of requirements. The business analyst needs to study this documentation to understand the business problem, the goals and objectives of the project, the scope, the environment that the new application will reside in,

[1]Building Requirements Consensus. Cook Enterprise Corporation. 2008–2009 http://www.building-requirements-consensus.com/index.html.

and how the new system will interact with and impact other applications within that environment.

By the time the user gets involved, the business analyst should already have a draft of context diagrams, workflow, requirements management framework, peripheral gap analysis, a high level draft of requirements, and a plan for how they will accomplish the work on this particular project.

Gap Assessment (vs. Gap Analysis)

Gap analysis is a small sliver of the work that comprises gap assessment. Where gap analysis analyzes individual gaps on a specific project, gap assessment takes it further and manages those gaps in the same way that issues would be managed. It provides a framework for the assessment of risks and impacts that are related to those gaps, and then draws links between the gaps and the areas that are impacted by each of the gaps.

Ambiguity Management

All too often, we speak before listening, or listen without hearing. In writing, the brain completes thoughts that are not written down, and in general, we tend to forget to look at things from other perspectives and get feedback from others. In requirements, these same types of incomplete processes create ambiguities. Evidence suggests that ambiguities are the leading cause of low project success rates, missed functionality, and unused features. In a nutshell, ambiguities are big risks!

The only way to ensure that ambiguities in requirements are exposed and addressed is to use a solid process for ambiguity management. The process must contain a clear set of steps that deal with each factor that causes ambiguities in the first place. Further, ambiguities as risks must be managed in the same way that other risks are managed throughout the project in order to reduce occurrence, and then to mitigate the impacts and effects when they do occur.

Requirements Validation and Facilitated Sign-off

During hundreds of interviews that I have conducted, I asked the candidates how they validate requirements. Again, 99% of business analysts say that they "go back to the user" in order to elicit requirements. The analysts are completely stumped when I ask them what *they* do when the user does not know the information that they need.

The fact is there are lots of proven tools and techniques that will support validation. The analyst just does not know what these tools are, and how to apply them to achieve the best result. They cannot see the value of using them when they are not sure how the tools work, or how it will impact the quality of their work.

Candid conversations with business analysts tell me that nearly everyone is struggling and learning "by the seat of their pants." This is a direct result of the lack of practice formalization. Few analysts will openly discuss this. Everyone wants to have some level of job satisfaction, to feel competent, and be seen as competent by one's colleagues. This means that business analysts are not necessarily going to ask for help and advice on which tools and techniques they should be using to validate requirements.

You can uncover this problem of the failure to ask for advice by looking at the number of projects within an organization that have scope creep, how many have users and stakeholders that are complaining about missed functionality, and how many projects are taking longer to develop than originally estimated. Another indicator of this problem would be that your break-and-fix cycles in testing are off the map. If you notice these patterns, my best advice is to work with the analysts to educate them and bring in a formal methodology that encompasses specific validation techniques. Any methodology that does not include a specific set of validation steps is incomplete, and not worth the money that you will spend on it.

Thorough requirements validation also requires something that some business analysts actually are doing, but are not necessarily doing well. It is facilitated sign-off. Many analysts, including the most senior, have asked me how I get stakeholders to read the requirements document. Despite all of the unknowns, this is one of the most significant challenges facing an analyst.

First of all, I boldly make the assumption that stakeholders will *not* read the requirements document, even though I give them enough time to do so. I also assume that those who do read some or all of it generally do not read it thoroughly enough to understand the details. That is okay—I don't need for them to read the details! However, I do need the stakeholders to understand the functionality represented by the requirements, and the best way for them to really understand this is to participate in a facilitated walk-through of the functionality to discuss how this creates the results that the business needs. I then have stakeholders sign off on it.

Quantifying Effectiveness of Requirements Activities

The final step that business analysts are missing is the compilation of quantifiable metrics that are associated with requirements in order to illustrate the effectiveness of the requirements activities. It is one thing to recognize that requirements need to change and to improve, and then another thing to have the ability to target exact areas for improvement and understand the full degree of improvements that are needed.

There is a lot of controversy on requirements improvement and traceability, but there does not seem to be a lot of discussion about how to measure and quantify those improvements. In order to understand the specific aspects of requirements that need to be improved, you have to approach it in the same way that any other improvement project is approached. First, determine the kinds of metrics that you can gather for requirements, and then analyze those metrics to determine and understand the starting point.

Setting these benchmarks allows you to illustrate the current situation, and then to determine the levels and types of professional development that the business analysts will need. Establishing milestones, by using these same metrics, provides you with the ability to perform a comparison at various points during the improvement process, and to determine the effectiveness and efficiency of your efforts.

In order to follow this process, it is important to understand the tools that will provide you with the metrics that you will want to use for assessing the requirements. Some requirements management tools will come with a couple of built-in metrics for traceability, but there is yet to be a single tool that will compile a full set of standardized metrics to support a true requirements improvement initiative. That means that without an adequate requirements management tool in the marketplace, you will have to generate metrics on your own.

At the basic level, you can easily identify the volume of requirements. Volume becomes more precise when you follow a standard numbering and classification protocol. Quite simply, it is a count of the documented low-level requirements.

The next, basic metric that you can gather is the amount of time that it takes to complete each stage of the requirements life cycle (as a separate subset of the software development life cycle). This will take some dedication on the part of staff to report if you are not using a tool that will provide timestamps at various points during the cycle.

During a typical life cycle, the next quantifiable metric that you can compile is the volume of requirements that are actually designed, built, and then implemented by the design and development team. Ideally, this information is available in a traceability tool, and traces back to both the mid- and high-level requirements and project scope. If it does not, it may take some wrangling and negotiating to survey the designers and developers to extract information from them.

Finally, in most organizations, you should be able to compile the volumes of passed and failed testing because of the nature of the detailed documentation created by the testing team. While this documentation will give you an approximate idea of how well the project did during the requirements elicitation stage, it is simply not detailed enough to help you understand the trends in requirements or in identifying the specific business analysis activities that should be improved.

So what do all these pockets of metrics mean? How can we compile, analyze, and compare them to understand exactly how effective the requirements practices have been? Well, you can use the volume of requirements divided by the time it takes to complete each step in order to understand how many requirements are completed in an average day.

However, in addition, compiling ambiguity metrics using a formal *ambiguity log* allows you to identify, understand, and monitor trends in specific types of requirements issues that crop up and then impact the overall quality of requirements. By adding this metric to the formula, you will be able to measure the full effectiveness of requirements techniques and activities.

Then, by comparing the metrics of individual projects across the organization, specific opportunities for improvement will become apparent. In fact, the understanding of organizational requirements effectiveness will enable targeted areas of development for your BA team, improve collaboration between project teams, and increase support for organizational agility.

All in all, missing any one of these critical steps not only increases the risks that your project will face, but it will add to development and maintenance costs, and then decrease the overall return on investment and benefits realizations. On top of this, you will not have the detailed information required to support focused requirements remediation efforts. Missed steps translate into a reduced ability to support your core business, and an inability to remain innovative and sustainable.

Opportunities for Improvement

As with everything else, if you can see the benefits, and if you have the time, money, and resources to capitalize on them, opportunities will outweigh the strengths of the current model. That is quite simply because we cannot improve on profitability and customer experience without also evolving the systems and technology to set the foundation. It would be like adding voice over Internet protocol without also improving the telephony hardware, or worse, adding SmartGrid and SmartMeter technology without first changing the underlying hardware systems. At some point, we would end up with a breakdown in the customer experience that would erode the ability to provide service, impacting profitability or ultimately causing a catastrophic failure of the business as a whole.

In general, the opportunities within business analysis management are to create greater alignment between the strategic goals and the business, create more customer-centric experiences, and reduce project failure rates. However, there is also the intrinsic value that is brought to resources whose confidence and sense of competence and job satisfaction suddenly increases.

By providing products that more closely align with strategic goals, customer needs, and business operation needs, analysts can change the ways in which customers are engaged. This, in turn creates an evolution of the business toward a more customer-centric experience, and increases the ability to better meet the needs of more customers with greater satisfaction, which ultimately increases profitability and improves the bottom line.

Next, consider that there is a cost associated to each lost opportunity. Just because the business is profitable right now, or even because it has a consistent track record of being profitable, does not mean that it is as profitable as it *could be*. Moreover, it does not mean that the business has not lost out on different opportunities that could have been used to strengthen it to meet challenges, such as an economic crisis. Not to mention that lost opportunities could also represent new products and services as customer needs shift and change, and the economy involves an increasingly global society.

In addition, there is an opportunity to improve the defect rate through the capture and definition of higher quality requirements. Within the industry, there is an emerging trend to standardize and formalize business analysis activities and deliverables to control quality and improve results, such as decreased defect rates among product families and projects. Formalized and standardized business analysis methods and management present an opportunity to capitalize on that trend and enable the business to move forward in an area where we have struggled in the past, even if you have not quite figured out that this is a source of many project issues.

No, it's not a flavor of the week! We simply cannot keep going as we have in the past, and then expect different results. As Marshall Goldsmith put it, "*What got you here, won't get you there.*" That means that it does not matter how we ended up coming to the conclusion that we needed to add a layer called business analysis between the developers, designers, and the business to capture and define more formal requirements before we started digging in and building something. We still have to formalize that role so that we can progress from where we are now.

Threats to Improvement

Finally, when we review the current model, there are threats that indicate the need for change as a means of creating and solidifying business continuity. Some threats include the distance that emerges between businesses and customers, sustainability and scalability of resourcing, increased role-based attrition, and a general inability to maintain compliance with external regulatory bodies.

Businesses have a fundamental need to interface more seamlessly with their customers and to satisfy customer needs. Without consistent resource pools and talent to draw from, this becomes a significant problem for businesses as they try to scale up production to meet business and consumer demands. In addition, delivering faulty products erodes not only customer satisfaction but their trust as well, and leads the consumer to seek the product elsewhere.

There is a real threat in the form of the availability of skilled and experienced resources because the growth of the practice is organic in nature and because it is directed by external groups with their own agendas.

We all need to feel competent and satisfied with our work, or we get to the point where we start to feel as though the job is just not worth doing. After all, it can be emotionally draining to do the same things over and over again, and not feel as if you are doing a good job, simply because the rules change on every project or you don't get along with your new project manager.

Without having a solid management model in place, other roles become more attractive and we start to see an increase in role-based attrition. Why? Quite simply, because humans like to move forward in an organized manner, and by-and-large, most people are followers, not leaders. Without leadership, people will gravitate towards roles that do have leadership because it engenders a greater sense of belonging, a need that we all have as human beings.

Another threat within the typical business analysis model is that there is an increased need for compliance to change external regulations, such as those imposed by government agencies. Companies must deal with government regulations, such as the Health Information Portability and Accountability Act (HIPAA), the Sarbanes-Oxley (SOX) Act, and utility boards. Unfortunately, a chief characteristic of government agencies is that they change regulations frequently, and the businesses that wish to remain compliant do so by adopting the changes within a specified period of time. Sometimes, compliance means changing project deliverables mid-project and then having to run through the change request process once the proverbial "other shoe has finally dropped," and the new rules have taken effect.

Without adequate management and governance in place, we really cannot claim any kind of compliance. Moreover, unfortunately, that also includes compliance to the much-touted Capability Maturity Model (CMM). Without managing your business analysts, you simply are not CMM compliant. With CMM, as with Maslow's hierarchy of needs, you cannot skip levels and then claim to be at the top if you do not meet the criteria for some or most of the lower levels.

The CMM levels indicate the maturity of an organization by the types of standardization, consistency, and formalization utilized within its processes, as shown in Figure 1.3. At the lowest level, you have poorly defined processes that are inconsistently applied, and sometimes processes that are even inappropriate for the organization altogether. At Level 2, processes are managed, that is, applied consistently, controlled, enforced, measured, and monitored on a regular basis. Levels 3 and 4 encompass both proactively managed and quantitatively measured processes that are designed

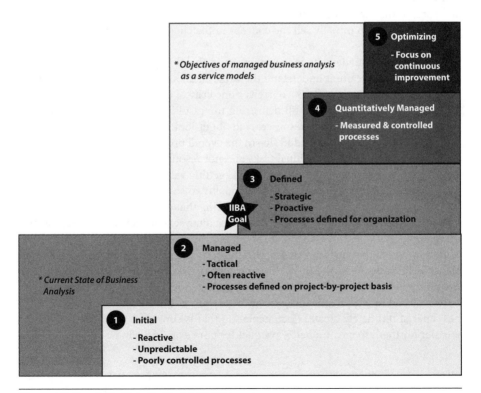

Figure 1.3 Capability Maturity Model (CMM) Levels

to support the organization over the long term. Finally, in Level 5, processes and governance are based on the principles of continuous improvement.

When companies claim compliance to CMM Level 2 and above, but then do not manage their business analysts, they are in fact failing to comply with the most basic criteria for true compliance to the CMM model.

Finally, one of the more recent threats over these last couple of years is the increased economic pressures to reduce waste and go lean. There is a common misconception that "lean" means the reduction of the numbers of resources; often, one of the first things done is to cut staff and then promptly start doubling up on the duties and responsibilities of the remaining resources.

I can recall a Fortune 500 ticketing client that let go of all of their business analysts in a downturn after the dot-com bubble burst. The client recognized that requirements were still needed for their new software projects, but decided that they would task the sales representatives with documenting and submitting the requirements to the development team.

By the time that the client called for help, the projects were grossly behind schedule and did not have any formal requirements because the sales representatives did not have the time, ability, or inclination to write the requirements. The development team was frustrated by not having any plans, requirements, or designs to build the new software, so they were forced to reverse-engineer from the animated storyboards that had been created to initially sell the concept to the client company in order to secure funding.

Again, without adequate management, and the ability to measure results in any one area, we really cannot understand the value chain and make any kind of assertion of being lean. Remember to ask yourselves one critical question in order to "go lean": Where can I save time while still delivering the results that my clients expect? That means it is not about cutting resources, but about looking for ways to trim the tasks (and related time) that do not add value to the overall process. We must also remember that lean is associated to individual tasks and not resource volumes, and then start to think in terms of ensuring that clients are still getting value. After all, clients are paying for a specific system and they do not want quality to suddenly drop.

Dropping business analysts and then insisting that others do their work is ridiculous. It is equally ridiculous to hire a business analyst that also does testing or programming. That does not save money or cut out the non-value added tasks; in fact, all it does is ensure that quality will drop like a rock. The way to make business analysis leaner is to understand the tasks that business analysts perform, and the value that each of those tasks provides to the overall project, and then choose which tasks are necessary and to what degree they are necessary to perform. Remember that the business analyst ultimately creates documentation that is consumed by others and makes it easier for them to create a better product to more exacting standards.

Right now, if you were to start measuring how much time business analysts spend being unproductive, or measure the work they are doing that is ineffective, you might be shocked! Some of them might as well be sitting around staring at the walls for how effective they really are; so if you want to make their world leaner, find ways to make it more effective. Once you do that, you will find that your whole project suddenly gets better, faster, and leaner.

Now we know the strengths, weaknesses, opportunities, and threats lying within the average business analysis model, but how do we improve it? How can we address the weaknesses, while taking advantage of the opportunities and reducing the threats to business continuity? Well, we do that by creating a sustainable management model for business analysis at the operational level instead of at the project level. Think *strategic* versus *tactical* here. The project level is tactical: Go forth and create.

You get your hands busy and mind occupied with building one small component or feature at a time. At that level, it is pretty hard to see if there is a common theme to the problems being faced by the business. That means you cannot see if issues that are uncovered are actually a part of a more widespread systemic problem that needs to be addressed. From a strategic level, you can see the whole situation and can actually diagnose any widespread systemic issues, to find the "cure" or the solution, and then push that solution down to the tactical level for build and implementation.

It is because of this dichotomy between the strategic and tactical levels that business analysis as a *service* must contain these two complementary layers (strategic and tactical), and that these layers be supported by the pillars of management, service delivery, and governance (see Figure 1.4).

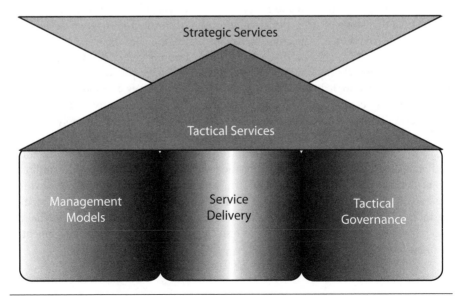

Figure 1.4 Layers of business analysis

Throughout this chapter, we explored some of the most common and pronounced attributes of the typical business analysis model, and then decomposed that model to illustrate the issues that need to be considered in order to generate a new model for the management of business analysis services. The decomposition highlighted a glaring lack of formalization and standardization among the practices and methods utilized within business analysis services, and the methods used to manage them. It also highlighted the lack of synchronicity between the requirements tasks and desired outcomes, as well as the disconnect between the roles of business analysts that results from the lack of formal management.

Unfortunately, one of the biggest hindrances to the establishment of complete services is the inability to understand and identify the nuances that affect the services that we deliver. Whether that is the limited nature of our own logic, or the fact that we tend to minimize so many of the smaller details and then discount those details, I cannot say. Nonetheless, we have to manage all aspects and factors that contribute to the quality of the outcomes.

We have to understand that factors that contribute to quality could be playing a more pivotal role than we realize, and until we start to measure and monitor them, we will never know just how much of a role they play. By taking the information from a SWOT analysis and detailed review of the current state of business analysis services, we will be able to establish practices that are more consistent and measureable, and more likely to lead to quality at the end of the process.

We can no longer bury our heads in the sand and hope that the problems with technology projects and poor requirement quality will go away as if they are merely an anomaly. We have to address this situation if we are to make it better, and in order to address it, we must admit that we have a problem. Once we do that, we can start a "twelve-step program" to make it better. I am convinced that once we are able to accomplish that, we will see exponential growth within the industry and develop the skills and techniques to create amazing new technologies.

Let's face it, 25 years ago, if you had told me that my cell phone would be more dynamic than my clunky computer, I would have thought you were dreaming. The point is, now I cannot help but think about endless possibilities. I cannot stop thinking about where we could be technically in five, ten, twenty, or even fifty years from now. However, I do know this is only going to be possible when we start to apply the same techniques that work well in other areas of technology to business analysis.

Any CIO or BA manager could utilize this information to evaluate the methods and practices that they currently employ under the business analysis services umbrella. An in-depth evaluation can aid them in firmly establishing a connection between business analysis methods and management to the deterministic outcomes produced by business analysts. An evaluation will also highlight the root causes of issues that are being faced on technology projects as a result of a lack of optimized management of business analysis services.

2

AN OPTIMIZED BUSINESS ANALYSIS MODEL

In Chapter 1, many issues and risks within the average existing business analysis model were decomposed by utilizing a SWOT analysis. However, some strengths and opportunities to increase ROI and the value of business analysis were also uncovered. Using that same information, an optimized state for business analysis services can be identified, along with how those services should be managed and utilized. In order to do that, we will take a look at an overview of the complete proposed and optimized business analysis model from end to end.

The overview also will offer insight into the primary elements of an optimized business analysis model and will provide the information that is needed to understand exactly how it is possible to optimize the overall use of technology, as well as to increase alignment of technology products, in order to better serve the client organization. This model supports the primary focus and purpose of business analysis as the process of translating strategic goals into tangible solutions to meet those goals.

Every task has been carefully positioned to support its focus and to help information technology achieve maximum results. Later in Chapter 3, you will see how the new concept of Business Analysis Stewardship is factored into this model and how it is uniquely poised to achieve the objectives of stewardship.

Where the previous chapter highlighted areas of concern within a loosely organized and coupled model, this chapter provides information about a specific, consistent and optimized business analysis services model that can be utilized to mitigate the risks associated with mainstream technology projects.

Business analysis is the enablement of the strategic plans of a company in that it is the process by which the corporate strategy is brought to fruition through the development of technical solutions, processes, and systems that produce the results that are

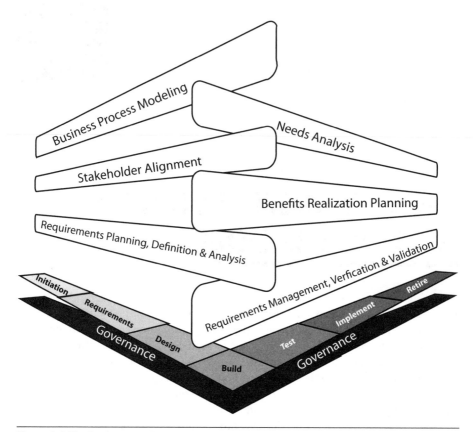

Figure 2.1 The business analysis model

mandated within the plans themselves. In this manner, a *business analyst* is a catalyst for the enablement of strategic plans and business continuity.

As depicted in Figure 2.1, the tasks for which a business analyst is both responsible and accountable encompass business process modeling, needs analysis, stakeholder alignment, benefits realization planning, requirements definition and analysis, requirements verification and validation, and governance. Each task is made up of a series of optional and compulsory activities that combines to create the resulting deliverables, as well as related artifacts.

It is the creation of the artifacts for each activity that provides the knowledge and information that the analyst requires. They utilize this information to build a complete set of deliverables. Unfortunately, many people, business analysts included, do not know the context or value for each of the activities, and end up missing key information that they require to produce complete sets of deliverables.

BUSINESS PROCESS MODELING

Business process modeling and engineering is the creation of visual maps and flow charts to illustrate the typical step-by-step workflows, value streams, and end-to-end processes utilized by the business. These processes extend across all of the roles that contribute to the entire process, so that the business analyst can understand the specific tasks performed, the business rules applied, and the overall processes utilized within the business in order to achieve particular work results.

The business analyst is most often involved in redesigning specific business processes in accordance with new systems, regulations, or policies, as a means of automating them, or to introduce new business programs. Business rule documentation, on the other hand, is the compilation and authoring of the rules by which the business manages and controls processes for compliance to specific governance initiatives and to achieve specific results.

Regardless of whether your organization utilizes separate roles for business process modeling and business rule generation, it is imperative that all business analysts are knowledgeable about the detailed processes, the associated rules, and the impacts that these will have on any solution that they will define requirements for. This knowledge extends from a full understanding of the existing business processes and rules to helping the business analyst to fully understand and identify the problem, as well as associated visible and invisible issues that are related to the processes. This knowledge enables the analyst to perform root cause analysis, either as a means of defining a solution or mitigating issues on the fly during a project.

It is crucial that the business analysis model you develop and implement includes parameters, best practices, and methods for the consistent capture, definition, and documentation of both business processes and rules, so that they become part of the corporate inheritance and knowledge base after a project has been completed and the resources have moved on. In addition, we must recognize the value of utilizing both business process and business rules documentation across projects.

Note that specific rules and processes supersede the individual requirements for any one specific project, as shown in Figure 2.2. While both rules and processes are instanced within the project documentation, both must be managed as part of the enterprise's content management systems. This reduces the risks of misinterpretation, incorrect application, and watering-down of the business rules and processes through dissemination and repeated capture and association with individual projects, as though they were tied exclusively to that particular project and its requirements.

NEEDS ANALYSIS

Once the business analyst has a grasp on the applicable and impacted business processes and rules, they can start to understand the needs of the business in relation to the solution being defined. Again, the business analyst is the catalyst for the

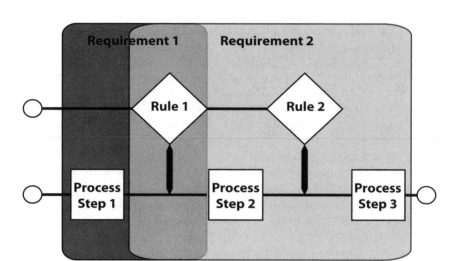

Figure 2.2 Relationship between processes, rules, and requirements

enablement of strategic plans so it is critical that every single analyst allocated to a project understand the problem or strategic goals and drivers behind the project. Their intimate knowledge of these drivers will provide them with the insight to know when the project is going astray or diverging from the required path and will not meet the targets.

By meeting with the sponsors and stakeholders to define the needs, the business analyst is able to review the identified needs against other trends, as well as the strategic goals and business objectives, and is then able to define a specific set of needs that will be met by the solution. While seasoned business analysts will definitely be more adept at conducting a needs analysis, all of the allocated business analyst resources must become conversant with the resulting documentation, as it will provide focus and enhance their ability to restrain the scope of the project to the specific targeted outcomes. Essentially, this will enable the allocated business analysts to support the alignment of the individual requirements to the predetermined outcomes, business goals, and drivers for the project.

Objectives, Stakeholder Alignment and Outcomes

Remember the example about the proposal for the testing solution mentioned in Chapter 1? Ordinarily, the senior business analysts were in a position to work directly with the prospective client to understand their needs and then to set a plan in motion to meet those needs. However, in this particular instance, the account management team told the delivery team that the client wanted us to demonstrate a specific testing technique called *logic modeling* as a means of providing testing for this project. After enduring eight long weeks of unsatisfactory deliverables, the bid was finally lost.

When senior management met to discuss why so much time and money had been invested into the client and the bid was eventually lost, the account management team stated that the prospective client had brought the delivery team in to demonstrate how we could test their product when other bidding firms were giving insane estimates. At that point, it became apparent that the delivery team had not been given a clear understanding of the client's real need, but only a specific interpretation of that need. It also became apparent that the intercession between the prospective client stakeholders and the delivery team only served to compound our inability to provide the requested solution, and to ensure that what we were producing was in fact aligned to what the client had actually requested. This story illustrates the critical need for all resources regardless of role and seniority to be well-informed about the needs expressed and implied by the client in the needs analysis.

STAKEHOLDER ALIGNMENT

Stakeholder alignment is closely tied to the needs analysis in that the business analyst has to work to balance the needs of the individual stakeholders, sponsors, and users with the needs of the overall business as expressed in the strategic plans. Quite often, this involves reigning in egos and personality, as well as political differences, in order to ensure that the solution meets the needs of the business and does not just appease a single stakeholder or user group.

Stakeholder alignment takes a lot of finesse and skill on the part of the analyst. It means that the underlying skills that are required to be successful in stakeholder alignment are assertiveness, mediation, negotiation, and conciliation. Each of these skills will enable the analyst to work with the various stakeholder and user groups from the business and to manage the needs of all groups, as well as the needs of the business, and to achieve positive results without leaving one group feeling excluded or jaded as a result of the interaction.

As with any group setting and dynamic, there will be a diversity of personalities to manage, work with, and engage in the project. That diversity means that there will be some stakeholders and users that participate because they were told to. They showed up and contributed because that is just what you do. Then, there will be those that want to be center stage and upstage the project in favor of their own agenda. Finally, there will be those that just will not participate, no matter what you offer them as incentive or motivation.

A *good* business analyst will be able to accomplish results with this latter group regardless of the levels of participation and interference of the stakeholders, but it will take time to accomplish this, which must be included in the estimate. A *skilled* business analyst, on the other hand, will be adept at identifying individual needs and will recognize the value of every person's contribution, working to create an environment where every stakeholder and user contributes in a directed and meaningful way to the outcome of the project. They can do this because they have strategies to empower and enable the contributions of others and support them in meeting their individual needs, even if they have to say "no" to some of the features that individual stakeholders or users want when they do not align to the business objectives.

BENEFITS REALIZATION PLANNING

Benefits realization is the planning, delivery, and subsequent management of positive benefits across the life cycle of a particular product that is derived from a specific financial investment. The latest trend within information technology is to attempt to capitalize on benefits realization planning under the auspices of portfolio management. This is where groups of related products and/or projects are managed at a strategic level instead of only a tactical level. This provides the business with greater ability to see the project or product within the context of the overall business and strategic objectives, and to ensure greater alignment of multiple systems and projects.

Benefits realization planning is important because it enables the business to measure and monitor returns on the money that it is spending. Essentially, it is planning to get benefits on a predictable schedule, and at a predetermined rate, from anything that the business buys and invests money in.

Chances are a lot of you out there (both men and women) have a closet full of shoes that are worn only once in awhile. You may even have a couple of pairs that you don't wear at all because they looked great in the store and were on sale, but the first time you wore them they pinched your feet and you got blisters, or you discovered another thing about them that rendered them impossible to wear. Yet, you still have them in your closet because you bought them and want to feel as though you have gotten your money's worth. If they were designer shoes that you got at a premium, you expected that you would wear them for years to come because, let's face it, quality costs more. Therefore, you planned to benefit from the purchase for several years by wearing them with specific outfits to certain events, and when that didn't happen, you had a hard time letting go of the shoes.

Maybe shoes are trivial, but you get the point. Every time we buy something, we exchange our hard-earned money and expect to receive something of value in return.

Companies are no different. Even when the money spent is in the form of operating costs or non-optional overhead, the company will still expect to see a benefit from whatever it is the money is spent on. If the company does not plan for benefits, it too may end up with a closet full of impulse purchases that are never used.

Now, think "software." How many software packages have your different departments purchased and installed that do either the same, or overlapping, tasks? They basically have the same features, but maybe look a bit different or perform the tasks differently. With benefits realization planning, you can look at all departments and consider how each one would benefit from a single product, and then plan to get the maximum benefit for the money spent. You would do this by calculating how much money will be saved from things like cutting support time for multiple individual products down to one; or how you can more readily move resources laterally because they will not need as much specialized training; or, how much easier it will be to share data and information across the whole company instead of having to find patches to convert it across multiple systems; and finally, how much less money will be spent on things like servers and network storage, and so on.

Once you have identified the benefits that you expect to see, you can plan how and when these benefits will be achieved by creating a schedule for migrating the data from other systems to the new one over a period of months or years. In addition, you can calculate the return on investment expected over the next five to ten years of using the new product. Again, the reason for doing this planning is simple: to make sure you are not just blowing your money on an impulse buy.

The Need for Benefits Management Exposed

An international insurance client initiated a project to improve their business analysis processes. Within a functional organizational model, one of the processes that came to light was that each leg of the company had its own information technology (IT) department. Several years before, the department that had initiated the process improvement project had decided to purchase an automated customer service cloud application to enhance the broker access portal. To say that it had "issues" would be an understatement. The business analyst that helped to broker the deal actually denied being involved when questions were asked about the documentation and benefits, as well as the vendor management elements.

First of all, the software application had not been completed prior to purchase. It was an idea of an application, and the insurance company had been paying for the development. The network crashed daily, and caused multiple fires and issues. Documentation for support was nonexistent and *no one* was accountable for it. Not only did they not want to remove it, but it also had functionality that other departments already had from a single solution that had previously been adopted by several other departments. There was absolutely no benefit to the company for having this application other than the fact that it had made someone feel as though they had the authority to purchase something substantial, and then had the authority to make other people use and support it. If the analyst (who by the director's admission had more experience and industry knowledge than he did) prepared even a simple benefits plan, the company would not be spending hundreds of thousands of dollars on a lost cause that they refused to dump. Furthermore, the fact that the application was sponsored by the VP of Finance for that division, who did not share a benefits plan (if there even was one), and did not care to hear about any of the issues or costs related to the application, made this a frustrating situation for all of those involved in the lower support ranks.

By preparing a simple benefits realization plan, the business analyst could have changed features requests, or shifted importance and priorities accordingly. The whole development and adoption, as well as the subsequent support, could have been much less costly. Not only that, the analyst would have been in a better position to talk to the VP and negotiate with the vendor on new features or fixes by having the knowledge needed to do so. As it was, the company was being held hostage by both the VP and the vendor because they were the ones responsible for the chaos.

While benefits realization planning could fall under the auspices of the program or portfolio management role, it is more appropriate under the business analysis role because individual business cases for specific projects are becoming increasingly complex. Many benefits simply cannot be identified without the engagement of the business community at large (and business analysts are uniquely positioned with the necessary skills and knowledge for this role), but it is also because of the detachment of the analyst from the outcomes of the individual programs and portfolios. Therefore, the business is better served when benefits realization planning is conducted by the business analyst during the course of their strategic role before pushing the solution down to a tactical level. In addition, because of the impact to requirements, the overall solution can be verified and validated more easily by the analyst team. Problem solving can be accomplished with less time commitment needed by the stakeholders because the analyst team is no longer solely reliant on those stakeholders as the keepers of the information.

Benefits realization planning is important for business analysis because it will enable the analyst to ensure that the solution created aligns to the strategic plans, the business objectives, and drivers, and that the resulting solution will, in fact, contribute to the overall continuity of the business. It impacts requirements in that it lends to scope, high-level requirements, and even detailed requirements for specific projects, as well as to the business readiness, and provides a solid plan for how the business will benefit (grow, advance, gain customers or market share, decrease overhead, etc.) as a direct result of the development and implementation of the project deliverables.

Unfortunately, this is an area that business analysts are reluctant to tackle, and project sponsors are equally reluctant to discuss it outside of the program or portfolio management realm. Why? Because the benefits realization planning role has not traditionally been a part of the assigned responsibilities of the business analyst. However, there is tremendous value in the inclusion of this task under the business analyst role because it significantly impacts his or her ability to deliver the right solution for meeting the long-term strategies of the company, and enables them to capture and define all of the necessary requirements for this to happen.

Once completed, the benchmarks and measurements roll up to the business case for the specific project, while individual requirements are encapsulated within the requirements and business readiness documents. This leads to the determination of a more complete solution and to the alignment of that solution to business continuity drivers, such as strategic goals.

While program and portfolio managers could also be conducting benefits realization planning across their respective programs and portfolios, and because these program-based benefits realization plans will impact both the business case and the requirements, it is imperative that benefits realization planning also be conducted at the individual project level. This effort ensures seamless alignment at a granular and tactical level with the highest-level services and strategic objectives.

Benefits realization planning requires a basic set of steps to be accomplished, so that benefits may be predicted across the life cycle of a particular product, as shown in Figure 2.3. These are:

- Identify the problem or need.
- Identify the desired outcomes and results.
- Define the benchmarks.
- Determine the priority of the benefits.
- Design and obtain agreement.
- Plan the new or changed capabilities.
- Plan any additional investments.
- Optimize the plan.
- Complete a risk/impact assessment.
- Consistently review planned vs. actual.

It is important to note that benefits are obtained from both the initial product and subsequent updates. Benefits also continue during the decommissioning process.

First of all, you have to identify the problem or need, or you must have a really intimate understanding of it. Before you can begin to understand and contemplate making a financial investment, you have to first understand *why* you are considering buying it in the first place. There must be some type of benefit that you want to get from the purchase. Alternatively, there must be some need that you have to justify the original decision to purchase the product or the skills to build a new product.

A need could be a gap that was identified by another project or solves yet another problem. The need could be a gap that was identified in the strategic plan from where

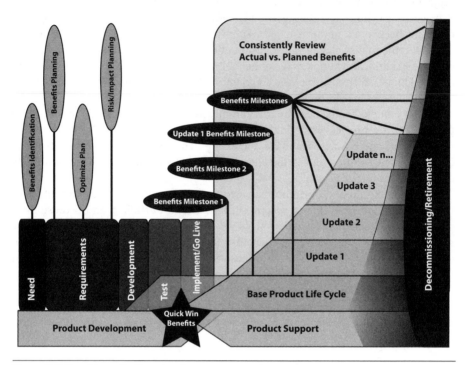

Figure 2.3 Benefits realization planning

the business is now to where it wants to be in five years, and what must be in place in order for it to get there. On the other hand, the gap might be something that is already in use and is either broken, outdated, or both. Whatever it is, you need to understand this before you can start any kind of benefit plan because the benefits have to align with this problem. The primary benefit should be that the current situation (no matter what it is) would be better because of the new system or solution.

Next, you will need to identify the desired outcomes and results, including return on investment (ROI) for the expense. In other words, you must ask yourself and your team a series of questions that enable you to determine the specific financial, service-centric, product development-centric, and emotional and team competency-centric benefits that you expect, want, or need to derive from the utilization of the solution or system.

In addition, the team will have to understand and identify what the business does *not* need, want, or expect to see for each one of these (financial, quality, service, products development process, team competency, and/or emotional) benefits. Benefits realization planning will provide you with information that will help you to assess (or re-assess), the solution that you are planning to put in place. Both the "wants" and "unwanted" attributes of the solution are equally important to identify and understand because the unwanted benefits are not only unnecessary, they can impact the adoption of the new product by the customers or business users. Unwanted "benefits" can actually decrease ROI and, in turn, negatively impact the benefits plan.

Next, you will need to define the benchmarks as well as the qualitative and quantitative measures for each benefit outcome. It is imperative that you have a way to measure and quantify each of the specified benefits that you have identified, so that you can actually determine if the product or solution actually measures up.

Small, But Costly Lack of Quantifiable Benefits Management

To illustrate the need for quantifiable measures in your benefits realization plan, I once worked with a small boutique firm, and one of the things that was blatantly obvious was that there was no firewall or security in place. It was obvious because every person on staff literally got nearly a hundred spam emails per day. When I approached the IT manager about this issue, he insisted that it could not be done and we "just had to live with it." Being one to take matters into my own hands, and having done an Outlook implementation early on in my technology career, I set up about a hundred rules to manage the spam, so that I did not have to waste my time dealing with junk mail. Not everyone was so lucky.

Think about the situation of 284 employees and contractors, each dealing with almost 100 junk emails per day. That is an average of 28,400 emails bombarding and overloading the servers unnecessarily, per day. Now, think about how much time each person spends dealing with them. They had to sift through regular work-related emails to find and segregate the spam before they could be deleted, so let's estimate about 10 seconds per email to accomplish this. The rough total number of hours spent by all employees per day was about 79. That is nearly the equivalent of two weeks of work for a full time employee! That translates to each employee spending about 17 minutes per day weeding out junk emails.

In the above example, the need for measurable benefits realization planning and management would have alleviated many of the headaches and costly lost time by employees. For most companies, wasted time on junk mail is not quite this dramatic, but it is still a task that we take for granted, never really thinking about how we could change the situation because the smallest unit of email seems inconsequential to us. We do not stop to think about how much time and money we could save by implementing a new solution until the smallest number becomes more obvious. It is like the dripping faucet, where lots of small drops add up to flooding the sink. In this case, however, the company employees were unproductive for a grand total of 20,540 *hours* per year. The same situation went on for five years, meaning that they were unproductive for more than 102,700 hours.

Next, consider that the average employee was paid well, so let's estimate the average salary was $80,000 per year, which is approximately $38.46 per hour. The junk email situation means that during a single year, the company paid employees roughly $789,763 for wasted time. Even at about half of this number, the company could not only have saved money but also hired various other staff and implemented some simple solutions to fix the email problems.

The trouble is that the company never once looked at how much was being spent, and how much they stood to benefit by implementing something as simple as a firewall. That is exactly why we need to understand what the benefits are and assign quantifiable metrics or measurements to ensure, over the years, that we get the benefits we expected, needed, and wanted.

The types of things that we want to measure for each benefit are not just how much they increase, but also about how much they will fluctuate or decrease over time. Measurement can be especially difficult when we are attempting to assign metrics to things like the emotions of employees because they are largely intangible. However, there are real, tangible things that we can measure that are associated with emotions. These could include employee or customer satisfaction, attrition and retention, absenteeism, loyalty, performance, individual customer purchase rates and buying habits, and application-based usage rates.

However, analysts have to bear in mind that over the years, benefits and how much we benefit from each of them, may depreciate. That means that we have to plan, measure, and monitor the benefits, as well as how much we need to benefit, before we start thinking that it is time to pull the plug.

Once you have figured out measurements that you are going to use to monitor and assess the benefits against, the analyst will need to determine the priority for each of the benefits against others on the list. This will enable them to set appropriate schedules for the benefits realization across time and in consideration with other factors, such as the priority of other needs and projects. The benefits will need to be communicated to business stakeholders and sponsors, so that they can collaborate, design, and obtain agreement on a tailored benefits realization management approach for the investment.

To accomplish benefits prioritization, you will need to define how often the various attributes or benefits will be measured, what criteria constitutes success or failure, and the escalation plan, as well as the backup plan, and responsibilities and accountabilities matrices. Let's face it, once you implement the new system and drop everything else, you may not be able to simply "pull the plug." You may have to reroute everything else to the new, alternate path, validate it, and then make sure that it delivers the needed results.

Once you have an accepted management approach, it is time to start planning the details in order to ensure that it will actually happen. You will have to start planning the new or changed capabilities necessary to realize the benefits and, where applicable, include resulting requirements in the scope and/or high-level requirements for the new project. To do this, you will need to understand if you need new resources, new skill sets for existing resources, or other infrastructure (physical or virtual) that must be in place for it to be successful.

I can remember getting a contract to work with a large international computer consulting firm. Even though it took over a month for all of the "on-boarding" procedures, when I arrived, I did not get an access card, a laptop, or even my own desk. It was very frustrating because I literally had to share all those items with another resource and use paper the rest of the time. It took more than two weeks for me to get the laptop and an access card (I never did get a separate desk). You would almost think that they weren't expecting me; it did not make me feel great about working with them. When we think about the things and resources that need to be in place before we can see the benefits, think about this: was I able to work effectively for two weeks? No. So, in order for the company and their client to see the full benefit of contracting me, they had to first ensure that they had some simple things in place in order for me to perform as they had hoped, and to produce the results and benefits that they needed.

The next step is to plan any additional investments (such as automated tools, full time equivalent resources, or equipment) to make the necessary adjustments to create or change the capabilities of the business. In the case of my needing a laptop and a desk, the company finally acquired and assigned the laptop, but had never actually planned for or allocated space for me to have a desk. Of course, it was more than just going down to a store or ordering online to get one; they also needed floor space, which meant lighting, heating, air conditioning, and other facilities investments in order to provide me with a desk to work.

Later, I actually heard a story about an entire department that was scheduled to move to a new office location. The new office was remodeled and carpeted, and moving day arrived. The employees showed up to the new location, and so did their furniture and boxes. However, someone forgot to request and set up both telephone and networking throughout the space, so they had to move right back to the old offices. No one had a phone outlet or Ethernet connection because they were never installed!

What analysts will need to do is to ensure that the right sequencing of events is planned, and that each of those events can be implemented as seamlessly as possible. In the case of the employees showing up with furniture and boxes, and then having to move back to the old space, the phone lines and network should have been checked and verified as installed before anyone showed up. Had this been done, they would not have had to move back, even temporarily.

Sometimes, something as simple as forgetting to budget for resources beyond six months can be the issue. Whatever the case may be, we need to ensure that we not only plan for the items that are needed, but also plan for how we are going to pay for them and how they will impact the benefits that we are trying to manage.

In another example, I had a friend who bought a used car. She spent her entire budget on the car and did not account for things to go wrong, like a repair that was bound to be needed. A few days later, she was quite happily driving along when the car stopped dead in the road. She called the dealership and they basically told her, "*caveat emptor*" (buyer beware). It took months of haggling and arguing back and forth for the matter to be resolved. She did, after all, forget to budget for problems (and basically anything other than fuel).

Once we have all of the pieces of a plan together, we can start to evaluate and optimize it by utilizing value stream mapping and other lean management techniques in order to reduce waste and ensure the appropriate resourcing levels, and the accuracy of time and budgetary estimates. Again, a mistake that we make when evaluating value stream maps and optimizing processes using lean principles is looking to reduce resources instead of looking at the element of time. Make sure that you account for *how long* a task takes, and how that can be decreased instead of cutting resources. Dropping resources does not mean that there is less work to do; it means that you have less people to do it.

So far, a prevailing theme in the stories that I have been sharing is to "understand what you are up against." You will need to complete a risk/impact assessment in order to develop mitigation strategies and to identify acceptable levels of risk. By understanding what can go wrong, you can plan for it.

Murphy's Law states, "If anything can go wrong, it will." It is an old adage, but definitely appropriate to business analysis. We do not want anything to go wrong, and I think most of us are naturally optimistic (even when there seems no reason to be). Unfortunately, most business analysts are not very good at planning for something to go wrong. They forget that use cases must also document what the system must do when only some of the criteria are met (and in what combinations), or none of the criteria are met. A big part of planning for something positive is to plan for something negative to also happen, and come up with strategies for how to manage the impacts or what else to do instead.

The final stage in the benefits realization plan is to continuously review the impacts of the planned vs. the actual implementation on the benefit measures, and to utilize consistent improvement techniques. Watch it, measure it, keep it on track, and then improve it where and when you can.

REQUIREMENTS PLANNING

Requirements planning is preparing, organizing, and establishing the foundation for the requirements activities to begin. We have to understand some of the key elements about the work to be accomplished, and how it will be done, validated, and managed. Each of these elements dictates that we plan and then prepare for the successful completion of the work by applying key techniques and undertaking specific tasks. Unlike benefits realization planning, which plans for the business to realize specific results across the life span of the product, requirements planning is essentially the work needed to achieve the results defined by benefits realization plans.

It is important to plan the requirements activities in advance of starting the work because the planning will refine the estimates and establish the foundation for the real work of requirements to occur. In other words, the estimate for requirements activities goes from being a ballpark figure with a rough estimate of tasks and resources to a detailed and defined set of activities, work products, and deliverables. The details lend greater accuracy in requirements, and provide analysts with opportunities to become more involved in estimating by applying their expertise into the effort estimates for those tasks. Related considerations that have to be made for requirements during planning are shown in Figure 2.4.

The foundation of requirements typically refers to the customization and/or creation of the templates, specific processes, reporting elements, naming structures, requirements storage, and traceability components before the work begins. Planning and establishing these components upfront minimizes the number of changes to the techniques, templates, and "systems" utilized for the requirements activities as the team starts to perform the work.

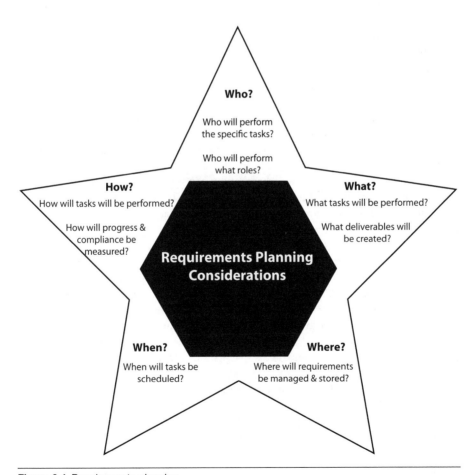

Figure 2.4 Requirements planning

Requirements planning sets the stage for a streamlined effort across the requirements phase and enables analysts to focus on the tasks of eliciting, analyzing, specifying, and validating the actual requirements, instead of the so-called "housekeeping" items that are associated with the work. This improves resource productivity and effectiveness because they can just work without having to manage the tasks in the midst of also having to perform each one of them.

I would argue that requirements planning enables the analyst to create better deliverables and artifacts because the distractions associated with an unplanned effort (such as naming and numbering conventions or file storage issues) are eliminated. In addition, requirements planning establishes clear parameters for what deliverables and artifacts are expected, and to what degree of detail, so that the analysts no longer have to struggle with the question about how much detail they have to go into in the individual requirements.

In order to understand the work to be accomplished, we must first understand the environment in which that work will be done, the role the work products will play in the environment, who will use it, and why it is being done. Unfortunately, many analysts are known to skip simple research about the existing systems and architecture because they believe it is outside of the scope of their role. What happens as a result is that they end up missing requirements altogether or have requirements that are logically incomplete.

Analysts cannot expect the architecture team to figure it all out and fill in the blanks when it comes to requirements. The solution is to work with the entire team so that analysts can build a single, complete, and logically consistent requirements document. The business analysts do not need to know how to program or design it, but they do need to know what data flows where, and when and how that data gets reported out, so that they can use that information to complete the requirements.

Consider the following requirement; would you be able to interpret it? *"System A must utilize data from system B to generate the following results..."* What data? What if system B generates more than a single type of data, how would you know which data element(s) to use? If the analyst was no longer available, who would you ask? You would have to assume and many of us already know what happens when you assume!

To understand how the work will be done, we need to determine the tasks, activities, and deliverables for each piece of work. Then we need to determine how long each task will take, how much time there is to accomplish the work, how many resources are available, and how their skill sets contribute to the accomplishment of the work, as well as how the team will cooperate and collaborate to achieve the work. Finally, we will need to determine what templates are available for each of the deliverables.

When it comes to allocating resources, do not make the mistake of simply grabbing someone "off the bench" without first determining if they are qualified to do the work. Many companies make this mistake because they think they can reduce the cost and time delay associated with having to find and recruit new, qualified talent. What they are not considering is the cost of errors made by "newbies." Unfortunately, outsourcing firms are rampant with new staffing to almost epidemic proportions. Maybe this type of back-sourcing can be excused away because people do not know enough about business analysis to adequately determine who is qualified and who is not. I am not trying to scare you away from outsourcing firms or damage their credibility. I just want analysts to understand what they are really getting into in order to take an active role in fixing the situation.

The next element we need to understand and determine is how the work will be *validated*. It is not enough to say that it will be tested; we must also consider how we will verify and validate the deliverables (requirements) so that they are clear, complete, consistent, and correct.

To accomplish the validation of deliverables, there are a variety of techniques for assessing the requirements for specific attributes such as logical completeness, use of concise and appropriate language, and verifying that the requirements are actually the right requirements. These techniques include an ambiguity review, use cases, and decision tables among the best ways to complete the litmus test for requirements.

If you worked in retail grocery, you would not forecast the needs for perishable items such as dairy products or fruit every month. This is because you need to understand how much is being sold on a daily basis, and therefore, you can tailor your orders to meet this. We know this reduces waste because there are less perishable products sitting in coolers and on shelves. We know that we have to do this in order to maintain saleable items in conditions that are appealing to consumers. With an industry track record of garbage coming out the other end, in order to understand the issues in the process, we have to also measure and verify health of the requirements "products" along the way. Only then can we ensure that we are able to pinpoint areas where we can improve the overall process.

Finally, we need to understand, plan, and prepare for how requirements will be managed. To do this, we need to ask and answer basic questions about the requirements themselves:

- How will requirements be captured?
- Where will individual requirements be stored?
- Who will have access to edit these requirements?
- How will each requirement be traced back to the corresponding processes and business rules?
- How will each requirement be traced to the corresponding design(s)?
- How will each requirement be traced to the corresponding test plans, cases, and scripts?
- How will other teams (design, development, and test) report on consumption of the requirements and implementation into the product?
- How will issues uncovered later during design, development, and test be reported and managed?
- How will requirements changes be made, managed, and reported back to the teams?
- How will requirement quality be quantified?

- What metrics and benchmarks will be utilized to measure the activities them-selves and the results of those activities?

Once we have answered these basic questions, we can set up templates and systems for the business analysts so that they can focus on the content of the individual require-ments, instead of trying to answer these questions on the fly and then establish each of the pieces. If this process was code, the resulting product would be an *ad hoc* system that looked a lot like spaghetti code.

To illustrate how important it is to answer the basic questions about a project, I want to share a story of a project that I had the opportunity to be a part of several years ago. Two significant things happened on this project that demonstrated a clear need for planning before any of the work occurred. The first event I will call the "binder incident," and the second I will call the "database incident."

What happened in the binder incident was that we were organizing a conference for approximately 200 stakeholders from across the five companies that made up an oil and gas conglomerate. The project sponsor and the project manager wanted to report on how far we had come over the two years since project inception, and how much progress had been made in achieving SOX 404 compliance. They both had decided that there was a lot of information that needed to be given to each of the attendees, and so binders would be the most useful way to do that. Then, the project sponsor went out of town to attend two family crises and to take her exam for an MBA. She was not thinking clearly, and left it to the project manager to plan and oversee the creation of the binders.

One of the analysts was then asked to put the binders together. After an hour or so of working, he advised the project manager that there was a lot of work and that a couple of temporary clerical staff should be brought in to do the work so that we could save money, but that did not happen. It took three full days (at a substantial contractor rate) to put them together, and by the last half of the last day, both the project manager and the other business analyst were also working on them. At the team meeting imme-diately after the end of the conference, the project sponsor sat there flipping through papers and stated, "I can't believe how much I just spent on putting binders together. I got in trouble for this."

While the binder incident may seem like a trivial and isolated incident, the reality is that it is all too common on projects and in organizations where business analysts do not have a functional manager to report to outside of the project. In our SWOT analysis we explored how confusing it can be to resources and processes when there is only direction coming from the project manager and that direction is not augmented by direction from a functional manager that can help ensure that situations like these don't happen.

Unfortunately, in the same way the boutique firm lost hundreds of thousands of dollars because of the lack of an email spam filter, many companies are also los-ing money where less important clerical tasks (like binder creation) are being done by high-paid contractors rather than by a clerical resource, simply due to a lack of planning.

In the database incident, there was one month left on the project before the project manager determined that we needed to set up the knowledge base for the process library. It was established in CARDMap, and as we started to configure it and enter some of the process names and descriptions, the project manager announced that she wanted to extend the contract by another six months, at substantial cost, because she had just realized that the thousands of process flows, which had been mapped out during two years, had duplicate names, and that this must be corrected before the process flows could be catalogued into the process library.

Both the "database" and "binder" incidents showcase the need for careful planning and the establishment of some basic infrastructure prior to the execution of the requirements and the real work because it alleviates large and compounded headaches later on. In this case, had some simple housekeeping questions been asked and answered early on, the project would not have required an extension to clean up the deliverables and artifacts.

Not yet convinced by the need for planning? Well, how about this situation: You have newly joined a project that has been ongoing for two years. The day before you joined, the project team had finally implemented the first phase of the project (a year and a half late), and things blew up. I'm not just saying that the system that was built and implemented crashed; I mean all of the other systems it interacted with blew up as well. This included billing. Finance was not very happy about having to perform weekly manual billing for about 60,000 customers.

Therefore, it is up to the whole project team to figure out what went wrong and fix it. Trying to read the requirements document is pointless because it is over 200 pages of ambiguity, and there is no traceability and no requirements management tool; no one on the team seems to know what was built and implemented. It is a total nightmare! Trying to find answers, you pick through team emails and spend countless hours and days trying to find clues. Once the gap analysis has been completed, you discover that the development team completely ignored the requirements documents.

Here is what was supposed to happen: The company had an insurance risk program that was out dated, and the automated systems running it had always been broken (it was hobbled together). So, they decided to transition to a new program that would replace it. The new program would run in parallel with the old program for two years while the customers in the program transitioned into the new one through renewals. A completely new system was to be built to run and automate the new program. Nevertheless, that is not what happened.

The development team looked at the old system and determined that some of the existing functionality should be duplicated and reused in the new system. Again, this did not happen. The first thing to go wrong was that the main server that the old program resided on was decommissioned, and the code for the program was segmented onto four new servers. Then, the team did not actually duplicate the code; they integrated the new program and its code into the old code. Before doing this, they did not create a backup in case the new system had to be backed out.

They were more than a bit surprised when it broke. Well, it was broken to start with! They went into "blame the BA" mode when they had to halt the project to fix the 396 bugs that were discovered in testing. It was not until a heated meeting between business analysts, developers, and the project manager that the truth of what happened came to light. At that point, the business analysts insisted that we be allowed to review the functionality of the old program in order to continue. The project manager was defending the position to keep it out of the scope and refused to let the business analyst team review the old program. The business analysts told the project manager it had to be brought in for the team to be able to do their jobs and fix the broken program, and to define requirements for the next iteration.

In this same scenario, the business analysis team lead prepared the biggest gap assessment package that she had ever done. Sometime later, during a meeting, business management asked the project manager pointedly about it, and she said that she would investigate the full extent of the root cause of the issues. The project manager asked the development lead how much of the new program had been integrated with the old program, and the response was: "All of it. It is fully integrated."

Where were the answers? It took a lot of digging to figure this out and find answers in the root cause analysis. Planning requirements could have prevented much of this situation because the team would have been prepared for things to go wrong and known how to mitigate the expected issues that could arise. As it was, the project was grossly over budget and long overdue, and no one was prepared to find and fix errors; because of the lack of traceability and requirements planning, no one really knew what they were looking for.

The Golden Rules of Requirements

While there are many opinions about how to achieve requirements success, one thing is certain: each of those opinions is based on a set of basic principles and a "rules" to follow.

However, this is where principles and rules usually stop. It is not so much what the rules are, but rather, how they are implemented. I think most experienced business analysts can agree that the basic rules are:

1. Identify and define the objectives.
2. Define and document the requirements.
3. Verify the requirements against the objectives.
4. Validate the requirements (apply scenarios and use cases).
5. Review for consistency and ambiguity.

So, why do we still struggle if we are following this basic set of rules, even if we are implementing them differently? In part, the struggle is due to the fact that not everyone is actually verifying and validating the requirements.

I recall, recently, that someone asked me if you still had to validate and verify stand-alone requirements. Well, yes! Why build *anything* that does not align to the business objectives or is wrong?

I think we are all writing requirements the way that most people diet. We are looking for a quick way to get the job done without having to do any of the heavy lifting involved because it is too difficult. We substitute various tools and iterative or compressed techniques the way some people go through diet pills. The reality is that it should not matter what tools you are using if you know, understand, and apply the basic and fundamental workout behind requirements definition. That means understanding why certain tasks are done and the value that they add to the project, as well as where they fit into the rules.

Nevertheless, you also have to take some time to learn and hone the underlying skills like muscles to flex (such as effective listening, facilitation, and assertiveness), so that you can apply and utilize them more effectively. Only then can you become adept at applying the rules of requirements in a way that gets the job done as proficiently as possible.

REQUIREMENTS DEFINITION AND ANALYSIS

Before we can really begin to reshape business analysis, we have to fundamentally change the way that we think about *requirements*. The evolution of business analysis has changed requirements from the core of what business analysts do, to one item of the many on the task list that an analyst is assigned. While it remains true that many of the tasks performed by business analysts are intended to define, analyze, and clarify requirements, there is more to it. In addition, we have to shift the way that we think of the requirements themselves.

In the past, requirements were a collection of business needs and wants clustered together into some kind of fashion in an attempt to paint a picture of the business solution at a granular level. Today, however, requirements are more like *decomposed* business needs. In this way, they have changed from user-centric activities and depictions to business-centric, needs-focused solutions at the micro-level. Why is this distinction important?

Well, the business analyst is no longer tasked with discovering and documenting wish lists from users and user groups, but resolving specific issues and problems, and creating specific results for the business. In order to move from wish lists to results-oriented solutions, we have to understand that there is a fundamental difference between needs, wants, and expectations.

Needs are the things that are necessary for the business to create or put into place in order to achieve the necessary or essential results, whereas *wants* are really just the desires of individual users and user groups. Wants and needs are often in conflict. The wants can be asynchronous to the long-term objectives of the business, as they tend to meet only a limited set of criteria under a specific set of circumstances, and are neither forward-looking nor focused on the bigger picture. Expectations, on the other hand, are the set of criteria determined by the business and the stakeholders that determine how the needs will be met.

This means that requirements are now driven by the needs and results of the business as a whole, instead of driven by the desire of individuals within the business. In itself, this shift in thinking changes the way in which requirements are exposed, defined, analyzed, and then validated.

In high-level terms, *requirements* are the detailed systems and process specifications that are used by the project team in order to create the solution(s) needed by the business. The architecture team utilizes these specifications to design new systems or create enhancements to existing systems. The specifications are also utilized by the development team in order to build a system, as required by the business. Finally, system specifications are subsequently used by the quality assurance and testing team(s) to test and validate the solution against the requirements, to ensure alignment of the solution to the defined components, and to meet the business needs.

The process by which requirements are compiled and documented (often referred to erroneously as "gathering") is the uncovering of business and functional specifications (features) that define, dictate, and determine how the new system, process, or application must behave in order to meet the business needs, goals, and objectives. As shown in Figure 2.5, the general process for requirements tasks are:

1. Elicitation, research, and analysis;
2. Elaboration and specification; and
3. Verification and validation.

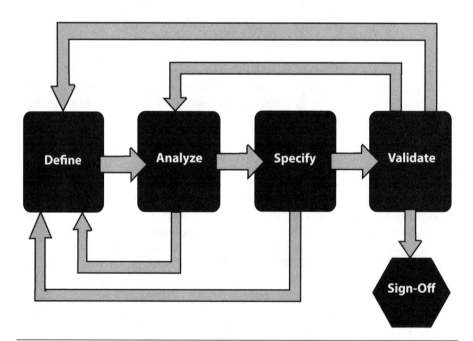

Figure 2.5 Requirements tasks

For each stage, there are key activities that must be performed in order to be successful at creating the right solution for the business and to ensure that it aligns to the business' overall strategic goals.

Within elicitation, the analyst spends time working with key stakeholders and the general business user groups in order to understand the needs and the problems they want solved, but also to find out the primary results that they are looking for in a solution. This requires the application of various techniques, and that specific skills and characteristics are utilized, in order to accomplish this work. Not every analyst can do these sets of tasks effectively and efficiently, and as a result, the business often completes some or all of this work themselves or brings in a project manager or consultant to uncover the needs and outline the problem and the solution.

Unfortunately, when this happens, the analyst is not available to provide business insight into the alignment of the project plan to the strategic plan or contribute other information that they may have about either the business or the industry. Quite often, a solution gets pinpointed, and the project to develop and implement it is commenced without adequately reviewing viable alternatives and how they might create the results that the business needs. This is quite simply because others tend to focus on the immediate problem or stated need, instead of the *results* that the business wishes to achieve now and in the future.

Within research and analysis, the analyst spends their time working to analyze the information they have collected from the stakeholders and general business user groups in order to make sense of it and to create a cohesive set of specifications that can be consumed by the other teams downstream. That means they typically utilize critical thinking, problem solving, and analytical thinking skills that will enable them to create a picture from the puzzle pieces that they have accumulated.

Unfortunately, this is an area where the typical analyst may rely simply on gap analysis, instead of finding and applying other comparative techniques that would enable them to evaluate the information and plan the solution more effectively. As a result, incomplete requirements are often missing vital information and critical data that is required for the other teams to perform their work effectively. Instead, these downstream teams are left to "assume" or fill in the blanks on missing information, and hope for the best.

Recommended techniques for analysis include decision tabling, scenario planning, and workflow and data flow mapping in order to ensure that all pieces are accounted for and all possible scenarios are planned. It is also important that the analyst renders the data and information in multiple ways so that any gaps can be exposed through the various types of depictions.

Analysts cannot simply apply one validation technique and consider the deliverables to be a complete and accurate set of requirements. Looking at data and information from all angles is one of the few ways of discovering areas of potential misunderstanding by others and ensuring that no important information is missing.

The next stage is the elaboration and specification of the requirements into the actual document deliverable. Again, to accomplish this task, the analyst requires a set of skills that enable them to write well and be able to edit the work of others critically. This requires both planning and organization, so that the understanding of the analyst can be systematically and logically documented in such a way that the information is easy to digest by the document consumers.

Here, the most common errors that analysts make are the use of jargon (e.g., nicknames) and the use of "$10 words" instead of "$2 words." In other words, they use flowery, "Shakespearean" language meant to be impressive instead of simple language that is easy to read and consume. Consider that most daily newspapers are written at the 8th grade level. This is because the average reader can read and process the information at a faster rate than they can with large, less commonly used words.

The Seinfeld Approach to Requirements

Software industry stats clearly show there is an urgent need for dramatic and immediate improvement to the way we develop IT products. Only 32% of software and technical projects are successful; of the successful ones, only 7% of the implemented features are used all the time, and 45% are never used at all![1] With some math applied to those numbers that means that only 0.22% of all proposed features are actually implemented and used!

The single-most common reason for those alarming statistics is the requirements. A lack of practical formalization, and lack of a holistic view of the causes and effects of failure, have led to the "shotgun approach" to requirements. Periodic successes with this approach have, in turn led business analysts to believe that the fault lies elsewhere in the process.

In a nutshell, we approach requirements the same way we approach any other communication or conversation. Most communications and conversations are one-sided and egocentric. The TV show, *Seinfeld*, was an excellent example of multiple people carrying on conversations in the same room without either listening to each other or being heard. Translate this same situation into requirements gathering and you get ambiguity, miscommunication, and missed requirements.

The solution is that we need to streamline the requirements process and follow the SMART ideology. The process must be specific, measureable, achievable, repeatable, and timed. Think of requirements like a recipe. If the recipe called for flour and a little bit of sugar, then said to "cook until done," could you possibly make the recipe? Not unless you took the time to go through countless trial and error cycles and created a prototype in each cycle. Wait, that sounds like the average development project!

We would have better luck creating recipes and requirements in the same way that we conduct a science experiment: Define the expected outcome, determine the specific measures we will use, and verify the results. At this point, I realize that you are going to argue that we verify during testing. The fact is that testing verifies the product against the defined requirements. When they differ or the requirements are wrong, we have testers pondering if they should be testing the product as it was developed, or

---

[1]The Standish Group. (2010). Chaos Report.

testing it against the defined requirements. The truth is that if you develop the product defined in the requirements, there is nothing left to wonder.

Unfortunately, what happens is that when requirements are poorly defined, validated, and communicated, development occurs based on the misunderstood requirements and testing exposes the gaps between them, causing struggles in reconciling the differences.

During the requirements activities, you need to start the traceability process so that when you face issues and ambiguities later on, you can follow the thread and fully understand the differences between functional and nonfunctional requirements.

Many analysts use traceability solely to find issues in requirements once they have been identified down the road in testing, but the real function of traceability is to follow the line from the strategic plan and business goals—to scope, requirements, and developed product—through testing to implementation to demonstrate that the strategy has been implemented. This means showing that identified goals were met, how and where they were being met, what issues occurred during development, and how those issues were dealt with and ultimately resolved.

What is frustrating in interviewing business analysts is getting the same uninventive responses from about 90% of them. Typically, when I interview analysts, I ask questions based on my skills matrix and their résumés. However, there are two questions that they are guaranteed to get. The first is, "How do you define requirements?" Disturbingly, the single most common answer is, "I go to the user." When I get this answer, they are guaranteed to get the second, follow-up question, "What do you do when the user doesn't know?" and several people will get that wrong because they get stumped. At that point, they had better prove they are going to be ready and open to mentoring and display some value that they would bring to the table.

Unfortunately, far too many business analysts assume that the user knows the technical details of the project and what they want. That is exactly why we need to redefine requirements as the specifications for delivering the necessary results for the client. These results should be androgynous to the solution until the solution has been defined, and even then, I would argue that we should not hang onto it too tightly in case it turns out to be the wrong solution, or it is just not feasible or practical to implement.

It is one thing to gather and document requirements, but that is really only half of the task. We also have to verify the requirements before we start the design and development process. When you consider that 60 to 80%[2] of the cost of rework in testing is used to fix requirements, and that the cost of fixing requirements can be as much as $1000 for 1 requirement[3] when you get to this stage, you could potentially save 1.43% of the project budget for each requirement by performing due diligence up front.

---

[2] Lawhorn, B. (2010). Presentation on software failure. Adapted from Meta Group research.
[3] King, T. & Marasco, J. (2010). What is the cost of a requirement error? *Sticky Minds*. Retrieved from http://www.stickyminds.com/sitewide.asp?ObjectId=12529&Function=edetail&ObjectType=ART#top

REQUIREMENTS VERIFICATION AND VALIDATION

The question of how deeply you dive into requirements before you hit design snags is the subject of much debate with developer colleagues. The problem is that they do not seem to understand that requirements are not merely the result of business analysts making notes during short, sporadic meetings with stakeholders and user groups.

Requirements are a collaborative effort between business analysts and developers throughout the project. High-level requirements start with scope and drill down to the next level of detail. Business analysts tend to make the mistake of attempting to get as much down on paper as they can and write really detailed requirements upfront.

The fact is that high level requirements are basically the same list as the scope and work breakdown structure. They are quite simply the next level of detail from scope. Most analysts will not do a mid-level set of requirements as they conduct research and analysis to extract greater levels of detail. They jump right from the high level to the very detailed. Unfortunately, not enough analysis can occur here to provide designers with adequate details to create a thorough technical design.

Validation of requirements is a team sport, and I do not just mean the business analyst team. The single most effective tool you can use for validation is the ambiguity log for tracking requirements ambiguities. That means your team should be distributing the unfinished requirements document to the developers, designers, and testers for review. Ask them to log their ambiguities in the main ambiguity log. This gives the analyst team items that they need to address in requirements. Pay careful attention to the sentiment, what it is the others don't get or understand. This is pushing the responsibility for understanding onto the developers that basically only know what they read at this point and forces them to communicate what they don't understand.

Once the document deliverable has been created and reviewed by the analyst team in a peer review, it is imperative that the contents of the document are verified and validated. To verify the requirements, the analyst is essentially confirming that the solution meets the business needs by creating the results that they expressed at the start of the project. They then complete a set of activities that requires the analysts to apply a set of specific techniques in order to ensure that the document and contents are clear, consistent, complete, and accurate. Next, the analysts work with the architecture, development, and quality assurance teams to ensure that the requirements are understood as written, that there is sufficient detail for them to complete their work without assumptions and that there are no critical system or data elements missing.

Again, the analyst utilizes a set of techniques that enables them to render the information in multiple ways in order to expose the gaps and holes in the information and the language. One of the things to remember here is that when we write any document, whether it is a letter, or a book or technical requirements, we may not always write in complete thoughts, but when editing them, we may not see that it is incomplete because our brains fill in the missing information. That is why it is very important to conduct a peer review. During this peer review, we should be looking for and exposing gaps in thought as well as gaps in information and the best way to do this is by applying the principles of an ambiguity review. This type of review highlights and exposes basic language that can cloud the meaning of the words and leave the author and individual readers with multiple interpretations of the same set of requirements.

Verification and validation is a critical part of business analysis activities because it ensures that what has been specified actually aligns to the needs and will indeed create the desired results, but also because it ensures that the language is clear and the thoughts and logic within those thoughts are complete. Unfortunately, this is an area where many analysts struggle because of the lack of consistent formal process and the understanding of how to achieve this outcome at this stage.

Many believe that interpretation is solely the responsibility of the architects, developers and the testers and that they have no role in ensuring that what they *intended* to write is actually interpreted by the readers. This would be true if this were poetry, where one phrase can have multiple interpretations and it actually lends to the feelings evoked in the reader every time they reread it. But this is not poetry, and the analyst is solely responsible for ensuring that what is interpreted is actually the message intended. Again, the ambiguity review and workshop sessions are the ideal setting to create this understanding by walking through the requirements "brick by brick" in order to discuss the meaning and expectations of the individual requirement sets.

In order to ensure that business analysis is conducted effectively, with quantifiable and qualified outcomes, the analysts must follow a standard process that involves these principles and basic sets of techniques for both requirements development and management.

REQUIREMENTS MANAGEMENT

Requirements management is the set of activities that are performed in order to manage the requirements deliverables from the start of the project to implementation, as shown in Figure 2.6. Both individual requirements elements and collective requirement sets are managed to ensure that if and when changes are necessary, they can be made easily, and that each requirement and its collective requirement set can be traced back to the goals and drivers of the project to ensure alignment of the solution to the business needs.

Managing requirements is important not only to account for alignment of the solution and to reduce the time to make changes or corrections (Figure 2.7), but also to ensure that the benefits are realized by the business through the production of the component features that will deliver the proposed benefits at the rate at which they are expected. In this way, requirements management is more than just identifying the requirements and placing them in a document or other storage bin, but it is also an extension of benefits realization planning.

In my earlier example of the insurance project that was to automate a new risk program, the second thing that would have prevented some of the major issues that arose would have been management of the requirements. As it was, the development team ignored the requirements but this was not discovered until a new resource was

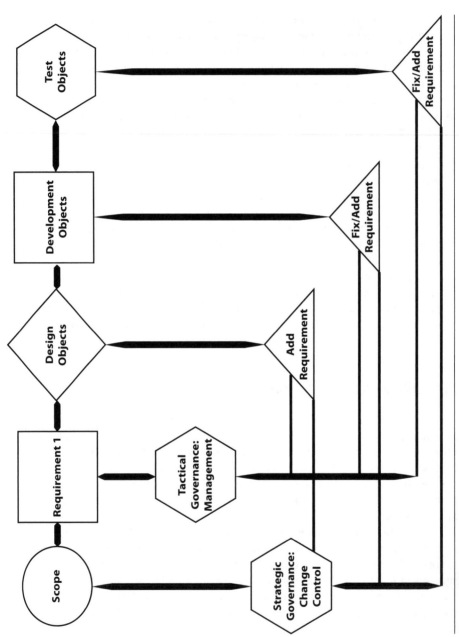

Figure 2.6 Requirements management

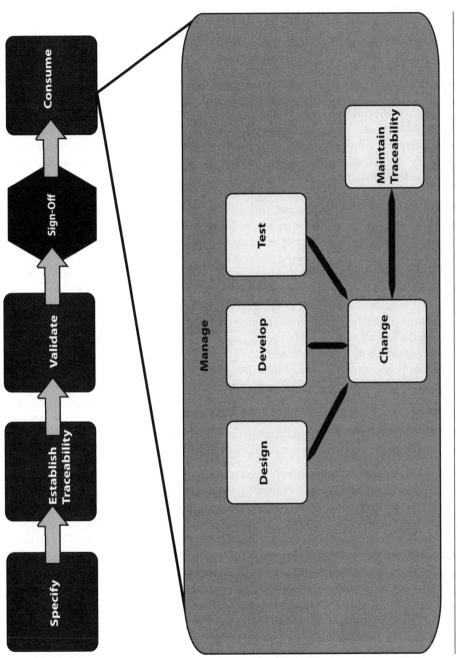

Figure 2.7 Change control

brought on board and that resource dug around to find out what had been developed and implemented in order to establish traceability and report back to the business. That new resource would also not have wasted hundreds of hours picking through countless email threads just to establish what the project was trying to accomplish and how, if only requirements management had been in place.

Adequate management of requirements greatly improves the effectiveness and efficiency with which business analysts are able to perform their tasks. It does this by providing the means of capturing, indexing, searching and making changes to requirements across the project life cycle and frees the analyst to focus on the content and accuracy of the requirements themselves instead of all of the trivial housekeeping of trying to keep them sorted and coherent.

At a tactical level, requirements management should look like the early establishment of the templates and systems for the capture and ongoing management of the individual requirements elements. Once the requirements elicitation activities have begun, it should look like a complete end-to-end system (whether that is manual or automated in a tool), to ensure that there is a common repository for collection of the individual elements as they are captured and exposed, a set of common tools and tasks for analyzing the requirements for logical consistency, completeness, and ambiguity.

In addition, management is the ongoing measurement of progress and quality against the established benchmarks in order to monitor issues and identify trends that impact the overall requirements process and resulting quality. It is the coordination and organization of resources in order to achieve a specified outcome through work. That means you must not only control the work being done, but the pace as well. This implies that there is a set of quantifiable attributes that we can observe as the work is being done, and that there are specific factors that will either positively or negatively impact the work and progress being made.

In order to benchmark and quantify the work being done and the progress being made, some of the metrics that can be collected include:

- How many requirements are being captured from all sources?
- How long has it taken to capture these requirements?
- What types of requirements have been captured?
- What types of issues have occurred during design, development, and test?
- How many requirements have been changed or modified as a result of issues?
- How many requirements were successfully developed and implemented?
- How many requirements were modified as a result of ambiguity?
- How long did it take to correct issues?

Each of these questions can be answered to establish a benchmark for requirements before they are passed through subsequent phases of development and be tested in order to understand and identify trends in development, as well as trends in requirements issues. Having this understanding will enable the tactical team to better plan for and prepare for ongoing requirements techniques and will enable them to correct issues as they arise.

Metrics and benchmarks should be built into the management system so that they feed into the governance system automatically when requirements are entered into the system by analysts. While they must be established as a part of management, they must be monitored as a part of governance, and the bulk of what the analyst team sees and does to contribute to both management and governance is to enter their requirements and changes per the protocol of the system to ensure traceability from scope all the way through to testing.

A specific factor that is less quantifiable, but nonetheless will have a significant impact on requirements, is the level of team communication and collaboration. In the absence of consistent and specific communication, we can end up with false assumptions and misinterpretations that cause costly errors down the road. Through the establishment of a communication and collaboration framework, we are able to ensure that the teams communicate and that we are all accountable for contributing information that will lead to the development of the right solution.

BENCHMARKING REQUIREMENTS

It is one thing to recognize that requirements need to change and improve, and completely another thing to target exact areas for improvement and understand the degree of improvement needed. There is a lot of controversy on requirements improvement and traceability, but there does not seem to be a lot of discussion about how to measure and quantify those improvements.

To understand what aspects of requirements need to be improved, you have to approach them in the same way that you would any other improvement project: Determine the kinds of metrics that you can gather for requirements and then analyze those metrics to determine and understand the starting point.

Setting a benchmark allows you to illustrate the current situation and determine the levels and types of professional development your business analysts will need. Establishing milestones provides you with the ability to perform a comparison at various points during the improvement process and to determine the effectiveness of your efforts.

To set both benchmarks and milestones, it is important to understand the tools that will provide the metrics that you will use for assessing your requirements at key stages such as starting (benchmarking) and subsequent checkpoints (milestones). Some requirements tools will come with a couple of built-in metrics for traceability, but in reality, there is yet to be a single tool that will compile a full set of standardized metrics to support a true requirements improvement initiative.

At the basic level, you can easily identify the volume of requirements, which becomes more precise when you follow a standard numbering and classification protocol. Quite simply, it is a count of the documented, low-level requirements.

The next basic metric that you can gather is the time to complete each stage of the requirements life cycle (as a separate subset of the software development life cycle).

This will take some dedication on the part of your staff to report if you are not using a tool that will provide timestamps at various points during the cycle.

During a typical life cycle, the next quantifiable metric that you can compile is the volume of requirements actually designed, built, and implemented by the design and development team. Ideally, this information is available in your traceability tool, and traces back to both the mid- and high-level requirements and to project scope. If it is not, it will take some wrangling and negotiating to survey the designers and developers to extract this information from them.

In most organizations, you will be able to compile the volumes of passed and failed testing. While this will give you an approximate sense of how well you did over-all during requirements, it is simply not detailed enough to help you understand trends in requirements and identifying the specific activities for improvement.

So what do all these pockets of metrics mean? How can we compile, analyze, and compare them to understand how effective your requirements practices are? You can use the volume of requirements divided by the time it takes to complete each step to understand how many requirements are completed in a day.

In addition, compiling ambiguity metrics using a formal ambiguity log allows you to identify, understand, and monitor trends in specific types of requirements issues that crop up and impact the overall quality of requirements. By adding this metric to the formula, you will be able to measure the full effectiveness of your requirements techniques and activities.

By comparing the metrics of individual projects across your organization, specific opportunities for improvement will become apparent. In fact, this understanding of organizational requirements effectiveness will enable targeted areas of development for your business analyst team, improved collaboration between project teams, and support organizational agility.

TACTICAL (TASK-ORIENTED) GOVERNANCE

Tactical, or *task-oriented, governance* is the ground-level monitoring and reporting of the metrics that indicate and measure compliance in the application of the strategic level processes and policies to ensure that the end solution aligns to the business need, and is developed in a manner that is financially responsible and sustainable.

It is important to monitor compliance to the established protocol at all levels, and to be able to pinpoint issues at a granular level, so that they may be resolved, as shown in Figure 2.8. One way to monitor compliance is by utilizing metrics as an indicator of key attributes, such as how often things are done, quality of results, effectiveness of the activities, time spent, and productivity of the team.

Governance impacts business analysis by ensuring that the end product aligns with the strategic objectives of the company, the product is sustainable through financial responsibility, and the team is financially accountable for the effectiveness of the practices used to create it. In other words, this is how a company establishes and

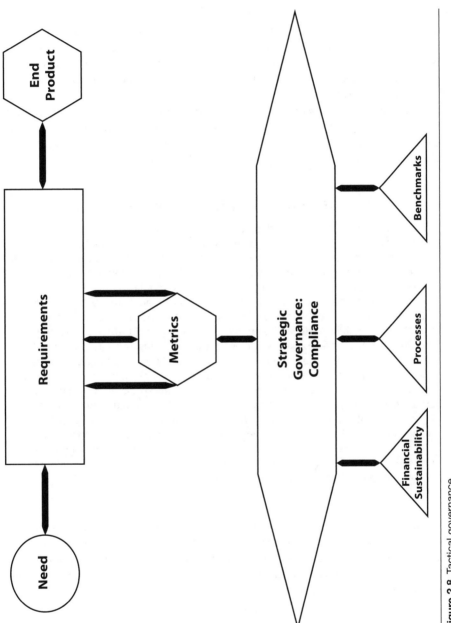

Figure 2.8 Tactical governance

maintains lean management principles within business analysis. Without this view, it would be difficult to quantify the value that business analysts bring to the table, and companies might double up roles or make cuts by role in order to save money. Governance leads to the formalization and establishment of consistent processes and measures that indicate the levels to which roles and tasks are being performed to produce the needed results.

From a business analyst perspective, monitoring follows the established protocol without shortcuts because there is accountability at the tactical level to do so. There is a chain of responsibility in place to ensure that people do not cut corners when they are tired or frustrated, or they simply don't know how else to get it done.

Governance In The Real World

Kosher butchery industry practices are an example of governance at its best. Traditional Kosher laws are very specific about the way in which an animal is to be butchered for eating. The laws are in place so that the animal does not suffer, and the people eating the meat can be assured that no shortcuts were made simply because they were more convenient for the butcher.

For starters, there are always two individuals present: the butcher and a rabbi. The butcher is the person who applies the specific techniques to kill the animal instantly and painlessly, while the rabbi is there to ensure that if the animal does suffer or linger for even a little bit, the meat is not used for a Kosher diet, and in many cases, is not used for human consumption. Next, the two people work together to ensure that the meat produced is high quality and adheres to the strict principles of Kashruth, Jewish dietary law. For many consumers, this type of close monitoring not only means that they can enjoy a humanely obtained meal, but also that when it says "beef" on the package, it means beef. Mechanically separated beef, chicken, pork, and/or other ingredients of a meat-like substance, are guaranteed to be absent. The point here is that the requirements, combined with oversight (governance), ensure the quality of the final product are preserved end-to-end.

This overview of the model for business analysis services provides a high-level look at the specific tasks that comprise an end-to-end services model. By detailing the steps and stages of business analysis, the model serves as a reference point for the remainder of the discussion and enables us to shift the perspective on the position and contributions of business analysts.

The model also demonstrates the full value that business analysis brings to the technology discussion, and in this way, business analysis is no longer just a medium for the transcription and relating of requirements from the business to the development teams. According to this model, business analysis services are major factors in the alignment of the technology solutions to the business strategy and provide the vehicle for business continuity.

In fact, each element of this model supports the premise that business analysis is the enablement of strategy. Each task, as well as the underlying activities for each task, culminates in the analyst's ability to bring strategic goals to life through the development of specific solutions and requirements. It is the overall governance, planning, and management of these tasks that ensure that the deliverables align to the goals and needs, and actually create the requirements deliverables that are necessary for the other groups in the project team to develop the right solution.

In the next chapter, the relationship between careful planning and management of business analysis services and business analyst resources is further discussed, as well as how that can be used to ensure that business analysts are meeting their objectives and obligations to the business, ultimately leading to business continuity.

3

BUSINESS ANALYSIS STEWARDSHIP

This chapter discusses the impetus and obligation of business analysis services to protect the interests of the business, while serving as a key enabler of business strategy. It outlines the connection between the planning and management of methods and resources to the achievement of the strategic goals of the company, while remaining accountable for financial sustainability throughout the process.

Where business analysis is the process of translating specific items identified in the strategic plans into tangible systems and applications or into business protocol and automated processes, Business Analysis Stewardship is the careful and deliberate planning and management of the business analysis resources.

Business Analysis Stewardship accomplishes one primary objective, as shown in Figure 3.1. That objective is to safeguard and protect the interests of the business during the development of its technological tools and products, which is accomplished by:

- Ensuring that solutions that are developed preserve the financial sustainability of the business.
- Positioning the business to maintain its existing business operations.
- Positioning the business to expand through new opportunities.
- Helping the business remain competitive.
- Helping the business achieve or maintain compliance with specific mandates or regulations.

Business Analysis Stewardship, as with other types of stewardship, is in place to ensure that the organization is financially stable and accountable, and the organization utilizes planning, management techniques, and strategies to ensure that its processes are affordable and sustainable over the long term. Effectively, *Business Analysis Stewardship* is a partnership between the technology organization and business

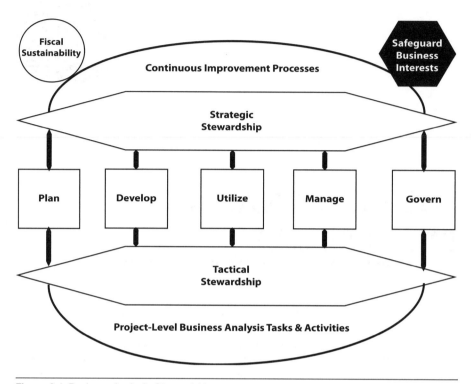

Figure 3.1 Business Analysis Stewardship

analysis services organization to ensure fiscal responsibility, compliance to corporate objectives (vision, mission, policies), and quality outcomes so that the practices, processes, and management utilized in the development of technology-based products support the long-term sustainability of the business.

The concept of Business Analysis Stewardship aligns both directly and indirectly to the business analysis model presented in Chapter 2. The model represents the direct and implied business analysis tasks that must be accomplished in order to comply with the objectives of Business Analysis Stewardship. The specific tasks that align directly to the business analysis model are needs analysis, stakeholder alignment, benefits realization planning, and tactical (task-oriented) governance. Stewardship is demonstrated indirectly through the business analysis model within the various requirements tasks.

Within each of the aligned tasks, it is demonstrated that employing clear and deliberate tactics and processes that are predetermined and planned will minimize wasted time and effort, while increasing the quality of end results. To achieve this, within each activity that comprises a given task, the deliverables and tactics employed are consistently measured for quality and productivity; the ongoing measurement and application of each tactic is diligently monitored; and the data from these stewardship tactics are rolled up into a well-established and consistent improvement process.

From an operational perspective, the organization has implemented stewardship strategies by developing task-specific processes for the planning, management, auditing, optimization (re-engineering), and utilization of the techniques at a strategic and tactical level. Business Analysis Stewardship changes the way in which the organization supports, sponsors, and utilizes business analyst resources. The organization is responsible to stop hiding its bad practices and poor management like unorganized clutter in the closet that no one really wants to sort and throw out. Taking responsibility in a Stewardship model unites the company with the technology organization in a close-knit marriage that is mutually beneficial and respectful, without the traditional competition of who is leading who. It is support and interconnectedness that enable divisions of the company to understand the vision and mission of the entire company, and how that will be accomplished through strategic planning. Then, each party can contribute to the long-term goals and health of the organization with new ideas for technology that will meet the strategic plans.

The Business Analysis Stewardship model makes the business analyst a mediator and conciliator because s/he has the skills and position to provide counseling to both of the parties that will make this happen, the company and the technology. You could say that analysts are like the neurons between two halves of the brain whose task it is to transmit messages back and forth to bridge a divide that would otherwise exist.

In any case, Business Analysis Stewardship affects the ways in which everyone works, including business analysts. Stewardship is really an obligation that we all have to be accountable for the organization's health and finances. It changes the ways that analysts do their jobs because there is suddenly more accountability. As analysts, we will know that we are not in the working relationship merely to please others or make them feel good about themselves by taking orders.

Again, Business Analysis Stewardship is performed at two levels, strategic (operational) and tactical (task-oriented). From an operational perspective, it is a strategic role for a senior analyst to audit and then optimize the business analysis practice area by developing the techniques, activities, deliverable templates, management, and governance processes that will be employed by the organization to oversee business analysis and ensure the support and financial responsibility of the whole organization. Everyone at the top of this chain, once implemented, is practicing Business Analysis Stewardship because each person is responsible for ensuring the ongoing maintenance, alignment, accountability, and optimization of the practices over the long term.

From a tactical level, Business Analysis Stewardship ensures alignment of the individual program or project to the overall initiatives by making sure that all program or project resources employ and apply the specified techniques and that each component operates in accordance to the operational goals. For an analyst who is on the team (a tactical resource), Business Analysis Stewardship ensures that their performance complies with the mandates and directives of the governing body. This means that they will employ and apply the techniques as directed and report the results back to the body for ongoing governance and improvements.

Tactical business analysis resources achieve stewardship on a project-by-project basis through specific activities that have been defined in the business analysis model, and through careful planning and management of those activities as they are being performed. Therefore, Business Analysis Stewardship is the responsibility of both the organization and the tactical business analysis resources to properly plan, develop, utilize, manage, and govern techniques for performing business analysis activities. This ensures that current business analysis processes are strategically aligned to the business objectives, and that they are applied at the tactical level to create alignment between the individual solution and the specific objectives derived from the strategic plans.

On a strategic level, Business Analysis Stewardship is the planning and management of the business analysis resources themselves. This ensures that the tactical resources are held accountable and maintain compliance throughout each of the activities.

By planning and managing the processes and techniques utilized in the performance of business analysis activities, the business analysts ensure that the outcomes are both financially affordable and sustainable over time. The implication is that the business analyst is obligated to collaborate with the stakeholders to proactively protect the interests of the business, through the responsible use and protection of the client's resources, by utilizing sustainable development practices. It also implies that the business analyst is responsible for the quality of the deliverables that are consumed by the other teams throughout the development process.

In this way, the senior business analyst that practices Business Analysis Stewardship can be working full-time with a program manager to measure and monitor the ongoing health of individual programs and to support project initiation when change is needed. However, it is more likely that the senior business analyst will employ the stewardship tactics while they are leading a team of other analysts.

You see, the team lead is really like the navigator on a ship. S/he ensures that the ship sails towards its destination in the fastest time possible and that it avoids unnecessary obstacles. The crew then complies with that navigation plan and ensures that the ship remains on course unless and until it either changes course or the ship reaches the destination. In business analysis, this means that the analysts work with the techniques mandated by the governing body to accomplish the goals of the project, but also to ensure that the individual project is actually going to meet the objectives and maintain alignment to the company's strategic goals. The critical thing to note is that it is not about keeping the team lead happy and appeasing their ego. Unfortunately, egos can be the biggest barrier to proper Business Analysis Stewardship because individual analysts are segregated from each other and thus can become more concerned with keeping an individual happy rather than meeting the business objectives and ensuring that the project is set up for success. One issue when appeasement happens is that the person giving the directions may often give directions that are biased towards themselves, and therefore, compete with or be in direct contradiction to the objectives of the company.

Remember the binder story described in Chapter 2? In that example, the higher-cost analyst created the binders in order to appease the ego of the project manager, and for no other reason. When it was suggested that temporary, low-cost resources should be brought in to accomplish the work, the project manager felt that her judgment was being questioned and wanted to enforce her authority, so she refused to bring on clerical staff. In the end, such a costly maneuver was not in the best interests of the company. Unfortunately, the project sponsor did not hold her accountable, and instead took full responsibility for the decision.

Unfortunately, this incident is really only a smaller example of widespread trends when it comes to time spent in housekeeping tasks. All too often when we calculate the cost of requirements, we only consider the overall cost of the resource per hour. When we look at ways to improve costs in business analysis, we are not really performing any type of real value-stream mapping, we just accept that the nonautomated tasks or even the housekeeping tasks that could be done more cost effectively are the "cost of doing business." However this case highlights an overall lack of Business Analysis Stewardship because stewardship demands that all of those who practice it are accountable to the organization for meeting the overall objectives and are also responsible for utilizing financially sustainable methods and resources, thereby implying that stewards are assertive about the needs of the organization.

To be successful with stewardship, business analysts must also demonstrate and possess key competencies. The competencies will enable them to perform the two primary responsibilities within stewardship: conduct business analysis in ways that meet the objective, and manage and hold analysts accountable for their performance of tasks and overall alignment to the objective.

The competencies outlined in this book defined as soft skills and personal traits are really those competencies that predispose individual business analysts to success in Business Analysis Stewardship. The specific competencies that align to successful outcomes and performance in stewardship are assertiveness, conflict resolution, change management, and negotiation.

Overall, Business Analysis Stewardship permeates the business analysis model, the functional management model, services delivery models, and engagement models presented in this book because it provides a guiding objective for the entire business analysis profession. Business Analysis Stewardship provides both context and focus for business analysis services as a key enabler of business strategy. It is a means of maximizing technology investments through the planning and management of business analysis methods and resources.

The information gained from stewardship can be utilized to reposition business analysis services for both the business and technology organizations to effectively maximize information technology spending, and achieve close alignment between the products and the needs prescribed by the business.

In summary, the main concepts discussed in this chapter were:

- The objective of Business Analysis Stewardship
- How this objective translates into higher quality deliverables
- The role of planning and management in both business analysis methods and resources in the achievement of strategic business objectives
- How Business Analysis Stewardship can be demonstrated at both the operational (strategic) and task-oriented (tactical) levels of business analysis

Where the previous chapter outlined a new and appropriate model for business analysis services, this chapter focused on the roles that planning, management, and fiscal responsibility play as key drivers for authentic success in business analysis.

4

FUNCTIONAL GOVERNANCE

A key area where technology fails outright is the governance of business analysis services. Many would argue that failure happens because business analyst roles and resources are still immature. However, I disagree.

If you have a mature organization, and it begins to segregate duties and create new roles, then it must also adopt and employ the governance techniques that it employs in other areas of the business to ensure that the new roles are profitable, adequate, and can be monitored and managed in the same ways that all other roles are. Without this adaptation, there can be no justification for the elimination or combination of roles simply because there are no established criteria for benchmarking value or time spent on the various activities.

Governance is the process of verifying performance and compliance to established protocol in order to ensure consistency, standardization, and optimization of processes, and alignment between the business objectives and outcomes (results) of the work being performed. To accomplish this, governance frameworks contain elements for step-by-step processes and templates for common deliverables, as well as measurements and benchmarks for quality, quantity, effectiveness, productivity, performance, and consistent improvement.

In reference to Business Analysis Stewardship, *functional governance* is utilized by management to hold task-oriented business analysts accountable for meeting the primary objective of stewardship (safeguarding the interests of the business), and for compliance to the processes and methods established to support this objective. Where management's role is to manage both the allocated resources and support compliance to governance protocols, they may or may not dictate the elements, as the elements are typically an extension of the overall business (i.e., how the business has determined that it will manage and govern its activities on a daily basis).

Governance is important because it supports the resources to perform specific work under particular conditions in order to produce predetermined results. This reduces chaos in the work environment by defining "who does what" and "whose job is whose," and by providing a set of standard guidelines for resources to follow every time they perform a given set of tasks. This guidance enables consistency that reduces not only chaos, but also stress and oversight by the management team because they are then free to focus on planning, organizing and reporting more than directing and re-directing. Resources essentially know what to do, how to do it, and what results should look like. When they face issues in performing the activities, they can escalate smaller fires to the manager for resolution and make sure the whole team is on the same page. Business goals are achieved faster and the team evolves as a cohesive unit instead of individual personalities who are constantly competing to look better than each other.

One hallmark of a lack of adequate governance and compliance to governance is micromanagement. Often, micromanagement happens because the manager has to become heavily involved in the daily routines of the resources due to either a lack of protocol to follow or because people do not know what to do. Unfortunately, micro-management brings in a host of other problems that decrease morale and increase the attrition rate. To that end, I would like to explore micromanagement through this problematic lens because it impacts our ability to contribute effectively and can be a damaging factor to governance initiatives.

THE ORGANIZATIONAL IMPACTS OF MICROMANAGEMENT

Micromanagement is a corporate illness. The symptoms are employee attrition, sup-pression of innovation, absenteeism, and loss of productivity. The impact of each symptom is far-reaching and affects both the top and bottom lines of a business.

Jim Rooney,[1] people skills expert at People Smart Tools, describes micromanage-ment as "excessive involvement by a manager with an employee in regard to their performance. In short, it is imposing work standards and behavior expectations that meet the personal needs of the manager, not the employee. It is to control a person or a situation by paying extreme attention to small details." The manager may have good intentions to assist the employee in fulfilling his or her duties, or have self-serving strategic or political motives, or be emotionally insecure, or be a narcissistic control freak. However, regardless of the manager's motives or intent, the employee feels dis-empowered, not trusted to complete work properly, and productivity falls drastically.

Scope of the Problem

One of the biggest problems with micromanagement is the collusion that occurs as the rest of us sit by and watch it happen. We do this for two primary reasons: we want it to just go away and/or we are afraid of becoming the next target. In reality, the micro-manager often targets one person at a time until they each leave or become disengaged.

---

[1]Rooney, Jim (2009). http://biznik.com/articles/from-micromanagement-to-mentoring

Micromanagement is also a form of bullying, which at the very least exposes your organization to risk. No organization would tolerate an employee who sexually harasses another employee. We know that it is clearly wrong. However, micromanagement is not as cut and dry, despite the fact that the organizational symptoms are strikingly similar. At heart, both are control issues and lead to conflict, which impacts retention, innovation, absenteeism, and productivity. It should be noted that these impacts and results could also be seen among the team that is not directly involved, but witnesses the controlling conduct on a daily basis.

The primary reason that workplace conflict results during these symptoms of micromanagement is that we are all basically afraid of conflict; we are endowed with a fight or flight response, and just want it to go away. What ends up happening instead is that we tend to adopt the "see no evil, hear no evil" policy and view the victim as the instigator because they are calling attention to the situation. The victim is shunned and punished for speaking out, and often ends up being forced out.

Jane's Story: An Employee's Perspective

Jane worked for a company for two years. During the first year and a half, Jane was the star, and it seemed she could do no wrong. She got rave reviews from every client and team that she worked with. The corporate executive loved her work, and she was constantly praised for her talent and value to the company. She was known for her innovative work and ideas. She was promoted shortly before Ralph, a new manager, was brought onto her team.

Within a week of starting to report to him, Ralph declared that Jane was incompetent. He inserted himself into a project she was on, insisted on screening all of her deliverables, and requested that the project team only communicate with her *through him.* Ralph told Jane that there was a history of complaints about her work, despite the rave reviews she had received from clients and coworkers and the fact that she had consistently achieved her performance targets early and had gotten quarterly bonuses as a result.

Jane, being anxious to improve her work, approached the people who had reportedly complained. She approached them from the perspective that she had been advised they had some input and feedback as to how she could do her job better. To her surprise, none of them could offer anything but positive feedback, and she was given the direct impression that they had not complained at all. By the time she contacted the third person for constructive feedback, she was called by HR, told by HR to stop making the calls, and told not to call it "bullying" as she was "raising eyebrows." She resigned. Jane was in a perfect position to sue the company because the collusion that had occurred amounted to constructive dismissal.

The Micromanagement Cycle

Sometimes, the micromanager will target direct reports one at a time until each leaves. This void leaves an opening, and when the new person joins the team, the cycle continues. Unfortunately, this cycle costs the organization money to recruit and train new talent and to try to keep them motivated. This cycle also comes with the cost of lost corporate knowledge—knowledge that goes straight to your competition.

Where does this cycle start? Let's look at Jane's scenario. The first thing that happened when the manager started declaring her incompetent was that Jane lost confidence in the job she was doing, even though she rationally knew that she had been doing a good job, and she questioned the reports of long-standing complaints. She suddenly started spending her work time justifying her competence and job to her new manager, instead of doing work. Because she was no longer focusing on her work, she was no longer able to be as innovative as she had been. Essentially, she was no longer productive.

Jane did complain to HR about the treatment, and started taking more time off work and calling in sick. She was too stressed to deal with the manager's consistent verbal attacks on her character and work. Her absenteeism increased. Jane was moved from a manager's role into a functional role in another department (she was given a demotion without a real demotion). As a result, she resigned.

When she was asked by close colleagues why she chose to leave the company, she explained what had happened, and that the manager would target person after person until they left too. Jane later heard similar reports from others as this manager did indeed target people until they quit one after another, and replaced them with those who were complacent. He not only continued to be employed, but also took on increasingly senior roles. There was no one left to challenge him.

Rita's Story: A Micromanager's Perspective

I once had a manager tell me that micromanagement was her "style." For the sake of discussion, I will name the manager Rita. The problem with that style is that *micromanagement* is the inability to trust or relinquish control to others, and is a manifestation of fear and insecurity. By declaring micromanagement as her style, Rita was basically saying that it was a choice. However, insecurity is not a choice; it is a position of resignation for those who do not know how to change.

Rita declared that micromanagement was her style simply because she was afraid of admitting that she was insecure about how well she performed in her job. Because of Rita's own insecurities, she not only micromanaged the team that reported to her, she berated and publicly humiliated them. By doing this, Rita gained a feeling of control and superiority; however, she stifled the progress of the team and the ability of individual members to contribute. As their ability to contribute diminished, and the quality of their work declined, it only served to reinforce Rita's perception that she needed to micromanage them.

The impact of Rita's insecurities and subsequent micromanagement on the project was that it took longer to complete and escalated conflict on the team, resulting in significant cost increases. In Rita's case, she had never managed a successful project that met its deadlines or came in on budget. In fact, her projects averaged over double the expected cost and delivered so little of the requested functionality that none of her projects were ever implemented.

The Trap of Self-fulfillment

Unfortunately, for teams under a micromanager, the impacts of micromanagement on productivity, focus, quality of work, and motivation become a self-fulfilling prophecy. It is not that each team member really believes they are incompetent and need to have their hands held for every task, but their perception becomes that if they do not defend and prove themselves, others will believe it. This is exactly why they tend to divert their attention from their work, and ultimately, these negative impacts become self-fulfilling.

People claiming injury by another that we later learn was self-inflicted in an effort to gain sympathy due to that person's deep need for attention is often an example of a mental disorder known as *Munchausen syndrome*. Munchausen by proxy is where the afflicted person causes physical harm to others (typically their own children) in order to gain sympathy and attention for themselves. I have long held that there is an undiagnosed form of Munchausen by proxy that impacts relationships, which I call "Emotional Munchausen by proxy". With Emotional Munchausen by proxy, the person creates conflict around them so that they can gain attention and importance.

They create conflict by manipulating others and micromanagement fits the bill. They gain attention and importance by being the one who resolves the conflict, and in the case of micromanagement, appearing to be the one in control of the chaos, deflecting problems onto others and then calling attention to those problems, thus creating the perception that they are the most competent person in the room. Others actually start to believe the micromanager's rhetoric about where the source of a problem lies and it becomes self-fulfilling.

The best ammunition to provide your own employees is knowledge and assertiveness. These will raise their level of empowerment and provide them with the skills and confidence to continue working at a similar pace, delivering the same quality of work, and continuing to innovate. You can show your support by creating an open door policy. This will enable your employees to work and communicate openly without fear of repercussion, and more importantly, leave no room for manipulation.

Cost to the Company

It is easy to see in our case examples where Jane and Rita's companies spent money and got no return on investment. Jane's company paid her more for the same tasks performed previously since she became less productive. Eventually they had to recruit, hire, and train her replacement. In this case, they were lucky that Jane did not sue.

However, more than this, Jane lost her zeal for doing the work that clients loved. She lost her team that she loved working with and they lost a leader and mentor whom they respected. Because Jane had been innovative in her work, her company lost the ability to transfer this innovation to the team she had mentored.

According to people skills expert Jim Rooney, "Micromanaged employees become disengaged, and contribute very little to the success of their assignments. Disengaged employees tend to drag down other employees and customers."[2] It is estimated that the annual cost of disengaged employees in the U.S. is 250 billion dollars per year![3]

Identifying Micromanagement

In retail, if you have an employee theft problem among shift workers and need to pin-point the culprit, you move employees to various shifts and alternate the people they are working with and watch what happens. After a while, you begin to see a pattern emerge and you are able to identify the thief.

Similarly, how can you tell who your micromanagers are? There is the obvious check for complaints, but the best way to recognize micromanagers is to look for teams with high turnover and low productivity. Study how those teams work together, conduct a survey of their job satisfaction, and begin tracking their productivity. Shift the manager that appears to have the most conflict surrounding them with another person known for their leadership ability for an extended period, and then conduct the same survey two more times at one- and three-month intervals.

Compare the results against your benchmark and the previous results, making sure to include changes in productivity as well. If your employees' productivity and morale improve dramatically under the new manager, then you had a micromanager. Of course if you want to be 100% certain, do the same survey and tracking for the micromanager's next team because further verification will be seen when the same pattern emerges.

Executive Assertiveness Is Key

You do have a few of options once you recognize who your micromanagers are. You can move them into a role with limited authority, mentor and train them, or let them go. There is no in-between or waffling, hoping the problem will resolve itself on its own. Make no mistake, you need to intervene and act (no matter how uncomfortable it is). If you do not act, the rest of your employees and ultimately, your company, will

---

[2]Rooney, Jim (2009). http://biznik.com/articles/from-micromanagement-to-mentoring
[3]Kabachnick, Terri (2006). *I quit but forgot to tell you.* The Kabachnick Group Inc.

suffer. That means more than not being named on the list of the best employers to work for!

It is more than just a corporate responsibility to act regarding micromanagers; it is an individual executive responsibility to address this issue because it will significantly and directly impact governance, and anyone and everyone in the direct chain above the micromanager. Everyone has a personal responsibility to the company, themselves, clients, employees under the micromanager, and yes, even the micromanager.

When you address this issue be decisive and lay out a clear plan of action with consequences for not following through. If you are going to move the micromanager and limit their authority, consider whether they have the potential to add value to your company, and then outline where and how. Next, institute a mentoring and leadership program that can realign them with the organization's values. If the person does not add value and has no potential to add value in the future, consider letting them go, but be quick and decisive about it, and do not negotiate your position. The respect of the rest of your organization is depending on it. Once you lose the respect of your employees, it will only erode the authority you have and it will be difficult, if not impossible, to turn that around.

Many micromanagers only work well when they are *being* micromanaged. This will make your job of managing, mentoring, and retraining challenging. Make sure you choose someone you believe is motivated for mentoring and retraining, or the same issues will continue despite your best efforts. In conflict resolution training, "the power you use is the power you respect."

Micromanagement is not just a hallmark of poor governance; it is an indicator of poor management. Left unchecked, it will undoubtedly lead to crisis, but addressed, it will become an opportunity for growth that everyone in your organization will benefit from. It is important to recognize that people have a keen sense of fairness, which is closely tied to how well an organization enforces the rules through governance activities. By not governing any given role or resource, we can leave the door open for all kinds of highly subjective and potential legal damage. That exposure both impacts and affects everyone in the organization.

Micromanagement is one extreme symptom of a lack of governance, but it certainly is not the only symptom. To date, many companies have not managed their business analysts or provided them with a formal governance process. This may be due in part to the utilization of outsourced resources, but it is also due to the lack of formalization with which the role has been created within technology organizations. In other words, who has created the role within the organization, and the protocol of the organization for creating new roles, impacts what those new roles will look like and in turn, how they will be governed.

When you have a CIO that simply adds business analysts to the roster, and permits project managers to start hiring them, there will be little framework in place to manage the resources and govern the activities that they perform. Unfortunately, this creates chaos and impacts the work deliverables, morale, and attrition rate of the individual resources, and this in turn impacts the overall success of projects and the business at large. This is because resources have their own way of doing things, deliverables are inconsistent between resources and even projects with the same resources, and no one is measuring what really works.

From a business analyst perspective, a governance model (Figure 4.1) contains standardized processes for doing the work; established segregation of duties; key performance indicators for deliverable consistency and quality; templates for deliverables; and ongoing improvement protocol to enhance the processes and results as the role within the technology organization matures. Without these basic elements in place, the role of the business analyst, and consequently the work that they perform and the results that they produce, will never mature and improve.

One of the biggest arguments to imposing governance on the role of a business analyst comes from the technology organization because there is a false belief that adding the governance layer simply adds overhead without adding value. However, without benchmarking and progressive measuring, we cannot say that it does add cost when it might simply be moving budgetary dollars from the cost of training and mistakes, to the cost of doing it right the first time, and governing that.

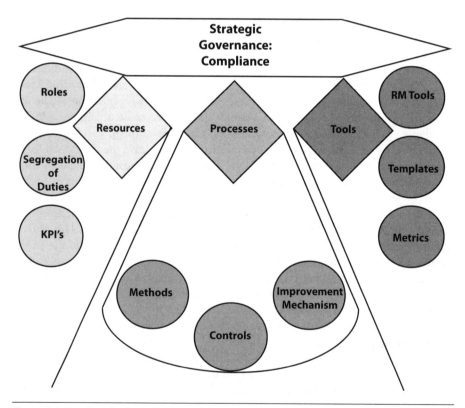

Figure 4.1 Functional governance

CRISIS AND OPPORTUNITY

The technology industry, as with the global economy, is facing a state of crisis. In reading the numbers, the technology industry is improving at a snail's pace when compared to other industries. What is interesting to note is that according to the average learning curve identified by Boeing, for every time that output volumes double, we should actually improve by about 80%. Yet, that certainly has not happened within technology, and we cannot point to ever-changing technologies as the cause for this severely stunted improvement rate.

For a smart group, we are far behind when it comes to continuous improvement. We seem to have a blind spot when it comes to a source of the largest number of issues. While we have identified poor quality of requirements as being one of these sources, we seem unable to wrap our heads around how to make a significant impact.

There is an irony in business analysis. While recruiting, screening, hiring, and teaching others for and about the role of a business analyst, we demand and filter for technical and academic skills. Yet, once hired and in the role, we insist that the business analyst's job is too volatile and uses too many soft skills to be measured. We further assert that these factors alone deem that the measurement and benchmarking of requirements activities, progress, performance, quality, and even effectiveness cannot be accurately pinpointed and evaluated.

The key obstacles to our ability to improve include a lack of scientific method, our own egos, and an operational infrastructure that has not quite caught up to the job. We all know that the key to continuous improvement is following a carefully structured and recorded process that measures the inputs and outputs, and tests for positive changes to the results (scientific method). Part of that structure is *control*, and quite frankly because of the slow evolution and adoption of control by the business analysis practice, the operational and organizational infrastructure simply has not caught up. Unfortunately, our egos have created this blind spot that limits our ability to see the true value in creating an infrastructure, and we have been slow to adapt. The result is an almost nonexistent continuous improvement process.

So how do we change into a continuous improvement structure? We start looking at the *Chaos Report* by the Standish Group as an opportunity instead of a crisis. That means identification and adoption of operational infrastructure that establishes clear processes for requirements, and manages those processes in a controlled manner to really start seeing wide-scale industry improvements.

In this chapter we discussed the importance and benefits of governance and examined governance of business analysis services from both an operational and functional (or strategic) perspective, as well as how it influences business analysis and technology as a whole.

We exposed some of the risks of not utilizing governance practices to manage the methods across the business analysis function. We dug deep into one of the hallmark symptoms of a lack of governance and indicator of poor management common to many firms and why and how it must be addressed. We discussed the lack of formal governance in many organizations, identified some of the other barriers to widespread adoption of governance models, and discussed the concept of turning potential crisis into opportunity through continuous improvement.

This information can be used to identify some common problems and issues within your organization as root causes, and help remove barriers to establishing functional governance programs within technology as a means of managing the methods of business analysis.

CONCLUSION

In this section, we took a revealing and no-holds-barred look at business analysis as it is today and how that affects projects and ultimately the business. This look uncovered an overall lack of substantive management, quality control, governance, and performance management. The commonly accepted practices of coordinating business analysis resources and activities were decomposed to reveal serious flaws that wreak havoc on the quality of the deliverables and outcomes that business analysis provides. Unfortunately, these outcomes are being consumed by downstream teams that design, develop, and test the products that technology projects create.

Through SWOT analysis, the extent of the problem and how that impacts the overall effectiveness of technology as a whole was discussed. A new optimized model was proposed that repositions business analysis, the technology organization, and the business for success. The new optimized model, also explored in subsequent sections and chapters, has a singular, core focus for all of business analysis activities. That focus is to enable strategy and safeguard business interests.

It is through repositioning that the future of the business we serve can be ensured by applying cost-effective and sustainable strategies to improve the results of technology based on the ability to increase alignment to the strategic objectives of the business. The new optimized model asserts the obligation of the business analyst to perform tasks, such as benefits realization planning and governance of requirements activities, in order to meet the overall objective of safeguarding the interests of the business. This is done through the development of solutions that enable strategic objectives to be met while remaining accountable and responsible for applying financially sustainable methods.

This information can be used to create a new understanding of business analysis, and forge the foundation of solid partnerships between the business and technology through business analysis services. It is the consistent application of stewardship principles to the practice of business analysis that will enable the business to profit and the business analysts to cement this partnership. Stewardship underscores the successful relationship and execution of the tasks that add value and ensure business sustainability.

MANAGING BUSINESS ANALYSIS SERVICES

Basic functional management models are organizational frameworks and infrastructure that assign the responsibility for ensuring efficiency in business operations through resource allocation and effectiveness in meeting customer expectations. This is done by coordinating and by utilizing the least number of resources needed for any given set of tasks or work to be performed. In essence, functional management, in and of itself, is concerned with managing the overall process that converts materials, labor, and energy into goods and/or services.

As we can see in Figure S2.1, three core elements form the nucleus of the functional management model in order to ensure that resources are coordinated effectively at all stages. Typically, standard functional (operational) management models include a very specific set of key elements (as depicted above). These elements are organizational structure, resource management, and performance management. Each of these elements is crucial to the success of the organization because of the unique role that each plays in the success of the individual resources and their ability to apply the standard techniques and comply with the governance protocol in order to achieve consistent and predictable results from the work.

Organizational structure provides the framework and infrastructure for career progression and opportunities for growth within the organization and creates a structure for the management of resources that closely aligns the accountability and responsibility for the achievement of operational goals related to that particular group.

Resource management is responsible for coordinating and allocating resources to fill needs across the customer base. This includes capacity planning and planning for fluctuations in staffing levels as resources move across transition points of their career.

Performance management is responsible for the establishment of benchmarks, competencies, and key performance indicators based on the role that has been defined and the associated tasks for that particular role. The development of these attributes and elements ensure the success of the analysts in performing the work and that there is a consistent measure for assessing both competency and performance on an ongoing basis.

Business Analysis Stewardship pertains to the concept of all business analysts being responsible for and ultimately accountable for safeguarding the interests of the business by employing fiscally sustainable methods, and translating strategic plans into tangible solutions. This is accomplished through the careful planning and management of business analysis resources.

In effect, the trifecta of organizational structure, resource management, and performance management are the key enablers in the planning and management of business analysis resources. The combination of these three management structures ensure that business analysis is performed in a controlled manner so that the results and quality become predictable and consistent across all resources and projects.

This section illustrates the practical application of Business Analysis Stewardship through the implementation of a functional management model that includes organizational structure, resource management processes and performance processes. It will demonstrate how to plan and manage business analysis resources within the context of the overall organization and the functional role that the analyst performs. It also demonstrates how the organization and coordination of those resources can be completed in such a way as to support the achievement of both the objective and primary function of business analysis.

Figure S2. 1 Functional management model

Finally, the functional management model depicts competencies and key performance indicators that complete the management model and identifies the skills and measures for ensuring the realization of Business Analysis Stewardship objectives through the development of competent resources to perform the work in compliance with exacting standards and measures.

5

ORGANIZATIONAL STRUCTURE

Organizational structure is the arrangement of human resources into departments and sections in order to perform work. It affects organizational life and work in two main ways: It establishes the base on which standard operating procedures and routines are founded, and predetermines which individuals are permitted to participate in particular decision-making processes. It is participation that determines the extent that the views of these individuals shape the organization's actions and identity.

While there are several types of organizational structures, we will be reviewing the primary elements of two common types: functional and matrix (also known as divisional or cross-functional). A comparative snapshot of the primary differences between these two types of structures is shown in Figure 5.1, depicting how resources are organized.

In a functional organization, resources and the organization are segregated into departments and divisions by job function, such as human resources or finance. In a cross-functional organization, the resources and organization are divided into divisions according to the types of services or products offered. Within information technology, the most common divisions are between hardware, software, and networking.

Companies utilize organizational structure as a means of orchestrating and coordinating work through a chain of command. Coordination of work requires an understanding of leadership, career planning, and properly defining and allocating resources.

The chain of command gives us both accountability and responsibility toward the organization as a whole, and provides the protocol for reporting and monitoring the other elements. An additional aspect that a chain of command provides is the ability to escalate issues to the appropriate levels of accountability and authority to address them in a timely manner. If this breaks down, we suffer from a lack of governance and the issues that are related to that lack of governance.

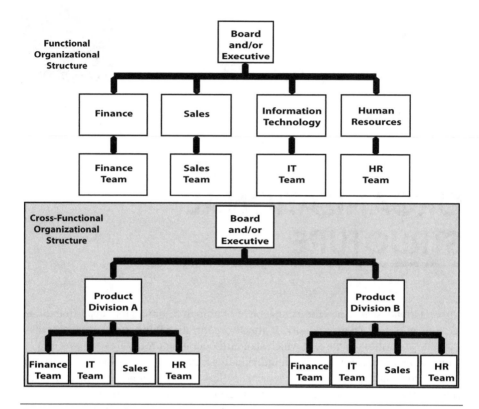

Figure 5.1 Types of organizational structures

As human beings, we have an innate need to be organized and part of a social order—a pecking order—if you will. We create organizations that are fluid and ambiguous; we follow instead of lead. Something that we have discovered through the ages is that an organization is not just about control, it is about being productive and simultaneously effective. In other words, we are not content just to move blocks around a room, we are compelled to move the blocks in synchronous patterns so that our paths do not impede the work of others or get impeded by their paths. This is not to imply that we are all obsessive/compulsive about structure, but we do tend to seek order (consciously or unconsciously) to reduce the feeling of stress and anxiety that we get when things are not orderly.

Years ago, when I was a student, I worked with physically and mentally challenged adults. It does not take long to see that the need for order and routine is innate. There was a need to reduce stress here, too, and a realization of how stress can be caused by the mere act of changing a daily routine.

In the book (or the movie) *The Lord of the Flies* by William Golding, the boys in the story did not create a social structure merely because one of them had a megalomaniacal complex, wanted to rule the world, and finally got a chance. The boys created a structure from a combination of necessity and impulse. They needed work to be done, and with the dangers present on their island, it would not have made sense to have everyone do the same thing or to create tasks that did not need doing.

Organizational structure gives most of us something we crave: order. It is within order that we find confidence, and we may even find varying degrees of job satisfaction and feelings of competence and self-worth. We all pride ourselves on doing a great job, so much that our perception of how well we do at work can influence our personal identity.

Scott Ginsberg, well-known author and authority on identity and approachability, considers what you do for a living to be part of the initial formalities of getting to know someone new. He also considers learning what people like best about their job as a good way to get to know someone or build a relationship. Ginsberg clearly suggests that we take what we do in our careers very personally. It is part of our identity.

In fact, in a brief Internet search about the first questions to ask someone new, the top listed sites mentioned "job questions" right up there. As you may have observed, when people introduce themselves, they often state their profession right upfront in conversation (sometimes even before they mention if they are married or have kids), especially in a professional setting.

So, how does knowing how people identify themselves affect business analysis and make us better at doing our jobs? Well, knowing about personal commitment and self-identification makes us better at change management for starters because it enables us to connect and develop rapport faster in a project setting. Further, it allows us to understand where everyone fits within the organization.

Having organizational structures in place gives us feelings of confidence and competence, and enables us to get work done effectively and efficiently. Business analysts are no exception. Nevertheless, analysts have been treated as exceptions in many cases because (as described in Chapter 1) when we expose the existing model to scrutiny; we learn that so many business analysts do not belong or have a real organizational structure.

Not having structure in place means that we are constantly tripping over others, trying to get work done that has not been allocated properly on projects where we are being evaluated. This is exactly the kind of scenario that business analysts face within their projects. Direction is limited, subjective, and inconsistent without organizational structure.

The end result is that we have inconsistent deliverables from resource to resource and project to project, resource attrition, and there is general confusion about what to do and when. Thus, business analysts stay up late posting questions on Internet discussion boards, hoping someone else will have an answer that they can live with and apply in their situation.

From a practical standpoint, organizational structure enables the resources themselves to move about and complete their tasks in an orderly and effective manner because it tells us who does what, when, and for how long, as well as what success looks like. It also tells us how we can move around. Organizational structure essentially sets the "batting order" and the strategies for coordinating the resources to get as many points as possible and win the game. This includes career planning, resource allocation, role definitions, and clearly marked exits.

An effective organizational structure should define who reports to whom, how and when they can move up or across, and the criteria for those moves. It gives us clear indications of qualifications for success because it defines success and enables analysts to focus on doing what they love to do most: business analysis.

The best structures that you can put in place are a functional or divisional structure for coordinating resources, and a Center of Excellence, which generally has a cross-functional team structure. A Center of Excellence will provide and foster the skills within all of its members, and will encourage individual business analysts to internalize the formal structure and processes.

LEADERSHIP

As part of the natural order described above, some people rise to the top and become leaders and managers, and others do not. Many people simply become complacent and stop striving for a coveted, top position. However, even young children can opt to follow instead of lead. There is an innate need for order (as previously discussed) and that for people to abide by that order, many simply do not try to become leaders.

According to subject matter expert Don Clark, leadership means that in order "To inspire your workers into higher levels of teamwork, there are certain things you must be, know, and do. These do not come naturally, but are acquired through continual work and study."[1] I think we need to understand what a leader *is* before we can really understand what they *do*.

I believe that a *leader* is any person that sets expectations for themselves and others, and then creates the environment in which to meet those expectations. These can include expectations for attitude, respect, behavior, deportment, performance, strategies, and goals.

If we use this definition, then *leadership* is basically the act of communicating the expectations, providing the support and guidance, and motivating as well as controlling the pace and momentum that enables successful performance and leads to the accomplishment of goals and activities.

Leadership, as we all know, is not the same as management. You need to have a balance of both in order to have a successful model. For example, you can have multiple leaders and a single manager. In fact, leaders support management and are a critical part of any team. Leadership utilizes techniques such as personal recognition, respect and assertiveness, active listening, encouragement, and negotiation to create and manage the environment.

---

[1]Clark, Don. http://www.nwlink.com/~donclark/leader/leadcon.html.

It is not enough to say that a leader is a person who uses influence or so-called "powers of persuasion." The reason that you need both is to extend the reach of the manager and to increase the connection of team members to each other and to the management model. Leaders reinforce the strategies, goals, and policies of management by creating the environment for successful accomplishment and contribution.

Great managers can tell you who their leaders are, and have great relationships with them because they support the leaders in their roles. The leaders, in turn, extend that support outward to the other team members. Great senior managers tend to be great leaders as well.

Without leaders, business analysts are like anyone else: we look for them, even when those leaders are outside of the role and may be inappropriate for giving us advice on how to complete a task, what success and failure look like, or even what should be done and when. That lack of leadership creates chaos and leaves business analysts where they are in the average model we see today, subject to the whims and biases of individual project managers and stakeholders with no real firm targets to hit or standards to follow.

Impacts of Conflicting Leadership on Resources

As a case in point, many years ago, I took a job as a receptionist in an engineering firm. I liked the president (and owner). He had some specific ways that he wanted things done, but was always approachable and I could talk to him. The office manager, on the other hand, had a completely different perspective on how things should be done, and she was not a very pleasant person if you did not do it exactly as she had directed.

The president wanted all office mail, including magazines, to be stamped in the upper right hand corner, and the office manager wanted them stamped on a sticky note and then posted in the upper left hand corner. While a minor issue, when I went into his office, he would correct me and tell me to do it his way, and when I went into her office, she would direct me to do it her way. This type of inconsistency was quite common at this firm. Think of my position—she was my manager and had the power to fire me, but he signed my paycheck.

I explained to the president what the office manager had instructed me to do, and I explained to the office manager what the president had instructed me to do. Later that same day, she called the president into her office and stood over him, wagging her finger at him. After that, every time he went out of town, I did the stamps her way, but every other day, I did the stamps his way.

This situation is similar to the one that many business analysts find themselves in due to a lack of leadership and consistent standards or guidelines to follow: pulled in different directions and trying to appease everyone because they have to be kept "happy" in order for us to get a good evaluation. Unfortunately, this creates an unhealthy environment for business analysts as they spend more time trying to appease egos than meeting the needs of the business. For this reason, leadership is absolutely crucial to having a happy, healthy, and productive team of business analysts.

Leaders do something even more. They make us feel comfortable and confident so that we can ease up on second guessing ourselves and set about getting the real work done. Maybe it is because we know that if we have a question or a problem arises, we have a leader whom we can turn to for help.

Leadership is only truly effective when the other elements are also solidly in place. That means that a leader and their team must also know that there are defined roles, and that the overall structure exists to coordinate the resources both effectively and efficiently.

A primary issue with a project-focused approach to BA management is that there is an overall lack of career planning and development. Unfortunately, this leads to a gaping hole in the promotability of business analysts. That means they have only two promotion options: move onto another track like project management, or continue on and slowly gain relevant experiences from the roles they find. This is exactly where I started to identify role-based attrition for business analysts and noted that the rates were higher than for other groups within technology.

Having options and the opportunity to advance is so important that many of us are motivated far more by advancement than money. I have accepted lower paying roles that called for lower qualifications if I knew that I had one of two opportunities there:

1. The ability to learn new skills that I could apply later on at other positions.
2. The ability to advance my career.

I know that I am not alone. Advancement opportunities are one of the most asked questions by candidates during job interviews. A clear career path does more than just motivate people, it gives them confidence. They know the path that they are on, and how to get from one place to another along that path. It is that feeling of confidence that enables people to focus on the job at hand because they do not have to worry about how they are going to advance and move themselves forward. Learning more and becoming a better business analyst is okay, but not a real incentive nor a career path. It is like saying that when you finish this work, if you do really well, I'll give you more of the *same* work.

Career Path Development and Myths

One of the biggest misconceptions that I see on Internet discussion boards is the idea that you have to learn business analysis purely through experience. This is only partly true. Recently, I read that the difference between academic knowledge and specialized knowledge is the degree to which you are also trained to organize and apply the knowledge that you have learned. In a way, I have been saying this same thing for years. I have postured that while universities may teach you the information, they do not readily teach you to *apply* the knowledge. Do not get me wrong—I believe that both have their place, and should be equally valued. It is just that one cannot exist without the other. I have met MBA graduates without any real-world experiences and met people in business with little or no formal academic education or training. If I had to choose between the two, I would probably choose the person with real-world experience simply because they will have knowledge that I may not have the time or the inclination to teach, while the MBA graduate would have to learn how to think and apply the knowledge that they have learned only in theory.

However, ideal business analyst candidates have both formal academic education and real-world experience. Here's why: the candidates would arrive with a diversity of knowledge that I could show them how to apply, the real-world experiences will teach them what to do with that other information, and it will begin to all make sense without me having to teach *everything*.

To be honest, the argument of academic education vs. real-world experience reminds me of how people once thought that the world was flat. I'm sure if they had the Internet back then, we would have seen a diversity of arguments pouring in over this debate. Most business analysts today received a lot of knowledge from the "school of hard knocks" after they spent years in university or working as developers and testers, but that does not make it right, and it does not mean that others have to follow in our footsteps. Today's educational and certification programs (such as the IIBA) were not around when most of us were honing our craft. We created them so that the rest of the analysts would not have to keep putting their hands on the proverbial stove to know it was hot and could learn from our past mistakes.

My suggestion is to take advantage of programs like the IIBA, so that business analysts do not have to take the long road to success; instead, they can take a short-cut and be better off for doing so. Through these types of training and certification programs, analysts can acquire all of the precise knowledge and skills within a shorter period of time, with fewer mistakes and headaches.

The motivation to advance and improve is absent when people do not have a clearly defined career path to follow. That means an increase in stress, a decrease in overall job satisfaction, and general de-motivation to do a good job. Not only that, they have to exert their own effort to create a plan for themselves and then map out exactly how they are going to get there and what that looks like when they arrive. That is time they could be spending on creating a better solution or higher quality requirements. Instead of being focused on the task(s) at hand, they are focused on the journey and can become complacent about producing in the "now" unless they can see how it is going to benefit their long-term plans. A career plan outlines the journey, stages, and criteria for each stage, and shows people how each task that they do now in the current role leads to that future they want.

Inasmuch as a career path should outline how an individual gets from here to there, it should also summarize where they have come from to get this far, because that itself influences the path. Not everyone coming into business analysis arrives with the same type or level of knowledge. Therefore, an ideal career path for business analysts should outline how they would converge and move forward, so that at some point, there are formal standards and consistent results from the work being done by all of the individuals filling a role, regardless of how they got into the role in the first place.

When you consider business analysis, there are five starting points for people moving into the role. That is, they will have a background in at least one of five key areas before they become a business analyst:

- Testing
- Business
- Systems analysis
- Development
- Recent MBA graduate/campus recruit

Each candidate can be categorized by the skills that they have that will contribute to their success as a business analyst. Based on my experience, I would put the most ideal candidates in Group A and less ideal candidates in Group B, as depicted in Figure 5.2. This is not to say that I would not hire candidates in Group B. It is just that their ability to jump right in and start the role with only a small amount of handholding is lower than that of Group A. When I have hired candidates in Group B, I have invested more

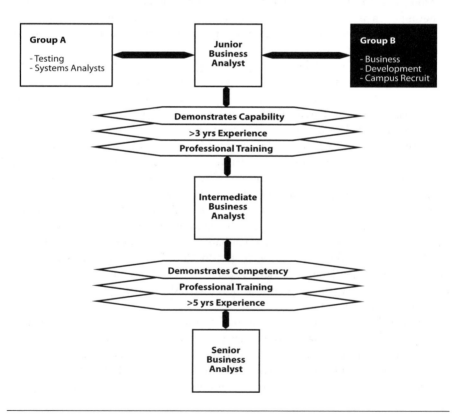

Figure 5.2 Career path

time and energy into them personally to ensure that they were successful. That being said, the groupings are:

Group A

- Testing
- Systems analysis

Group B

- Business
- Development
- Recent MBA graduate/campus recruit

Each candidate will need differing amounts of training and handholding based on who they are and where they came from. We cannot assume that just because someone has applied for the role (or claims to have done it before) that they have an aptitude for it, or that they are any good at it.

How do we move each group of candidates toward Business Analysis Stewardship and leadership on the same career path? First, we have to define the basic set of training and experiences they will need to accomplish in order to get there. They are categorized so that you can develop only two sets of training plans instead of five and spend money wisely. After all, you are probably not running a university; you are running a technology organization and you have to maximize the investment that you are about to make in the candidates. You can do this by understanding that the candidates in Group A probably already have an idea of how to analyze things and what the results should look like. Let's face it, testers may or may not know how to elicit requirements, but they will sure know how to scrutinize them and know quality requirements when they see them.

Group B candidates will have the least amount of experience and knowledge, and have a barrier to overcome no matter where they personally came from. Developers do not think or communicate like business people, and business people typically do not think or communicate like developers. On the other hand, graduates may not have enough hands-on, practical working experience in order for them to understand the context of business processes, and how and why things are done the way they are. These are hurdles that this group will have to overcome in training before they can start performing or learning the practical tasks of business analysis. Group A can almost start learning the tasks right away.

Once you understand where your candidates are now, you will have to understand and determine how they will get to new levels and what those new levels are. There are basically four levels along a BA career path:

- Business analyst (junior, intermediate, and senior)
- Team lead (intermediate and senior)
- Solutions consultant (senior)
- Manager (senior)

You will need to outline a plan to help business analysts move toward team leadership, because there will be times when you are going to have a team of business analysts and they will need a leader. To that end, it will be best to determine what qualities and competencies you want in that leader, as well as the tasks that you will expect them to perform so that you can build a credible and realistic path to get there.

The business analyst (junior, intermediate, and senior) is the resource that directly performs the work of business analysis that is primarily centered on processes, rules, and requirements.

The team lead (intermediate and senior) is the resource that performs tactical leadership, governance, and management of business analysis resources for a specific project. They report to strategic and project management on specific results and performance related to individual resources and techniques. In addition, this resource also conducts the benefits realization planning with the solutions consultant, manages stakeholder alignment, ensures that the project aligns to the overall objectives, and delivers the anticipated results and benefits through business analysis activities.

The solutions consultant (senior) is brought on to conduct a needs analysis and determine the results that the business needs, and then translates that into a solution for the project team to build. They ensure that the solution aligns to the Business Analysis Stewardship objectives and is financially responsible and sustainable by performing tasks such as benefits realization planning.

The manager (senior) manages the whole pool of business analysis resources, tools, techniques, and strategies from a strategic level in that they manage the group for the organization, instead of individual projects. This person ensures that performance is measured and monitored in accordance with corporate policies, key performance indicators are set, the business analysis service group is allocated appropriately (aligned with business objectives), and produces the value to the organization that is needed from the deliverables.

It may or may not be obvious that once you create a career path, you will need to align it to your organization's human resources (HR) model. That means that you may have to add layers such as business analyst I, II, and III in order to align the roles to bands of responsibility held by the HR group.

COORDINATING RESOURCES

Resources must be managed and coordinated effectively and efficiently. This refers to who they are, how many there are, where they will be deployed, and what they will do when they get there. It is a project manager's responsibility to build the foundation for successful projects by ensuring the coordination of all of the resources at their disposal, as it is the organization's responsibility to manage the resources at its disposal.

Remember the silly binder story from Chapter 2? Had the project manager and project sponsor recognized the benefits of bringing in multiple lower cost resources to perform the same work, it would have led to the work being done more cost effectively and efficiently in a shorter period of time. Why? Consider the capital that was spent on the resource that the project manager had to coordinate. She paid for 32 hours of work, plus her own 6 hours, and another 6 hours from the other business analyst, which totaled more than $2500. However, if she had paid for temporary clerical staff, she would have paid less than one quarter of the cost. It was not the number of hours that would have changed, but the cost per hour that was paid out. When you consider that the average contract project manager in oil and gas is paid at a rate of well over $100 per hour, her 6 hours only exacerbated the situation.

Therein lies the issue. Far too often, we think of the resources as individuals who have been allocated to the project and believe that we cannot bring on others to accomplish work because we think in terms of numbers of resources instead of the capital costs of those resources, or the time that it will take to complete the work.

Perception of Working Priorities and Estimating Time to Complete

One of the most consistent issues that I have faced on projects is working with employee resources who try to factor in things like social committees that they contribute to as part of the cultural work environment to their project schedule. In fact, in one such instance, I asked a business analyst team member to tell me how many hours of requirements work he had left to accomplish before the deadline.

He advised me that he had about 42 hours of work to complete over two full weeks, and that the work was to be accomplished by himself and another business analysis resource. By my calculation, they each had about 21 hours of work to accomplish in nearly 80 working hours. Then, he came back and said it would be late, and that it was impossible for him to meet the deadline. Huh?

I advised him we could not justify another extension. Based on the workload, I refused to believe that we needed one based on the facts that he had presented. I asked him to explain his reasons for wanting an extension, and it turned out that they also had a few social committee "obligations" to attend.

Of course, he was not happy when those obligations were pulled off his plate in favor of the real work that he was getting paid for. He actually told me that I was being unreasonable, but that the work still needed to be completed by the deadline.

In the end, not only did he get the work completed on time, but he came away with a much better understanding of estimating his time and workload. This made him a better business analyst and an asset to future projects.

Another important thing to consider is the direction and coordination of resources across the organizational structure. It does not do the team lead, project managers, or the business any favors to leave the team confused about what to do next. What can end up happening is an overall lack of consistency from resource to resource, or project to project, and in the long run, inconsistency creates more work for everyone, including the BA manager.

From a business analyst perspective, the effective coordination of resources is the distribution of business analysis tasks across the team in the most effective way possible to maximize the quality of the results and reduce the overhead costs of performing the work. Business analysts must start to accept appropriate roles, and companies need to do a better job of finding the most appropriate resources to perform the work.

My advice to business analysts has always been to carefully consider before accepting any role that is "BA slash (/) anything". Why? According to The Standish Group,[2] 45% of implemented software features are never used, meaning there is a universal breakdown in the requirements phase of projects. This lack of software feature usage that results from poor requirements planning can occur when BAs are also focused on testing or project management. They are simply not going to have enough time to do a good job detailing what software features are actually going to be used.

Another way that we restrict potential success is by considering the upfront resourcing costs, instead of the overall costs. Unfortunately, many project managers limit the rate per hour of the resource when they are sending requests for proposals to recruiters, and they end up limiting the resources that will apply for the role. These project managers are continuing to operate under the misconception that the overall budget is affected by the cost per hour, but they are forgetting about the cost of fixing mistakes and errors by contracting a less qualified resource to perform the tasks.

Consider this example: Project Manager A contracts a senior business analyst to perform 120 hours for requirements tasks. This business analyst is paid at a rate of $90 per hour, and s/he actually gets the work done in 105 hours. Therefore, Project Manager A has spent a total of $9,450 to accomplish the requirements tasks.

Project Manager B contracts an intermediate business analyst to complete a similar project with 120 hours of requirements tasks. This business analyst is paid $65 per hour, and gets the work done in 130 hours. Project Manager B has spent $8,450, but then during development they have to go back and change about one-quarter of the requirements because they are incomplete or incorrect. The project manager has to pay the resource another $2,112.50 to correct the mistakes. Finally, in testing, another one-quarter of the tests fail and requirements have to be redone. For these requirements alone, the project manager pays out another $2,112.50 to the business analyst to fix the mistakes. The grand total of requirements costs that have been paid to this business analyst is now $12,675, compared to the $9,450 that it would have cost for the higher quality work the first time around.

Let's face it, unless you live by the adage that it is "easier to beg forgiveness than to ask permission," you are better off going with the higher paid analyst because you are going to pay for fewer mistakes later on. Unfortunately, many companies are not tracking time to the degree necessary to identify these kinds of justifications, so all they "see" is the up-front cost in the rate per hour. It is much the same as when people

---

[2]The Standish Group. (2010). Chaos Report.

are buying a car. They look at the upfront costs that represent smaller payments, but do not consider that over the long term, they are paying a higher interest rate and actually shelling out more money. What seems affordable is a relative term and has a significant impact on the coordination of resources.

SUMMARY

The relationship between organizational structure, attrition, and quality of outcomes was discussed in this chapter. We explored the impacts of organizational structure on motivation, direction, and methods utilized by the resources. Some of the key issues that result from a lack of appropriate organizational structure were also discussed. The elements of organizational structure (both formal and informal) were highlighted as well as the issues that can arise when a structure is unclear or inappropriately managed and established.

This information can be used to identify areas of improvement within your own organizational structure, so that you can create a well-founded structure for business analysis services. The next chapter focuses on managing the individual and collective resources within that structure in order to efficiently achieve the most effective outcomes.

6

RESOURCE MANAGEMENT

The next layer of functional management that we are going to explore is resource management. *Resource management* is the organization's ability to coordinate and deploy (allocate) its resources effectively. This is primarily achieved through capacity planning. However, as Figure 6.1 illustrates, in order to perform resource management effectively, we must account for existing capabilities and forecasted need across the organization, coupled with the capacity of the organizational structure (represented as *opportunities*) to accommodate fluctuations in resources.

In order to be successful with capacity planning and models, we have to understand some key tasks:

- How to locate qualified resources and have a ready pipeline (talent acquisition, or finding and securing new talent).
- How to allocate resources as they advance in skills proficiency (promotion and advancement).
- How to replace resources as they leave a role or assignment (resource attrition), managing resource allocations, and maintaining staffing levels.

We have to recognize that resource management is more than finding skilled resources and assigning them to projects.

Many people care less about the current state of their role than they do about having the opportunity to advance. It is that career opportunity that a successful way of life is built upon. However, we need to realize that business analysts are a group of people who do not have other opportunities naturally built into their roles. With most other professions, there is an opportunity to advance oneself into supervisory and then management roles. This is usually not the case with business analysis because, for the most part, those roles have not been defined or they do not exist. This is because the management of their organization does not understand how to maximize the value that business analysts bring to the organization. Not to mention the fact

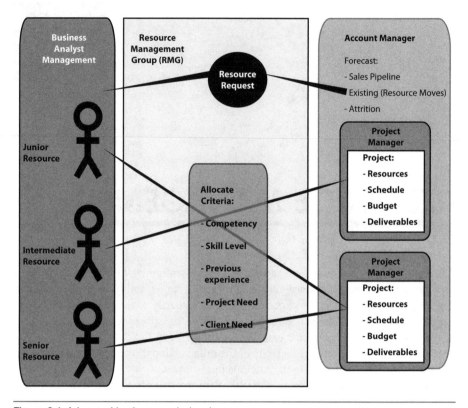

Figure 6.1 Advanced business analysis roles

that management at many organizations has little understanding of what analysts do, how to find good ones, and how to help them advance their skills. Frustrated, business analysts who want the opportunity to advance must move into another role. Figure 6.2 illustrates potential avenues for advanced business analysis roles that will provide growth opportunities for senior business analysis resources. Imagine that you are in charge of a company that has just hired a group of new college graduates. You have paid to put them into a program to train them regarding company processes to perform a particular job. Then, just as they have completed the training and are work-ready, they start getting and accepting offers from other companies to do the work that you just trained them to do. You are going to watch your investment walk out the door unless you have other work in place to keep them in the role long enough for you to benefit from the investment in their skills.

For starters, you will need to have a solid training bond in place to minimize the number of resources that leave, and you might also consider other incentives that will keep people on board. Remember that people are not always motivated by money; in fact, most people are motivated more by opportunity than they are by money. When

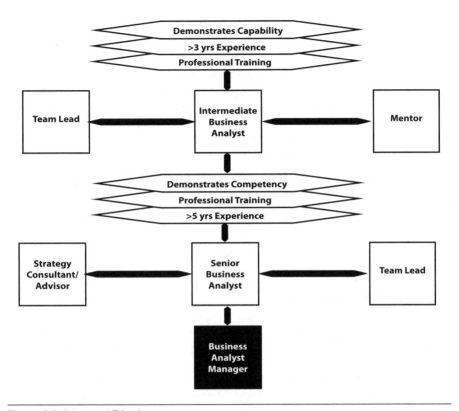

Figure 6.2 Advanced BA roles

you build a plan for your resources, you may not have to pay more, just provide more opportunity for role advancement.

That strategy involves advancing team lead and management roles as well as opportunities to contribute. At the end of the day, we all want to believe that we matter. Having chances to contribute to the organization and to other business analysts coming up does two things: a) it retains the investment that you have made in training the business analysts while they were working on your projects, and b) it makes them feel as though they are doing something that will make them matter and become important.

Retaining talented and trained business analysts means that other business analysts can learn from them, and you end up with an increase in consistency between projects and resources in terms of deliverables and results. The ongoing learning actually improves your ability to estimate projects because you will begin to know and understand the capability and capacity of individual resources, and know how to utilize them more effectively for the long term. You can augment their skill sets when you know that there is a need for other skills where they may not be as strong.

Again, a benefit in terms of managing business analysts is longer retention and increased motivation, especially when they can see that there is a "ladder" to climb by referencing clear-cut criteria for making it from one rung to the next. Meeting criteria enables analysts to set some of their own performance goals in line with the business objectives and expectations for performance, and lets them manage how rapidly they progress towards those goals. In the long run, performance is improved by using a resource management system because resources have the chance to compete against themselves to improve performance levels.

From a business analysis perspective, resource management adopts competency and screening criteria from performance management. These criteria include how resources will be assessed to be brought on board (talent acquisition), how they will qualify to be promoted and when (promotions and advancement), and how to define effective succession plans. There will be a key set of defined skills from the outset, methods for measuring and monitoring performance, and then criteria for terminating or reassigning under-performing resources.

CAPACITY PLANNING

Capacity planning is the anticipation and forecasting of resources that will be required to meet projected needs. It enables the business to prepare and adapt to changing staffing needs over time.

The most critical information that is needed to develop thorough capacity plans is project information (details, including type) and schedules (including volume of work to be done, i.e., estimates) as well as account information (see Figure 6.3). This information is compared against an ongoing "inventory" of existing resources, as well as those resources that are in the pipeline, so that the most appropriate resources can be easily located and moved into or out of an engagement rapidly. The ability to meet client needs on-demand is a crucial element in the success of staff augmentation and consulting engagements.

Once you have an accurate picture of your projects and anticipated account needs, you can identify the roles and tasks that will be required. This is used to locate available resources and prepare them to roll onto the project. Of course, there are some important considerations that you will need to make at a high level. These considerations will ensure that this step contributes effectively to resource management and are as follows:

- The complexity and range of services offered under the business analysis services model
- Organizational structure of the group, and how that fits into the overall organization (with respect to career planning)
- The structure of roles and performance management with respect to the establishment of the assessment framework that enables capacity

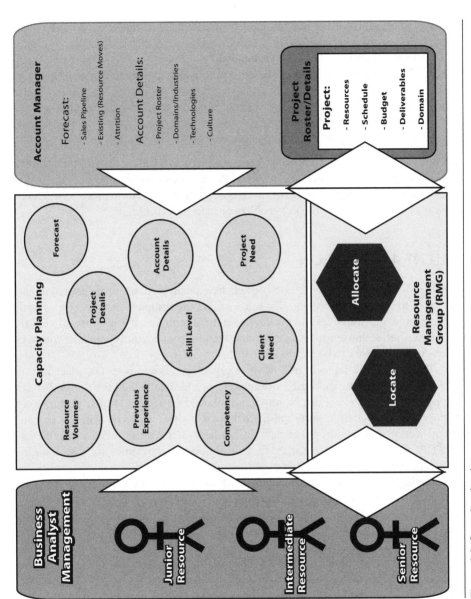

Figure 6.3 Capacity planning

- Expectations of the market, industry, and clients being serviced by the business analysis services group
- How existing needs will be maintained
- The projected future needs based on the sales pipeline and stage of the sales process
- Whether you can utilize any existing resources to shuffle them into new roles and then backfill their roles
- Who is coming off another engagement

All of this information is combined to create a picture of the capacity of the business analysis organization to meet the needs of its customers without lags or substantial issues in quality differences between resources. Again, performance management measures and controls are the key enablers of capacity planning.

TALENT ACQUISITION

Talent acquisition is the process by which new talent is discovered, attracted, and recruited to the company for specific roles, so that the company may achieve its goals through strategic initiatives and the development of products. It is important to ensure that we are attracting appropriate and skilled resources that will support the company and achieve the work to be accomplished.

There are big differences in how some organizations approach talent acquisition and retention. In some unionized workplaces, for example, one of the things that can happen is that employees can be hired and retained regardless of their performance history and willingness to accomplish anything in a given workday. However, in nonunion workplaces, resources typically do not have that kind of complacency to rely on. That means resources are more motivated because companies are always on the lookout for new talent to bring on board.

Having clear criteria for candidates with aptitude for the culture and the work will enable recruiters to spend less time making costly hiring mistakes and achieve a greater level of consistency in attracting the right talent. To do that we need to loop back to defined roles during the process of finding talent to ensure that we are looking for, attracting, and finding the right skill sets to meet the demands of those roles.

Having clearly defined criteria for new candidates creates a level playing field for business analysts and project managers in that it ensures that all new talent has a minimum starting point and set of skills. If the company is mature enough, they could also utilize this information to estimate and predict the success of their projects throughout the year, based on an average set of performance expectations. This means that business analysis will automatically have a minimum standard and will produce a baseline set of predictable and predetermined results.

How to Interview Business Analysts and Find the Right One

Unfortunately, the scenario of interviewer question pitfalls is all too common. In consulting, as a manager placing other analysts, I faced trying to educate clients about why the analysts I sent to interview were indeed the right choices. It is important for interviewers of business analyst candidates prepare questions that are open-ended, appropriate to the caliber of the candidate, specific to the role, complete, and without buzzwords.

I recently met with a prospective client to talk about an upcoming project. During the meeting, it became clear that he was not a business analyst and had no idea what tasks one should do. He did not ask appropriate questions for the role and he made some common interviewing mistakes that you will want to avoid.

The first mistake was not asking me open-ended questions. You cannot get enough information by asking someone if they have ever worked with a particular tool or technology. Asking closed-ended (yes or no) questions will likely only get you what you want to hear without adequate details, and you will not be able to make a sound choice in hiring. You should ask questions that make the person describe when and where they used a method to create a deliverable or solve a problem, and how they did it, or what issues they encountered. Only then will you know that they actually did create the deliverable and with what methods.

The next mistake he made focused on my skill set. After asking me if I had ever created any use cases and I responded affirmatively, he asked me *what* goes into a use case. This is a mistake in this instance because when interviewing someone with many years of direct experience, you do not want to ask about the elements; you want to ask them to give an example of a use case they have created and some of the challenges they faced. Alternately, you would ask them *why* the deliverable was important to the project (why they are created). The questions should be tailored to the level of experience claimed by the interviewee.

Another mistake that the potential client interviewer made was asking incomplete questions. At one point, there was a long pause while he collected his thoughts. Suddenly he asked, "What about functional requirements?" My response (not intending to be cheeky) was, "What about them?" As a seasoned professional with a great deal of interviewer experience, I asked for more clarity. "What exactly do you want to know about functional requirements and my experiences with them?" A candidate without an interviewer background would have likely rambled on by answering what she thought his question was. This is not open-ended questioning; it is simply vague and incomplete.

The other mistake that the interviewer made was focusing on buzzwords. It was clear he was not an analyst because nearly every question he asked used a buzzword. That tells me that there was no real depth to his knowledge. Worse, with his closed-ended questioning, it was clear he was content with a simple yes or no. He did not take the opportunity to learn anything about what an analyst does to improve his/her ability to interview or recruit new ones in the future.

One of my annoyances, which I suspect other senior level analysts share, is fielding calls and emails from recruiters who are asking me to apply for their roles, when they are really looking for junior and intermediate business analysts to work in a non-team lead capacity. So, why are they calling me? Quite simply, because they do not know what they are looking for and one analyst is as good as another.

To put this mistake into perspective, if you wanted someone to cook hot dogs in a vendor cart in the downtown area of a city, would you scan the online résumé section of the job board to find a professional chef? No way! Yet this type of recruiting and interviewing mistake occurs pretty often when it comes to searches for business analysts.

You need to ensure that you select the right caliber of candidate for the role and quality you expect. You will want to invest in quality, and opting for lesser qualified resources without also opting for a senior lead is not going to get you the level of quality that you are looking for.

Now let us say that you are looking for a senior business analyst and you come across an analyst with more than three projects under his/her belt and three years of experience. They might currently be in an intermediate role, but be qualified for a senior role and looking to advance their career instead of staying where they are. This could be a good choice.

When you interview someone and it is clear that the person has a lot of knowledge in an area, even if it is an area you share with them, it can be intimidating. The last thing you want to do is show how intimidated you are. It is bound to happen that, at some point in your interviewing career, you are going to interview others who are more senior than you are. Do not gush or appear ingratiating. Be professional and ask the candidates the same style and line of questions that are appropriate for their caliber. Ask for more details and examples, even if you do not know what they are saying and have no process for validating their responses. By asking for more detail and clarity in their responses, you may learn whether they are genuine. Since, in reality, great liars are hard to come by, when you ask for more details and ask the same question in different ways, you will quickly know the difference.

Another common mistake by interviewers is trying to intimidate and challenge the person whom they are interviewing. If you go into an interview with the attitude that you are going to catch them in a lie, or they are not as great as they seem on paper, my best advice is to either have someone else do the interview, or cancel it altogether.

A few years ago, I met with a prospective client whose president only sat and made eye contact with me for about two minutes of the interview. As he paced around the room, looking out the windows, he proceeded to tell me that he had hired MBA and Ph.D. graduates from Harvard and Oxford to come and work as business analysts. He blurted out that they had all failed. He demanded that I tell him why. Now, I know his real question was what makes you think that you will succeed when they failed, but that is not the question he asked.

I told him that I could not possibly tell him why without more details. I needed to know more about the individuals and work they had been assigned, and the processes utilized and the environment in which they worked, and the level of support (or lack thereof) that they received from management. I did not tell him that I was starting to get a pretty good idea why they had failed (some things you just keep to yourself), but when asked by the recruiter immediately following the interview if I would take the role if offered, I flatly said "No way!"

A good business analyst knows the needs of the business come first. That means that I am going to tell people things they may or may not agree with and tell them how to do their job better. Working for blatant bullies in a BA role is often a losing proposition, as I suspect the business analysts with doctorate credentials from Harvard and Oxford learned the hard way. Bully types can be impossible to please, making your odds of succeeding pretty remote.

The long and short of this discussion is before you ever get into an interview with a business analyst, know the caliber of the person you are going to interview. Read up on business analysis techniques and deliverables and write down some basic questions using the following caliber-centric guidelines.

Junior level candidates

When interviewing a junior level business analyst, you are looking for potential more than experience. That means you are looking for personal characteristics and academic knowledge more than detailed stories and explanations of where they have applied the knowledge. The types of questions that you want to ask are about the basic elements of the technologies, deliverables, and techniques. You want them to be able to tell you the elements, as well as why the deliverable is important to a project (why they are created). They may not have examples of how they have used them and challenges they have faced, so they need to know how and why you do them.

Intermediate level candidates

When interviewing an intermediate business analyst, you need to start blending your questions to include personal characteristics, academic knowledge, and experience. In general, you are usually considered to be intermediate at the three to five years of experience mark. That rule does not apply to business analysis. Years of experience does not necessarily correlate to specific levels of experience or even exposure to all deliverables, techniques, and tools. You could have worked for three years on a single project and never performed a particular task or created a particular deliverable.

In order to compensate for this, try asking questions about their ability to learn quickly and think on their feet because this will supplement their experiences thus far and still make them effective on your project.

Senior level candidates

When interviewing a seasoned senior level business analyst, you would expect that person to have worked on at least two projects, but in reality, most have actually worked on an average of 3.5 projects. You would also expect the senior level candidate to have had exposure to all deliverables and experience with most BA tools and techniques.

You do not want to ask senior level candidates about the elements of a given task, deliverable, or technique. Go in with the expectation that they must know these things if they are a senior level analyst. Instead, ask them to give examples of deliverables they have created, when and why they chose those ones, and then some of the challenges they faced on the project.

Above all, they must be able to explain the context of deliverables and techniques. That means you would ask them to tell you why the deliverable or technique is important to a project (why they are created). If you really want to challenge a senior level candidate in a positive way, ask them how they would improve the techniques, or what they do that makes them unique and more effective than their peers.

Uber-analyst candidates

Uber-analysts are those that other analysts envy and look up to. They have worked on ten or more projects across three or more industries and domains, and can provide strategic advice to the business from an operational and technological perspective.

The types of questions you should ask an uber-analyst in an interview are those centered on strategy, process, and the business. Do not ask them if they have ever used Microsoft Project and where, because frankly it does not matter if they have or have not. What does matter is their ability to adapt and adopt new techniques, tools, and technologies in order to get the job done effectively and efficiently, and to find ways to improve the overall project along the way. In other words, ask about what results they did achieve and how they achieved them.

It is really important to make the right choices for business analyst resources because making the wrong choices can completely derail your project. That means going into the interview with the right frame of mind, the appropriate set of questions, asking for details, and finding out how well the candidate will work with the team and business.

Depending on the complexity and criticality of your project, you will need to choose the right analyst(s) for the job in the same way you would choose the right tool for the job. In a toolbox metaphor, you would not choose a hammer if you had only screws to put some shelving together; you would choose a screwdriver and make sure that it fit the style of the screw. You would not try to make the screw fit the style of driver.

DEFINED ROLES

Defined roles can be considered an extension of the segregation of duties required by many regulating agencies. Having clearly defined sets of roles provide direction, efficiency in the performance of tasks, a layer of governance to ensure compliance, and prevent risks from becoming reality. In this case, defined roles prevent the costly mistakes of translation that occur when the business provides information about requirements directly to the development team, and then the development team goes and develops something else.

In this light, business analysis is essentially the governance layer to ensure that the business focuses on needs and results, instead of individual wants and desires. Having business analysts that are not dual tasked with testing or other activities also provides the ability for the analyst to produce results that are aligned to long-term business needs, goals, and strategies because they are not obligated to another role that can bias their approach and the resulting requirements.

The whole purpose behind defining the role of an analyst is to provide a clearly defined set of tasks, results, success/failure criteria, and performance measures that leads to a lean and optimized system.

The key element of any great organizational model is the coordination of resources to achieve a specific set of tasks. In order to be successful, every team member needs to know exactly what is expected of him or her, what to do, and how to do it. Defined roles are needed for each team and team member. It is a huge mistake to blur the lines on a technology project. You simply cannot get the quality that stakeholders deserve by doing so.

Remember the previous interview I had with the president of the company who was pacing around the room? One of the things he talked about as he looked out the windows was how they had no room for mistakes, and that people who made mistakes were "let go" immediately. Another thing he said that struck me was that I should not get too hung up on titles. In their IT department, they do not use titles—you could be programming one day, and testing or writing requirements the next. There is not a single human being alive who uses enough of their brain to be proficient at every single task available. The manager must segregate the roles and duties of each team member. When you do not, you set the stage for increased competition, team conflict, and duplication of effort. Why? Think back to why we do things like moving and stacking bricks in an orderly manner. It reduces stress. Have you ever developed a systematic way of doing something like loading the dishwasher, start to do it, and then someone else comes along to help? What is the first thing that happens? They mess up your "system" and get in the way. Eventually you have to tell them that you do not need their help or you move on and do something else and let them load the dishwasher.

Role definition improves the processes, attention to detail, and results. I have said it a million times: If you are a business analyst and you get offered a role that is BA/Anything, run fast in the other direction!

Each task that we business analysts do takes a certain combination of interest, aptitude, ability, and knowledge to do with any kind of proficiency. When we work on a project, we utilize these things to get the job done.

It is a rare circumstance that quality, productivity, and effectiveness do not suffer when you double up the role of an analyst with another project role. You do not reduce the amount of work by decreasing the number of resources; you are just decreasing the number of people you have doing the work. At some point, they are going to be physically, mentally, and emotionally drained, and quality is going to suffer. They are going to cut corners whether they are conscious of it or not. Why? If they specialize in another area, they may not even know that the corners exist.

A business analyst should always do business analysis. They should not be doing testing or also working as a developer. They should not also be acting as the subject matter expert, and they should not be acting as the project manager on top of that.

A business analyst must have a clearly defined job description and set of tasks and responsibilities, as well as a clear chain of command. Having these prerequisites will give the analyst the confidence, direction, and purpose that they need in order to work productively and effectively, without constant handholding.

At a minimum, the defined business analyst role must contain the following details: a list of key work products and deliverables and a detailed breakdown of the basic functional tasks to be performed. An example of products and deliverables, as well as tasks, could look like this:

1. Key work products and deliverables for the business analyst:
   a. Business processes
   b. Current and future state diagrams
   c. Benefits realization plans
   d. Verified and validated requirements documentation
   e. Use cases
   f. Object models
   g. Business rules
2. Primary functions and tasks for the business analyst:
   a. Communicate face-to-face, and through telephone, email, and web conferencing. The business analyst must be able to select the most appropriate means of communicating to ensure that they are able to perform all of their tasks and functions. They must be adept at both written and verbal communication, and have the ability to read and interpret non-verbal cues and body language.
   b. Conduct research to expose needs, high-level requirements, business rules, and processes. The analyst must have the ability to read both technical and nontechnical material, and extract relevant information that will affect the requirements, development, design, change management, and implementation of the end product. They must have the ability to locate and extract appropriate files or data as needed.
   c. Develop current state diagrams and process flow maps. The analyst must have the ability to illustrate and create a depiction of the current or present situation within the business. They will accomplish this through flow charts, context diagrams, storyboards, scenarios, and narrative documentation.

d. Contribute to the development of business rules to accommodate regulatory and corporate policy requirements. While the analyst is primarily responsible for capturing business rules, they may be required to create new rules for a new program, process, or application, based on inputs from internal or external sources.

e. Conduct joint application development (JAD) sessions. The analyst must be able to facilitate, lead, and drive the requirements sessions with assertiveness, confidence, and competence. The ability to provide leadership will significantly impact the overall project schedule, scope creep, and deliverable quality, as well as requirement quality, buy-in, involvement, engagement, and sign-off by the stakeholders and users.

f. Develop future state diagrams and process flow maps. The analyst must have the ability to illustrate and create a depiction of the future or desired situation (the results) within the business. They will accomplish this through flow charts, context diagrams, storyboards, scenarios, and narrative documentation.

g. Develop use cases. The analyst must have the ability to break down step-by-step interactions between the user and the system, and outline each step and task in a written document, or use this information to create a use case diagram. In addition to detailing the desired path, they must also demonstrate the ability to document and outline the alternate paths and extensions of use cases.

h. Elicit, analyze, document, and validate requirements. The analyst must demonstrate the ability to utilize various techniques, such as interviewing and facilitation, to work with users, but also to conduct research in order to compose requirements. They must also demonstrate the ability to analyze these requirements. In addition, they must have the ability to compose a well-planned, readable requirements document that targets the document consumers (architects, stakeholders, developers, and testers). Finally, they must demonstrate the ability to verify and validate requirements utilizing a variety of techniques that expose weaknesses in language, incomplete logic, and missing or incorrect requirements.

i. Lead and mentor business team members. Analysts must demonstrate the ability to lead and mentor others. This will exercise their ability to work with others across multiple types of teams and with various personality types. The ability to lead will influence the overall success of the project through a reduction in scope creep, and through product quality, alignment of the product to business needs, and schedule.

j. Make presentations to clients and project teams. The analyst must have the ability to create, organize, and conduct presentations to the business and project teams. They must be able to create a well-organized presentation, set up a meeting, establish an agenda, and manage participants and time effectively.

k. Manage priorities. The analyst must demonstrate the ability to manage priorities effectively in order to accomplish work in a criticality based sequence. This ability will also affect the analyst's ability to prioritize requirements according to need, readiness, and business criticality.

l. Work closely with quality assurance analysts. The business analyst must be able to work well with other members of the team, including the quality assurance analysts, in order to ensure alignment of the solution to the overall business goals and drivers, but also to ensure the quality of the final product before implementation.

The business analyst focuses on working with the bulk of the employee base up to mid-level management in order to discover and document the functional requirements of the "mass end user." The business analyst may also utilize surveys and historical issue management logs to identify areas of need and improvement, and use this information to develop or support the addition of requirements. The business analyst achieves this by conducting research, JAD sessions, and interviews with small groups, and through reviewing the gap analysis conducted by the process and systems analysts.

RESOURCE ATTRITION

Resource attrition is a symptom of a larger set of problems, and an indicator of an alarming trend that many people within information technology do not see. Unfortunately, resource attrition can impact the bottom line by increasing the cost to produce, and it can affect the top line by taking longer to develop products, which delivers reduced ROI over the product life cycle.

The unseen problem is that the numbers of business analysts that roll into and out of business analysis on a yearly basis is shockingly high. When a company has high employee turnover, it has a management problem. Either the managers cannot manage the staff and proceed to make them miserable enough to leave on a regular basis, or the managers are truly hiring the wrong people. Either way, attrition is a management issue and it must be dealt with as such.

Within a single role, it has been difficult to spot this trend. A lot of attrition blindness is due to the fluid nature of the relationship that most technology organizations have with business analysts. Since so many business analysts are contracted on a year or two (or less) basis, it can be difficult to see a pattern when we do not maintain a long-term relationship with individual resources.

Attrition is an important indicator of the overall health of the profession that must be taken into account, and must be taken seriously because the results that you can expect on your projects depend on it. Let me ask, would you consider hiring someone as an experiment on your multi-million or billion dollar project?

By the time that many business analysts are skilled enough to be considered good at what they do, many have decided to move on and are actively pursuing opportunities in new tracks. That means we need to look at management from a continuity perspective: continuity of the acquired skills and levels of expertise, and continuity of the very businesses we serve.

Why? Because when so many business analysts are not supported and continue to struggle, so too will projects, which ultimately leads to issues in the business because projects develop misaligned products and overspend at the expense of the businesses that we are supposed to serve.

This could be exactly why BA industry stats from 1996 to 2009 illustrate that project success rates went from 27% to a mere 32%[1]. That means that industry success rates progressed at a marginal pace of 5% over that time. If we used an average learning curve of a 20% increase for every time the volume of projects doubled across the industry, after doubling only twice, we should be at a 38.88% success rate; after doubling the number of projects a mere four times, we should be at an overall success rate of 55.99%.

So, why aren't the success rates better? Do the principles of a learning curve not exist in technology or business analysis? I believe that a high role-based BA attrition rate and the lack of formal BA processes and standards are hindering the growth in business analysis and success rates on projects.

In this chapter, we discussed resource management as a means of ensuring that we have the right numbers of the right resources in place to maintain existing client needs, and how to plan for and prepare to meet anticipated needs through capacity planning. The next chapter takes the discussion one step further and focuses attention on managing and measuring the performance of resources against the BA competency model. This yardstick supports resource management in that it provides information about the roles and competencies that enable accurate capacity planning and resource allocation.

---

[1] The Chaos Report. (2010). The Standish Group.

7

PERFORMANCE MANAGEMENT

Performance management works hand in hand with resource management in that it enables appropriate capacity planning and resource allocation. To accomplish this, *performance management* must provide a consistent set of metrics or key performance indicators, based on the role as well as the functional competency model.

BUILDING ORGANIZATIONAL CAPABILITY

Critics of Capability Maturity Model Integration[1] (CMMI) have suggested that achieving CMMI compliance levels is like walking a tightrope. If achieving CMMI compliance levels is like walking a tightrope (as it is exacting work to ensure that rope is taut throughout the trip), then maintaining compliance is like keeping a house made of crusted sugar from crumbling as it expands. It crumbles because as resources change and the business evolves, the level of CMMI compliance fluctuates. Unless compliance is controlled and our capability is tightly monitored, it cannot be maintained across the fluctuations. I have seen many companies give up trying to maintain CMMI out of frustration.

I have always been a strong proponent of CMMI, and consequently, a huge fan of Gartner,[2] one of the world's leading information technology research and advisory groups. The observations behind this model are sheer brilliance. However, I believe that the model is inaccurately labeled.

---

[1]Carnegie Mellon University, Software Engineering Institute; www.sei.cmu.edu/cmmi
[2]Gartner Research; www.gartner.com

Recently, I started to study and dissect organizational capability so that I could explain what I do professionally to others in a way that sells building capability as a service. Through my study, I discovered that there are components missing from CMMI. "Capability" is not just about maturity of processes that allow an organization to deliver; it is about its whole ability to deliver, period. Ability means infrastructure (processes, tools, etc.), environment (managing resources, culture, etc.) and resources (technical skills, soft skills, etc.). The current model is therefore a component of true organizational capability because it is merely a part of the larger equation that enables an organization's ability to deliver its products and services across its customer base.

Fully maintaining CMMI compliance is usually a snapshot in time, and is highly dependent on the organization to manage it as an entity as company growth fluctuates. Nevertheless, if we look at capability as ability, rather than the maturity of processes, it becomes more sustainable across growth fluctuations.

What is *capability* really? True organizational capability is the ability of an organization to deliver its products and services to internal and external customers, and ramp up or scale back those services as needed. In order to do this effectively, an organization must have the resources, framework, and environment to deliver those products and services. Without these, it will never matter how many people you have, or what you sell. You will never be able to adapt to meet customer demands as they rise and fall, or plan for those eventualities.

Building capability is more than just adding a few more skilled resources to the roster. It is more than buying them snappy tools to do their work. It is about understanding who you are as an organization, what you are selling, and how you will establish a company that lasts. It is about finding specific talent, managing that talent to produce as needed, providing them with the tools to deliver the services, and the emotional support to deliver the quality products and services your customers demand. If an organization wishes to be competitive and profitable long term, it needs to be able to answer the following questions:

- Why worry about building capability instead of conducting "business as usual" and,
- How do I know if my organization needs to build it?

In the technology industry the capability we have is clearly not working. For example, *The Chaos Report*[3] from 1996 to 2011 shows a slow crawl towards quality improvements while technology consumers foot the bill. Quite frankly, I wonder if we would be in our current economic state if corporations had been more fiscally responsible with their technology spending.

The fact is that if we build our organizational capability, we increase the ability to deliver products and services to customers. However, we have to be willing to go all the way. We cannot do this halfway anymore. That means if you have a technology organization, either internal or outsourced, and you use that organization to build

---

[3]The Standish Group; www.standishgroup.com

products or to reengineer process flows and infrastructure, you have to be willing to build capability across your entire technology organization. No amount of lean management or CMMI compliance can replace that capability.

BUILDING ORGANIZATIONAL EXCELLENCE THROUGH MANUFACTURED RESOURCE MATURITY

Building teams at all levels of an organization follows a fairly simple and standardized life cycle: hire, manage, promote, and terminate. Typically, when we hire an individual, they need to be trained and then spend time learning the assigned role. When we move into managing people, we expect to see an improvement in their performance because they have presumably learned the role. In order to promote individuals, we need to see that they excel in their career and believe in the organization. As we promote individuals, we expect to see them contribute more value to the business. Termination is a bit of a moving target because people can leave or be fired at any point in either the team life or career progression cycle.

Alternatively, the Resource Maturation Model (RMM), shown in Figure 7.1, illustrates an average progression that an individual will go through during their career: Learning, Improving, Excelling and Contributing. It aligns with the Forming, Storming, Norming, and Performing (FSNP) team development management model.

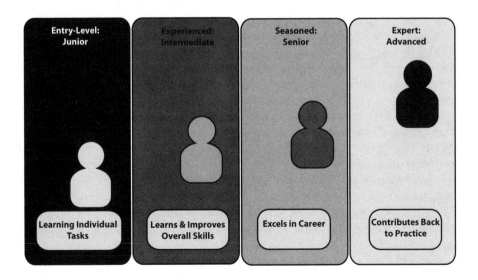

Figure 7.1 Resource Management Model (RMM)

As a person joins a team, there is always a degree of learning involved. They progress through the maturation model even if they are experienced; however, experienced people will progress at a faster rate. All new people also must deal with a new team, and so they will navigate through formation of that team and the struggles of storming, easing into the political culture of norming, and moving into performing the assigned tasks. The same is true of long-time employees who move into new roles or projects.

As people move through the maturity and the FSNP models, you can gauge an estimated timeline for when you expect to realize return on your investment in them (recruiting, advertising, training, etc.). It is important to understand that people are less productive when they are learning, and more productive as they become proficient, and that you want them to remain in a specific role or in the organization long enough to become proficient and start completing milestones. The more you support the success of your team through training and performance management, the faster you will achieve a positive return on the investments that you have made into analysts' careers.

Selecting or Hiring Team Members

In selecting or hiring team members, it is important to clearly define what you are looking for, and the role(s) that you expect them to fulfill, before you begin the recruitment process. If you have not already done so, I recommend analyzing the role and skills required to be successful, building a skills matrix and assigning a weighted 5-point rating scale to the functional elements of the matrix. Next, conduct an assessment of your existing practice area based on that matrix. The matrix will give you insights into the real capabilities and a measurement grid to see how closely capabilities align to your organization's goals and objectives. The matrix may also show that you already have the right people for the role, and that they can simply move into that same role or position.

Picturing your final team members can also give you the insights and the information that you will need to make more informed choices about new hires, training programs, and resource allocation. To select new people for your team, you will need to understand the career level of the candidate and his or her alignment to the capabilities assessment matrix. While this all sounds technical, leave room for gut feeling and perceived personality, and consider how these fit within the existing team and culture.

There have been many attempts to find the "magic formula" for hiring people. Companies have focused either entirely on personality tools, or on the technical ability of the candidate, but the truth is you must have a balanced approach. The approach that you take will depend on the people that you train and entrust with selecting and hiring new people.

I recently came across an interesting ancient Chinese saying about "walking on two legs."[4] The saying refers to taking a balanced approach to everything. You would

[4]Endicott, S. L. (1989). *Red Earth*. Toronto: NC Press Limited.

think it would be common sense, but it is not. For most people, the approach to many things, including the assessment or development of skills and competencies, is often riddled with biases adopted from one's own narrow perspectives. An example of taking a balanced approach in the development of competencies would be to create a weighted matrix and draw information from all areas that will benefit the person, increase their ability to perform a set of tasks, and ultimately produce the end results that are needed by the business.

Managing a Team

Assessing and analyzing team characteristics, qualities, and skills is not just something you need to do for recruiting new team members; it is also part of ongoing management and task assignment. It is a primary reason for monitoring performance. It is equally important to understand the needs and goals of individuals on your team because these will help you to plan future capability and drive training efforts to support team and organizational growth.

Managing a team is about understanding and recognizing individual team members, monitoring their performance, and providing opportunities for development. By understanding team characteristics, qualities, and skills, we can create an environment that fosters growth at a faster pace than simply letting people plod along in the same tasks for years on end. Yes, there will always be a group of people that will want routine. Moreover, there will always be a group of people that will never excel or contribute back. However, it is important to know who they are so you can set expectations for them. It can be disappointing to have a higher expectation of someone who will never deliver the work that is needed.

By adapting your assessment matrix to include key performance indicators (KPIs) you can create a consistent tool for ongoing performance management. Identification of KPIs is closely linked to the career level of the individual and their ability to perform given tasks with proficiency as they progress through their career. Assessment becomes an ongoing measurement of performance by evaluating how the resource performed the tasks against the KPIs.

The best way to measure performance is with a 360° evaluation. This type of evaluation provides a full view of the person's performance and supports realistic self-assessment that sets the stage for improvement. Consistent improvement is an ongoing individual and organizational need. Ideally, improvement is an ongoing process supported through an internal network mentoring program and nurtured by culture.

By building an internal network mentoring program, you are fostering an environment that empowers people to improve and set their own career progressions. This network essentially becomes a practice community that connects like-minded individuals who want to transition to new roles, improve their performance, share their knowledge, and contribute back to the practice through innovation.

The interesting thing here is that according to the RMM, you would expect to see innovation after a person has been in the role for some time and learned a thing or two. The reality is that juniors can also be highly innovative because they come in with an open mind, question the way things are done, and are eager to make their mark in their new roles. It is the refinement of innovation that comes from years of experience in the role that really matures the innovation to the point of being able to share and sell it.

The practice community also provides an excellent setting for organic mentoring and connections to occur as you bring together a cross-section of skill levels from wanna be's to senior people. These people will form cliques within the community and openly share their experiences and knowledge. By connecting these people, they can interact and begin to feel a sense of community. It is a sense of community that will nurture personal growth.

Manufactured Advancement

So, how do you use all of this information about managing teams to your advantage? By understanding that advancement is directly related to gaining knowledge and experience, we can manufacture advancement in an environment that provides both learning and opportunities to gain specific experience. Creating this environment provides the ability to speed up the advancement process.

When a resource has been assessed against the matrix and is shown to have the aptitude and drive, you can pair them with an on-the-job mentor and assign them to specific tasks that will provide opportunities for them to gain the specific experiences that they will need to advance successfully. You would want to manufacture advancement when you already have internal people that would be interested in and capable of performing the role. The only cautionary note is that, to work properly, you must establish the role of a mentor and provide the opportunity for experience. The mentoring needs to continue for at least six months.

Manufactured advancement does not mean that both people in a mentorship must be assigned to the same roles for the duration, but after the first few assignments, the mentor must remain accessible to the resource and maintain contact on a weekly basis. The mentor manages the performance of the resource and accepts responsibility for supporting their development into the role. This means that the mentor has to believe in the resource and their potential.

Promoting Team Members

Whether you have manufactured advancement, fostered the environment for organic advancement, or left it to individual people to self-manage, at some point you will have to decide to promote people into leadership roles. Moreover, while it is important to select people for the organization who will fit into your team and culture, it is even more important to promote people that personify the culture, and who will increase your ability to develop the skills of others and increase your organizational capabilities. Essentially, you would want to promote people who will extend your ability to manage your resources and provide continuity the organizational values.

In an ideal situation, we watch leaders rise within the ranks and provide them with opportunities to advance even farther. They become innovators and leaders that have the potential and ability to support your organization. Promoting leaders is a key differentiator between organizations that align to Gartner's Capability Maturity Model,[5] and those that do not. Organizations that do not manage and promote effectively tend to stay in chaos and find it harder to elevate themselves above it. It is possible to promote leaders without managing the process, but it will more likely happen by chance rather than by strategy.

The risks with leaving the emergence of leadership to chance are that you could end up with micromanagers, or people could be promoted to push the agenda of individuals over the organization.

Apples, Oranges, and Analysis

There is an irony within business analysis. While recruiting, screening, hiring, and even teaching others for and about the role of a business analyst, most managers demand and filter technical and academic skills. Yet, once people are hired and placed into the role, many of these same managers insist that the job that is being done is too volatile and uses too many soft skills to be measured. They insist that these factors alone make the measurement and benchmarking of requirements activities, progress, performance, quality, and even effectiveness impossible to accurately pinpoint and evaluate.

The reality is that we can build accountability into the system through process controls and governance models. Yet it is true that most governance models for the application of soft skills are the performance management system, policies, and practices in place.

Most performance management systems are typically highly subjective because the skills of the other people who are judging analysts may not be at their level. Company politics can play into their application of the system, and their perspective and interpretation can impact views of the same situation from different angles.

However, performance management assessments, coupled with metrics and clearly defined competencies, remove subjectivity (to a large degree) from the assessment process and provide both candidates and assessors a standardized set of criteria to work from. This means that the analyst can utilize criteria as goal posts to mark personal achievements and accomplishments. When using the same framework and criteria, the assessors and the beneficiaries of the assessments receive consistent results from all candidates.

In a recent discussion, someone quoted a business analyst "evangelist." The quote was, "The softer your skills, the harder it is to sell yourself." Well, I disagree. The more finely tuned your soft skills, the more assertive and able to negotiate you are, and the more effective your ability to communicate becomes. These are some of the hardest skills to learn. Don't get me wrong: learning the theory behind soft skills can be easy,

---

[5]Gartner Research; www.gartner.com

but learning the skills to the point of being able to readily apply them consistently is hard work. Actually, there is a longer learning curve for soft skills than technical ones.

One unique feature of IT is the diversity of work that can be done across a single career, especially as a consultant. Diversity of experience means that the person performs different roles, tasks and activities on each project (dissimilar), and often, performs those tasks different ways every time. In addition, many consultants experience feast and famine job cycles that impact the amount of experience actually obtained. When accountants say they have 5 years of experience, we know they likely have 5 years of similar experiences. However, when IT consultants work for 5 years, they may have held multiple roles and performed dissimilar types of work.

By performing dissimilar types of work, a consultant may not be able to claim the same amount of experience as those who perform similar types of work over the same time frame. A rough ratio is 8 months of performing similar work tasks is about 12 months worth of consulting experience. That means that when the average employee moves from junior to intermediate status after 3 consistent years in the same area, the typical consultant would make the same move at 4.5 years. However, with diversity of experience and feast and famine cycles, an analyst can go years (or even decades) without ever authoring a single use case, business rule, process map or requirement.

In fact, the nature of the analyst's work can make a résumé look more like a quilt than a solid, consistent profile. As shown in Figure 7.2, there can be large gaps between projects, and only some of those projects (with the stars) actually suggest some of the necessary experience to claim an iota of "exposure." However, that will not stop analysts from telling you that they have three years of experience, and are considered an intermediate when they would actually only be considered a junior. However, if a good performance management system with metrics and clearly defined competencies was in place to ensure that the quality of their results could be measured, then duration of time might not matter as much.

I recently saw an email from a recruiting firm calling for a Senior Business Analyst, which listed only two years of experience in business analysis as a requirement. The recruiting firm's desired performance level would be an issue because of the factors of diversity and the feast and famine cycles alone. Unless the analyst also came into technology with a long history in business or testing, it would be impossible for him or her to have achieved the performance level of a senior analyst, regardless of their level of intelligence.

From a business analyst perspective, performance management is a simple breakdown of the tasks that are performed to a granular level, deriving the competencies out of that granularity, and then assigning consistent quantifiable metrics to each competency, so that it can be observed and reported on consistently for each resource. Since we already defined the role of a business analyst, it is appropriate to start developing the details for each of the competencies before we get into the best scale for measuring performance.

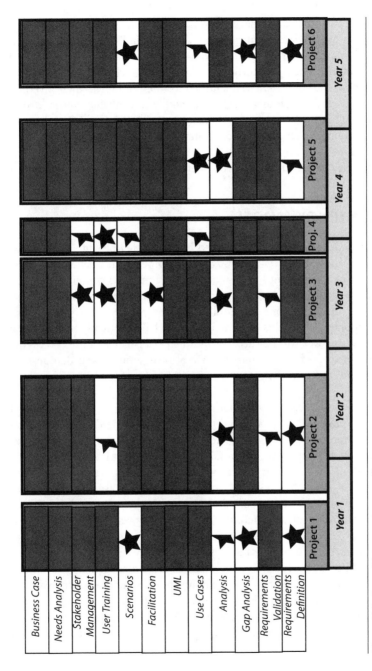

Figure 7.2 Consulting experience quilt

The other aspect that we have to consider is KPIs. Competencies and KPIs in combination provide a picture of how well a specific individual performs against the expected behaviors identified for their role, as well as against other metrics that the company identifies as being important. Typically, KPIs include not only a set of expectations based on the competencies identified for the resource at their given level, but other expectations for customer service and ability to contribute to the overall organization, as well as the amount of time that has been spent working with customers (the billable to non-billable ratio in consulting). KPIs are quantified and measured to portray a complete picture of the overall performance of the individual, as it relates to the role that they have and the company that they work for.

A COMPETENCY MODEL

Competency is defined as "a set of defined behaviors that provide a structured guide enabling the identification, evaluation and development of the behaviors in individual employees."[6] Therefore, competency models are frameworks comprised of the technical skills, academic knowledge, and behaviors that individual resources must possess in order to be considered for a given role.

The combination of skills, knowledge, and behaviors greatly increases the likelihood that the resource will be successful in the performance of the tasks required by the role. It is expected that resources must also draw upon and demonstrate these behaviors, skills, and knowledge sets during the course of their work at specific levels of proficiency.

Competency models are important for all resources as a means of reducing the time to train, ensuring adequate placement, increasing the chances of success, and decreasing the amount of money wasted in fixing errors and replacing lost resources due to attrition. Within business analysis, a key factor that I have noted is the desire of many analysts to move from business analysis to project management. One reason for this desire is simply because human beings are driven to be social and to follow parameters that make them feel confident and comfortable. When they have this drive at work their sense of job satisfaction increases and they are more likely to remain in the role.

Unfortunately, with business analysis competency models only now starting to emerge, there literally were no tangible parameters for how work was to be performed in the past. There was no idea of the behaviors that were needed. Moreover, there was no idea of the skills and knowledge that were crucial to success. As a result, many companies adopted a tendency to nominate business analysts from pools of either business users because they can use the jargon, or from pools of developers because the other developers think that they communicate well.

---

[5]*Wikipedia.* Retrieved from http://en.wikipedia.org/wiki/Competency_model.

The results have been catastrophic (although some people would dispute this). Nevertheless, when you consider that the success rates of projects have improved only marginally since the business analyst role was introduced, it is a wonder that business analysts are still around at all.

The most common mistake that companies make when creating a competency model is that they load the model with purely academic and technical skills instead of blending behaviors, personal characteristics, traits, and basic interpersonal skills, such as communication into the competency model. Unfortunately, when you load a competency model this way, you end up discovering personal traits and inconsistencies that make it difficult for the person to be successful at many aspects of the job.

Competency Based Assessment, Selection, and Management of Business Analysts

Choosing an analyst is much more than selecting the person with the most experience in a particular technology or domain. You need to find someone that is fairly agnostic of the applications and technologies within your environment, and someone who comes with the foundation that will make them a great analyst. You also want to ensure that the person comes with the personality to make them a great fit within your environment, and you want to find a person who meets the performance expected for the assigned role. Finally, you want to know the specific technologies that they have had experience with (unless there is a unique challenge coupled with an elongated learning curve). A great analyst has the ability to move in, learn new technologies quickly, and adapt to the new organization.

Domain knowledge presents a different angle than applications and technologies. While applications and technologies should play the least role in your decision to hire an analyst, arguments can be made for and against having domain knowledge. Typically, the knowledge of the intricate details of the project will increase with the amount of domain knowledge. The concern that I have with domain knowledge is that the emphasis is often misplaced because recruiters and hiring managers do not know what else to look for in a business analyst, so they tend to rely too heavily on domain knowledge.

If you choose to hire a person without domain knowledge, ensure that the person compensates with a personality that is open to learning and is results-oriented. Be cautious to understand how long it takes the average employee to adapt to your environment. If it takes a long time, hiring a senior BA without domain knowledge would be like hiring an intermediate person. This is because the level of performance that you will get will be similar to that of an intermediate while they are ramping up. I would reconsider this choice unless you are in a bind or the project spans a few years.

The Weighted Interview Matrix

In order to assess anyone for any task, you have to set criteria that are measureable, repeatable, and scalable, where the practical application between different people applying the same matrix yields the same result. Ideally, you want to get consistent results every time you assess a single individual, no matter who applies the matrix. The best way to achieve this is to define your criteria for measuring the skill levels of the analyst, and apply weighting criteria according to the skills you feel are most important to have in your organization. You essentially create a recipe for assessment by creating a weighted interview and assessment matrix.

Personally, I apply weighted criteria to the competency framework that I developed after working with, training, and managing groups of business analysts, and hundreds of hours of research into the roles that business analysts play in the technology realm. This approach allows the comparison of entire groups of business analysts to each other, assesses the capability of an organization through the skill levels of its resources, enables more effective resource assignments, supports more effective screening of new hires, and allows you to select new hires based on real need within the organization. Without weighted criteria, you are taking a shot in the dark on all of these items and you may essentially have collective chaos.

By drilling down into competencies and categorizing them, you can create a set of interview metrics that applies a 1 to 5 rating scale (where 1 equates to a new business analyst candidate with no experience and a rating of 5 equates to a strategic analyst or solution consultant). This set of metrics has supported the interviewing and screening of hundreds of business analysts with great success.

Competencies

With few formal professional standards governing the business analysis practice, how can we assess what makes a great analyst? How can we understand and assign a clear set of competencies to guide the hiring process? The best way to assess this set of competencies is to understand the scope of tasks and activities within the role, and then dive into the details of each of those tasks to create a practical set of competencies that are required by the person completing them in order to help them be successful.

A set of competencies can be categorized essentially into business skills, technical skills and soft skills, as shown in Figure 7.3. Within each category is a subset of skills, knowledge, and experiences that would give the candidate the ability to excel as an analyst.

Since the ability to perform a task is dependent on the person's ability to understand the business from both functional and technical perspectives, their level of domain knowledge, and their ability to collaborate with other people, it only stands to reason that competencies must include business skills, technical skills and soft skills. From my observations and experience, programs that do not include a full and holistic set of competencies consistently struggle and are plagued with challenges when it comes to the resources actually having the ability to perform the role of a business analyst.

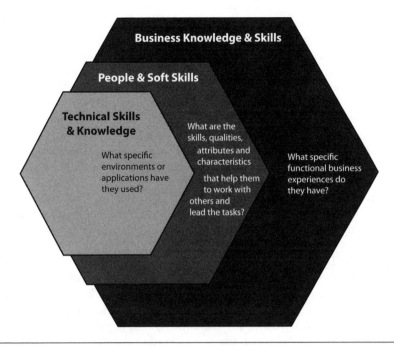

Figure 7.3 Competency model

Without a full competency program, projects are usually riddled with the symptoms of high client complaints, excessive scheduling slips, missed milestones, and missing or poor quality deliverables. So, exactly what are these competencies? Well, let us review some of the more common one.

Business Skills—An analyst is only as good as their knowledge of the business. It is, however, more critical that they have ability and a "10,000 foot high" view to understand that numerous businesses function similarly across industries. Yes, every industry wants to be unique, but there are so many similarities across business functions due to national regulations for individual professions (such as accounting and human resources), that the differences will lie more within the corporate and industrial culture than anything else. Having the ability to jump into any business and quickly understand the nuances that make it unique is a skill that can best be honed by exposure to various functional experiences such as project management, or just plain functional experiences within that particular industry.

Project management can be described as having the skill and ability to coordinate project resources to achieve an effective result for the client or stakeholders. What makes up an effective result? The project has been completed on time and on budget, and meets the target business goals and objectives outlined in the project charter. An optimal result would be a higher quality product delivered under budget and in less time. A challenged project is completed over budget and past the time line, and does not meet the targeted business goals and objectives. A failed project is cancelled because it is clear it will not meet the expectations or deliver any result for the money that is being spent. A good business analyst will support the project manager and work with them to coordinate their resources and deliverables to meet key milestones.

Domain Knowledge—This is the vertical knowledge and understanding that a person has in an industry. That is, a person going to work as a business analyst in a retail chain might have previous retail experience. This would be vertical industry experience.

Personally, I rarely put a lot of stock into domain knowledge unless there is a highly unique aspect to the industry that you must really know well. An average business analyst with domain knowledge will likely be able to work in the same industry that they know well and provide relatively decent results. However, a great business analyst will be able to walk into any client in any industry and provide effective or optimal project results. This means that they can tackle any project and learn it quickly enough to translate their learning into action as they work.

Ads on Internet sites looking for business analysts with specific domain knowledge are fairly common. In fact, many industries are notorious for being exclusive about the candidates having a specific amount of domain tenure as a business analyst. So why is domain knowledge often a requirement or hiring criteria? Part of the reason is because the recruiter or hiring firm does not really understand the value proposition that a highly skilled business analyst brings to the table, and the rest of the reason is rooted firmly in the functional complexity of the environment and the flexibility of the client to take risks in hiring someone who does not have domain knowledge.

Complexity impacts the type and number of requirements, not just from a functional perspective, but also from a regulatory perspective. It can also impact change control, size, and timelines when regulatory bodies make changes to their mandates and limit the time to implement the changes. In some industries, projects feel more like a tennis match with stops and starts, and routine changes in direction.

By asking for someone with domain knowledge, companies are really trying to address the functional complexity of the project. For highly skilled business analysts, this is not a real issue because they understand that business generally operates on the same principles, and they have the ability to think "on their feet." They expect change, and they plan for it. However, average business analysts are often just trying to keep ahead of the curve on a project, and do not look up often enough to be able to make plans for "what if" scenarios.

That is exactly why it is important to learn how to measure functional complexity before you start the requirements activities. It will make it easier to ramp up, estimate, and plan for the changes and implementation.

Technical Knowledge—This is the understanding that a person has of the technical (horizontal) aspects of the particular project. For example, a person going to work on a project to design a new point of sale (POS) system might have previous experience in designing a POS system for another client. It is the knowledge of the POS system that is considered technical knowledge, and the ability to apply that knowledge is a skill. Personally, I do put weight on technical knowledge, but not to the point of excluding analysts with the ability to learn and adapt quickly to whatever you throw at them. What I look for is a diversity of knowledge of technical environments and tools. This provides me with insight into the person's adaptability and ability to learn quickly. As far as individual technical skills go, the list can be as long as the list of projects. The best indicator of a business analyst's success is to have a basic understanding of how development occurs, how data is stored and retrieved, how processes are automated, and the basics of systems architecture. Each of these is a piece of a complex puzzle that they will be tasked with solving during the project.

People Skills and Soft Skills—For those who think you cannot or do not need to assess for soft skills, you might want to check with your clients because they are guaranteed to think soft skills are important. Soft skills are competencies and attributes that enhance job performance and career prospects and an individual's interactions with others such as coworkers and clients. As a number of soft skills pertain to proficiency of interactions with others, some are often referred to as people skills. To a large degree, they are simply intertwined. A listing of all potential soft skills would be extensive. So we will only discuss a representative sampling of these important skills. A listing of soft skills might include the following:

Interpersonal relationship skills are the ability to build trust, find common ground, and ultimately build good relationships with people. If a client does not trust you, the odds of you being retained are remote.

Communication skills are the ability to send messages to others in ways that are meaningful to the receiver. Communication is verbal, written, and nonverbal (body language), and all forms of it can be used to convey messages. Because people learn in many different ways, and since communication is a vehicle for learning about the world around them, it is important to provide messages in a variety of ways. By doing this, it will make it easier for your receiver to accept and learn the content of your messages.

Negotiation skills are the essential building blocks to becoming a good business analyst. High-end sales experience is one potential source for gaining a foundation in negotiation. This soft skill is needed because the analyst will be required to help a client understand if the requested solution is not the best solution, and they need to sell them on a new one and negotiate the right implementation in the environment to satisfy the client's needs.

Listening skills are needed to become even an average analyst. For example, how accurate will the requirements gathered on a project be if the analyst lacks the ability to listen and document what you have heard? If you were to learn one single thing that would enable you to collaborate better as an analyst, it would be listening. Often, we do not listen when others speak; instead, we are usually formulating our own response or counter arguments rather than listening first. We need to really hear what others are saying, recognize what they have said, and clarify it if necessary. Then, we can formulate a response and provide it appropriately.

Collaboration skills are critical for successful business analysts because they must be able to work with the business, stakeholders, developers, testers, project managers, and sometimes external vendors. They must be able to communicate verbally and on paper, and mediate and negotiate at all levels. Collaboration is as much a learned skill as it is innate. We learn by trial and error, and learn collaboration best when we are in tune with those around us. If you cannot collaborate with a client consistently, they will fire you.

Networking skills help form strong relationships or alliances with others. Networking is important in building connections across an enterprise. If you do not know something yourself, it's important to know who can help.

Teamwork skills allow you to work successfully in a group setting, including assuming the role of a team player, putting the goals of the team ahead of one's personal goals.

Critical thinking/problem solving skills pertain to one's ability to think critically and pull together data to solve a problem. One of the keys to being an effective problem solver is developing the solution to the problem in a reasonable timeframe. It is also important to be able to explain how the solution to a problem was solved in both a logical and systematic manner.

Innovation skills are the critical differentiator between analyst candidates. An analyst's willingness to think outside-the-box to resolve a problem with the best possible solution (without being hung up on personal attachments to particular solutions that do not cut it) is crucial. As an innovator, be prepared to describe what contributions you have made to past clients—these are achievements and the client or recruiter may want to hear them. Just be prepared to back up the claim, and be honest about how much of a role you had in it.

Facilitating skills are the ability to coordinate and solicit well-represented opinions and feedback from groups with diverse perspectives to reach a common, best solution.

Some additional examples of soft skills are influencing/persuasion, conflict resolution, interviewing, and presentations skills. The list could go on and on.

As mentioned previously, having people skills is about the ability to work with people of all career levels and developing positive relationships. It is necessary for an analyst to spend time with front line staff and developers, all the way up to executives. Having good people skills will enable them to do this in a way that makes the rest of their job easier.

In addition to competencies, there are other considerations for hiring. Two of them are career level and résumé.

Career Level

As discussed previously in manufactured advancement, as a person grows in their career, they move through various stages. The RMM illustrates the stages of learning individual tasks, improving at the overall job, excelling in performance, and contributing to the innovations within the practice. Not everyone will achieve all of these levels, but it is still important to recognize and understand the level that your candidate is at when you propose to hire them.

Hiring a new business analyst that comes in as an innovator does not mean that they will not still need some time to ramp up into the new role, project, or environment. They will need to get accustomed, so understand what you can do through training and orientation to mitigate and reduce that need.

You can use skill and career level of the business analyst to indicate the kind of participation that you can expect. This means more than handholding juniors and letting seniors loose in the shop. It means that you have to temper your project's needs with your budget and your ability to mentor, as well as your tolerance for risk. While interviewing, managing, and working with business analysts from newbie to off-the-chart advanced, I found the single biggest group of contributors was the junior to intermediate group. They were full of motivation to improve and open to being mentored.

The RMM shows that innovation and shaping the practice comes at a higher level, but this does not mean that people at lower career levels do not contribute. The difference is that the senior knows what they are seeing within the context of the project, practice, and environment and has the ability to document the innovation in ways that effectively transform the practice.

Résumé

If a business analyst cannot put together a well-formatted résumé, I would not consider them unless they were looking for a junior role. I am not saying they need to know how to navigate Microsoft Word with the deftness of a surgeon conducting brain surgery, but they should know how to use one tab to place text in certain places on the paper without hitting the space bar a hundred times. More importantly they should know how to put together a formal sentence or paragraph stating a clear message of what they are looking for in their new role, and be able to convey what they have done in the past.

Far too many business analysts' résumés focus on the wrong things or are written for the job they have, not the job they want. I eavesdropped on a business analysis Internet discussion board once, and read several threaded comments from an analyst who was complaining about sending out lots of résumés and not having gotten a single response. So, I told him that I have interviewed hundreds of analysts and have a solid reputation for selecting them, and that if he was interested, I could read through his résumé to see if there was anything that might be putting off prospective clients.

The analyst agreed, and within a couple of days, I was reading his résumé. It did not take long to spot the problem. It was not a business analyst's résumé at all, but a developer's résumé. He had an extensive list of all of the programming languages, software applications, and computer platforms he could work in. There was nothing noteworthy about his requirements experiences, results he had garnered for clients, or the projects that he had helped to implement. Honestly, if he had not told me that he was a business analyst, I would never have known it. A business analyst's résumé should never be limited to a list of programming languages and software. It should include mentions of the platforms and system types in order to explain what they did on a particular project and relevant accomplishments.

So much of the role of an analyst is about documenting processes, business cases, use cases requirements, issues, risks, and gaps, that if they cannot put together a résumé that reflects their ability to construct a well-defined document, I am not going to hire them.

It is important to remember that each project, situation, and candidate is unique. The fact is, like choosing any other employee for your company, if done well, the choice can contribute to the positive growth and evolution of your organization. Done incorrectly, the choice can turn into an unhealthy relationship.

KEY PERFORMANCE INDICATORS

We have previously discussed how KPIs can be utilized as a quantifiable framework for managing and assessing a team of individuals. Now, how to assign KPIs is further discussed to give you an idea of how to establish your own KPIs for your business analysis services organization.

KPIs are a combination of competency-based metrics and company goal-oriented measures that collectively provide a holistic picture of how well a specific individual performs (see Figure 7.4). They are measured at various intervals across projects and years of tenure in order to consistently measure and monitor an individual resource's progress.

Typically, KPI's are a set of defined and quantifiable performance metrics for a given role that enable you to measure and assess the performance of resources as either an individual or a collective group. Key performance indicators can be used to set expectations for growth, ensure that resources are consistently performing as expected when compared against their peers or other groups within the company, and show how that performance aligns to the strategic objectives. They are most commonly set by role and then by career level, so you would see a set of standard KPIs for junior business analysts, another set for intermediate business analysts, and yet another set for senior business analysts.

KPIs are important because they enable resources to self-regulate performance, and to work toward their own professional goals. This provides motivation for resources to improve, and supports the business' overall need to expand and maintain continuity. However, KPIs also support managers in assessing resources' abilities and on-the-job performance.

They support the allocation of the appropriate resources to the appropriate tasks in support of the business's overall goals by removing a layer of subjectivity and personal preference from the decision-making process. In the event that a resource is terminated, having a defined and managed set of KPIs can protect both the resource and the manager from repercussions stemming from a termination because they are tracked and monitored on a regular basis.

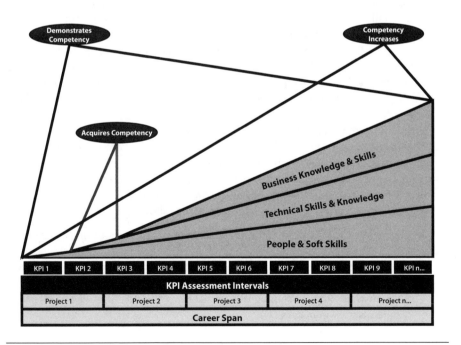

Figure 7.4 Key performance indicators

The type of KPIs that impact business analysis outcomes establish appropriate quality levels for productivity and effectiveness of the work. These indicators ensure that the business is getting value from the role, and that resources can be assured that they will be measured by more than just the like or dislike of a single project manager or stakeholder.

Unfortunately, there is often a disparity in the KPIs for business analysts. They are either nonexistent, subjective due to personal bias of the project manager or stakeholder, or set by the project management office (PMO). This disparity is one of the leading causes for the inconsistent application of business analysis methods between any two resources or any projects with the same resources. This same disparity is also a leading cause of frustration that can result in high, role-based attrition rates.

Where KPIs are nonexistent, business analysts have no yardstick by which to measure and self-monitor their own performance. This means that they are not able to set tangible and practical goals for career growth and development.

When KPIs for business analysts are subjective, the analyst's view of success is impacted by the likes and dislikes of the other person. This situation, in turn, can lead to poor references, an inability to secure the next project, and the promotion of other (incompetent) resources because of outright favoritism. For many business analysts, this means that their performance is not really rated based on whether or not they delivered on time and the client was "happy" with their deliverables.

A key issue with having KPIs defined by the PMO is that the defined indicators are usually inappropriate for the business analyst role, and do not adequately represent the competencies that they require to perform their roles successfully. Key performance indicators specifically for business analysts must be aligned to the core competencies defined within the competency model. Where the competency model describes what skills, knowledge, and behaviors are needed, the KPIs describe how well each competency should be demonstrated and how many are required for each career or advancement level.

Since KPIs are rooted in the competency model, and aligned to the overall strategic objectives, it makes sense that KPI matrices contain a cross-reference from the objectives and competencies to the skill level, and illustrate the proficiency with which you would expect to see the analyst perform each of the elements of the task. For example, where communication is the competency, it would be evident that an analyst is a good communicator if they can demonstrate the following:

- Responds to all forms of communication and provides input in a timely manner.
- Provides constructive input and feedback by focusing on positive results and how to achieve the goals and objectives.
- Demonstrates active listening in conversations and meetings or other settings where discussion occurs.

However, it is not enough to simply state that an analyst must be able to demonstrate each element of communication as a means of proving that they are good communicators. We must also consider the fact that people in general demonstrate varying degrees of proficiency at various stages throughout their careers. This means that we must also use a KPI model that depicts how well we expect each resource to demonstrate elements at each level. Therefore, if we look back at the communication example again, we must also state the level of proficiency we expect from resources across junior, intermediate, and senior levels like this:

- Responds to all communications and provides input in a timely manner.
    a. Junior: Consistent. Consistently demonstrates communication ability through the return of emails, voice mails, notices, and letters, as well as face-to-face conversations.
    b. Intermediate: Average. Not only demonstrates consistency in communications, but also demonstrates quality and a level of proficiency expected for an average resource after years of direct experience.
    c. Senior: Above Average. Not only demonstrates consistency in communications, but also demonstrates high quality and a level of proficiency expected for an average resource after years of direct experience, and is able to coach and mentor others in this skill area.
- Provides constructive input and feedback by focusing on positive results and how to achieve the goals and objectives.
    a. Junior: Inconsistent. Inconsistently contributes to ongoing discussions and provides some basic commentary on the work or subject.
    b. Intermediate: Consistent. Consistently contributes to ongoing discussions and provides appropriate, solicited and unsolicited commentary on the work or subject.
    c. Senior: Average. Not only demonstrates consistency, but also demonstrates quality and professionalism expected for an average resource after years of direct experience.
- Demonstrates active listening in conversations and meetings or other settings where discussion occurs.
    a. Junior: Inconsistent. Demonstrates the basic ability to carry on a conversation, but occasionally requires reminders to seek clarification when others are speaking.
    b. Intermediate: Consistent. Consistently demonstrates the ability to carry on a conversation and seeks clarification when others are speaking.
    c. Senior: Average. Demonstrates an average ability to carry on a conversation and seek clarification when others are speaking by making eye contact, paraphrasing, and confirming understanding or interpretation.

The above examples utilize a simple formula based on the consistency with which a given resource would be expected to demonstrate a specific element of the competency, while working on assigned tasks throughout the period covered by the KPI assessment. These levels of consistency can be mapped to the following definitions:

- Inconsistent—The resource applies the specific skill or set of skills in less than 50% of all related tasks assigned, and requires improvement in this area in order to advance to the next career level.
- Consistent—The resource applies the specific skill or set of skills in about 50 to 75% of all related tasks assigned, and requires improvement in this area in order to advance to the next career level.
- Average—The resource applies the specific skill or set of skills in about 75% of all related tasks assigned, and could use improvement in this area in order to advance to the next career level.
- Above Average—The resource applies the specific skill or set of skills in 85% of all related tasks assigned with a high degree of proficiency and quality. Practitioner may act as an SME or mentor in this area.
- Superior—The resource applies the specific skill or set of skills in at least 95% of all related tasks assigned with an exceptional degree of proficiency and quality. Practitioner may act as an SME or mentor in this area and qualifies to act as a strategy or solutions consultant in this area.

You can assign weighted metrics for each level to create a scoring mechanism. Depending on how valuable you think that communication is within the company, you may assign values to each level on a scale of 5 or 10. (I usually prefer a scale of 5 because it is simpler. See below.) In this case, each proficiency level would have a basic value, and the total of all values assigned to these levels should equal 13:

Level	Weighted Score
- Inconsistent	0.5 point
- Consistent	1.5 point
- Average	2.5 points
- Above Average	3.5 points
- Superior	5 points

The reason that you want to assign metrics to each performance indicator is to develop a weighted matrix of relatively nonsubjective standardized values that will make it easy to illustrate and evaluate the characteristics, qualities, and health of your business analysis team. If you were to conduct a simple assessment of your resources based on this example, you should reasonably expect to find that approximately 75% of your team falls into the category of Average proficiency, while approximately 15% will be Above Average, an estimated 7% will be Superior, an estimated 5% will be Consistent, and finally, about 3% will be Inconsistent.

If your numbers vary greatly from these estimates, you may have an issue to address in hiring. This is the approximate breakdown of skill levels you should find in many other practice areas if you were to explore them, as well. It all comes down to cost and necessity. Resources at either end of the scale tend to cost more, either directly to the resource or indirectly to manage them, while resources in the middle are the least expensive because they can be depended on to perform. How well they do is another story, but at least we can see that there is an aptitude and understanding in place.

From here, we can add other factors that have been derived from the strategic objectives. These would include customer satisfaction surveys, meeting targets for billable vs. non-billable time, as well as other objectives set by the company to ensure that the resource will do the job well and represent the company accordingly, contributing to growth and other goals of the company. For each skill, competency, and KPI, you want to assign a similar metric, so that the ratings can be compiled.

Another element that I like to add is a simple count and metric for domain knowledge, especially when it comes to business analysis. This metric will enable you to tap into specialized knowledge where and when you need to, but it can also indicate when you need to pull in others if you are short on a particular domain. It can also support capacity planning.

It is important to measure competency and key performance indicators so that you are able to monitor the size and capabilities of your team and make informed decisions about specific resource allocations, succession planning, and hiring. The metrics can be rolled back into human resources and financial reports that enable you to make policy and financial decisions, as well as to decrease the risk faced on individual projects.

SUMMARY

In this chapter, the functional management of business analysis resources and building organizational capability focused on three pivotal points: finding resources, promoting them, and replacing them. Gaps within the resource management process were identified, and how those gaps actually create disparities between the roles that an analyst must perform and the roles that they are directed to perform under the management of nonbusiness analyst managers was explored.

The information in this chapter provides an arsenal of methods for the selection and screening of business analyst candidates at various levels of their careers to ensure that the approaches to managing business analysis resources are consistent, managed, and controlled.

Performance management can be used to establish a proverbial yardstick to assess resource performance and competency against. Where resource management is all about creating capacity and the subsequent allocation of resources (deployment), performance management is all about the capability of those resources to perform specific tasks with a prescribed level of proficiency.

Performance management works hand-in-hand with resource management to ensure that the right resources are allocated to the right projects in order to yield the most effective and profitable results. In this case, KPIs and competencies are means of ensuring that you have the right resources. Competency models and KPIs can enable the development of a capability model. With a thorough performance management plan in place, your resources are positioned for greater success simply because they have a lot less on their plate to worry about. They do not have to be concerned with getting references for the next project or appeasing individual desires over the needs of the business.

When you consider that the role of business analysis is to translate strategy into tangible solutions, and the obligation is to uphold and safeguard the interests of the business while employing financially sustainable methods, it is the role of performance management to establish the competencies to make this happen. The role of the KPIs is to measure progress and outcomes. Once this understanding of performance management is internalized, and it is firmly established in the minds of every business analyst as well as embedded within the models for every business and technology organization, then the industry as a whole will experience an exponential increase in productivity. It will also equally accelerate a decline in the problems that are associated with inconsistencies between resources, poor business analysis methods, and informal standards, which enable resources to cut corners and employ methods as they interpret them. It is important to remove highly subjective management practices that focus the attention of the business analysts on the needs of the individual over the long-term needs and goals of the business. At that point, we will be in a position to create better outcomes for the business and ensure that any investment in technology carries with it a maximum return on investment with minimal risk.

IN CONCLUSION...

Who the heck created the ad hoc profession we now call business analysis anyway? Honestly, it reminds me of an old *Saturday Night Live* skit with Jon Lovitz.

"I'll create a new role. . . a new role to write up the requirements for software. That will make everybody happy. Yeah, that's the ticket!"

TECHNOLOGY ISSUES

For those of us in an industry that prides itself on strategy, metrics, scheduling and acquiring the next great certification, we did not bother to plan, set benchmarks, standards, communication and training for this industry-wide implementation of business analysis. It could be argued that the IT industry has been forced to adopt the business analysis role out of necessity in an attempt to fix the inherent issues in software development. Yet the fact remains that we have continued to forge ahead with this ad hoc role, and watch it gain strength and notoriety in an organic way despite the annual Standish *Chaos Report*[1].

Whether you believe the *Chaos Report* or not, it has consistently measured a set of metrics over the past fifteen plus years that paints a picture so disturbing that it could be said that those who openly dispute the report are actually in denial.

While requirements are not the only factor in struggling and failing projects, they are an area that individual business analysts can change because they have control over these tasks and elements. However even the most senior and competent business analysts have fallen into the pattern of organic growth while struggling to champion better

[1]The Standish Group; www.standishgroup.com

methods and techniques for all, because until the last ten plus years there were no formalized training programs, competencies, key performance indicators, job descriptions, assessment criteria, templates, and methodologies. It has been the emergence of university-accredited educational programs and groups like the IIBA supported by the innovative ideas of a few training and consulting firms that have made the push for widespread changes.

Nevertheless, even today, there are many band-aid solutions to get around and fix the problems with requirements such as Extreme Programming and Agile. However, at the end of the day we still have to fix the problem with requirements and not just the symptoms of poor requirements.

Essentially, we are approaching the problems with requirements in the same way that many people approach weight loss. We all want a quick fix so we can wake up and the weight is gone. We do not want to expend the effort, energy or commitment involved in working out and eating healthy so we invest great deals of money into quick fixes like dieting pills that promise big results literally overnight without any hard work or real effort on our part.

The *Chaos Report* is intended to draw attention to the issues that the entire industry faces. Yet sadly instead of doing the real work to change the situation, the report has lead to a widespread finger pointing and a focus on quick fixes. The industry as a whole needs to begin focusing on the issues, the realities of the situation, and not who to blame.

Based on interview results of hundreds of business analysts, those with fewer than three years of experience and less than two projects are struggling to do the job and steadily improve. Considering the fact that EVERY project and EVERY company is different, and the lack of consistent industry practices and formal methods and metrics in place, these results should not be too surprising to anyone focusing on the issues and the understandable realities of the situation.

Business analysts are so starved for support, standards, and formalized processes that they have resorted to meeting on sites like Linked In, Requirements Networking Group and Modern Analyst to connect with each other as if they are having a clandestine affair on management. The truth is that they need management as much as management needs them.

While we can see that the biggest consequence of this lack of management is that the industry faces dismal project odds, the real problems and issues are more far-reaching. We in the business and technology community are simply not addressing the issue of improper management of our resources needed to create specific, measurable, and improvable products that meet the needs of the consumer.

BUSINESS CONTINUITY AND SUSTAINABILITY

What does the improper management of resources that we just discussed spell for business and technology? It spells a lack of business continuity resulting from a lack of organizational capability. How? Business continuity is dependent on the consumer marketplace and the ability to consistently and repeatedly deliver products that meet consumer needs, as well as the ability to scale production up or down to meet fluctuating demands. If you do not have organizational capability, you can never have the capacity to create the factors that business continuity depends on.

PEOPLE + PROCESS + TOOLS = RESULTS

Organizational capability is the ability of a company or organization to produce and deliver its products and services consistently to its market with managed results by combining the elements of human resources, physical and material resources, and intellectual resources in an environment that is conducive to producing the desired results. In plain English, this means an organization's capability is really about having the ability to serve the needs of its customer base. As we can see in Figure S2.2 that ability is highly dependent on the skills of its human resources, the tools and processes they utilize, the framework to deliver that service consistently, the scalability of service delivery, and the support and framework in place to evolve that service.

Effectively, organizational capability is bound to organizational maturity in that maturity is a product of the evolution and refinement of capability.

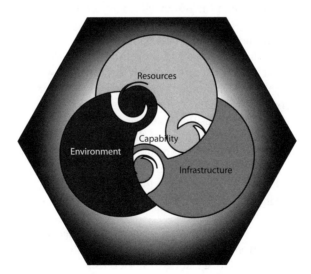

Figure S2.2 Organizational capability

Primary Issues Resulting from a Lack of Business Analyst Management

Now that we have a better understanding of what organizational capability is, let's look at the issues that undermine a business's ability to maintain continuity as a result of the lack of business analysis capability. In general, we have an inability to find, filter, place, manage, advance and retain business analysts as a direct result of our lack of functional management.

This is a direct result of our inability to consistently and concretely identify business analyst specific pipeline criteria, metrics, benchmarks, data and information, but also because of a lack of standardized role expectations, a lack of key performance indicators, performance metrics or benchmarks, competencies and career planning. What we see as a result, is that business analysis resource attrition rates escalate with tenure. In other words, the more senior an analyst, the more likely they are to move out of their role and the less likely they are to contribute back to the overall growth of others coming up through the ranks.

The general pattern that has been demonstrated over the past ten plus years of business analysis is that the management of the analyst resources drops dramatically after the hiring process has been completed and the resources begin reporting directly to projects. While there is some performance management on individual projects, it really is more of an ad hoc management that results purely from the specific issues that arise during the course of the resource's tenure on the project. In addition, it is subjective according to personalities and political agendas of the other team members, stakeholders, sponsors and project managers.

The reality of the situation is that as management decreases the analyst is expected to sink or swim, quite simply because they are forced to grow into their knowledge and abilities organically by combining their personal experiences on specific projects with little or no direction from a functional manager. Because of this, it can be hard to locate resources with enough consistent experience and ability.

In addition, because there are a lack of filtering measures and criteria, it can be hard to recruit and screen analyst candidates through any other means than simply using a desired skills checklist and scanning the résumé for key words. That does however change as the analyst's own ability to go into greater detail increases and they begin to educate the interviewer. Again, that only changes as the analyst's abilities grow organically.

Role-based attrition has always been a factor for business analysts because there is little or no direction from management and there is only so long that most people can sit on a drifting boat before deciding to abandon ship or take the helm. The rates of analysts using business analysis as a stepping stone to project management are still higher than they are with other roles, but it is getting better. To see a significant impact, we need to begin supporting our business analysts, motivating them, mentoring them, helping them to establish career plans, define real competencies that account for technical and personal skills, and really create a solid infrastructure for the management of business analyst resources.

In a subsequent section called "The Role of Management in Quality Requirements" it is proposed that business analysts need the supportive environment of upper management, project managers, sponsors and stakeholders to create quality requirements products. That section, which talks a lot about intangibles like motivation and support that we take for granted, should be inherent in every work environment. However, the truth is that they are not.

What I am talking about here, is really an extension of that social environment that enables you to consistently strive to improve and mentor others simply because you love your job, and the environment encourages you to do those things. I am talking about the infrastructure that management provides to help us navigate our own paths, yardsticks to measure progress against, and indicators that can detect early signs of either aptitude or failure. It is one thing to measure requirements efforts, but it is quite another to start measuring and directing the resources that perform the tasks.

That means that we have to understand that competency is not merely technical but social and interpersonal; that capability is not just learning more skills that are technical; that infrastructure provides a framework for continual capability improvement; and that environment shapes how the resources view their contribution to the organization.

The truth of it is that if we were talking about benefits coordinators, project managers, developers, testers, or any other role within an organization, we would get it. There would be no question that the benefits coordinators would functionally report to HR, or that the project managers would functionally report to the PMO before the project team.

Why don't we get it? Is it because the concept of the analyst is still so new that we still have this idea that they are the "Jack-of-all-Trades?" Well, you know what they say about the "Jack-of-all-Trades," don't you? "A Jack-of-all-Trades is a master of none."

That means no more doubling up resource roles: Analysts are not business analyst-slash-tester or business analyst-slash-quality assurance or business analyst-slash-technical writer or business analyst-slash-project manager or even business analyst-slash-developer.

Do we still not really know what an analyst does to add value to the product? If that were the case, that means we also need to understand not just what an analyst does but also what role the analyst manager would play.

Look, I could break them both down for you and tell you that an analyst bridges the gap between business and technology by interpreting business need into technical requirements, but let's assume you already know the myriad of little tasks that it takes to do that primary function thoroughly and accurately. I choose not to break it down because that is what infrastructure does. It provides the framework to perform these tasks and the benchmarks to measure performance against.

I could tell you that a manager sets and manages that framework and then creates the environment to motivate the analysts to adhere to and abide by the framework or provides the vehicle to support its evolution. However, that is what all managers are supposed to do, right? I take it that we are all in agreement on this point.

THE ROLE OF MANAGEMENT IN QUALITY REQUIREMENTS

It is a commonly accepted industry fact that problems in requirements manifest themselves in design and development and are later exposed in testing. However, it can hardly be said that development problems of this nature are purely the responsibility of the business analyst.

So where does quality and the motivation to produce quality come from? Well first, let's look in basic terms, at how a person moves through their career.

At first, a person takes on a new role and has to learn how to do the job (learning). Then they need to learn to do the job better (functionality). Next, they begin to advance to where they can show others how to do the job (supervising), and finally, they move to a point where they have done the job well for some time and understand it enough to be able to make changes to how the job is done. This is innovation.

It is challenging for organizations to attract and retain innovators unless they can demonstrate that they foster and nurture innovation in the next generation as well. It is especially difficult and almost impossible to demonstrate this in an organization that focuses on cost as the primary metric by which success is measured.

Nothing we do happens in a vacuum and business analysts are certainly no exception. Corporate management is just as responsible for deliverable quality as it is accountable. The truth is that innovation is nurtured in an environment that encourages it, rewards it and then fails at it.

Building quality is really an inherent part of the development process when you have innovators on your team. Nevertheless, do not assume that just because you hire better business analysts, you suddenly have a winning proposition. In fact, the best and most innovative resources (business analysts included) will wither and stop contributing in the wrong environment.

Some of the environmental factors that are closely tied to quality and innovation are the business model, company values, management styles and job satisfaction. This is because your employees are keenly aware of any discrepancies between internal and external messaging, how other employees are treated, and how well people are rewarded for doing a good job.

By sending the message (verbally or nonverbally) to your employees that they are expendable or that the bottom line is more important than talent, that individual contributions are not recognized, feedback and input is ignored, and where micromanagers are promoted and retained, you are creating an environment that breeds complacency, micromanagement, and disempowerment. Above all else, it shows up in the client relationships business analysts have and the quality of work these resources produce.

Management sets the tone for quality. There is simply no question that we limit both our organizations and ourselves when we foster the kind of environment that is complacent, disempowering and run by micromanagers, even if it does function on some levels.

As information technology managers, there is an opportunity to change and transform the business organization as a whole, through the technology that is brought in to support production of our core business products and services. Well-defined and managed technology unites and provides opportunities for collaboration at all organizational levels in a way that is unique, while poorly defined and poorly managed technology just becomes a money pit.

The information technology manager ensures the tools exist to create and deliver a quality product to business customers, and they ensure that the technologies and people who build those products integrate to form a streamlined business unit. Even in an organization that does not value or foster contribution, it would be hard to overlook delivery of better products and improved customer services that drive up sales for the organization.

In a way, you could say that the information technology manager's role in creating a positive and empowering environment supersedes other managers, because all other managers and employees are only as good as the tools provided to them by the information technology manager. After all, business success is hinged on right product, right place, and right time, and the information technology manager ensures that all of that happens.

We have discussed business analysis from a functional perspective and exposed some of the inherent issues with the existing services and management model. We have also discussed the role of management in the achievement of the overall objectives of business analysis. Again, where business analysis is the enablement of strategic plans into tangible solutions that create the desired future state, Business Analysis Stewardship is the objective to protect and safeguard the interests of the business through planning and management of business analysis resources. The functional management of business analysis resources ensures that stewardship is not just theory, but practice.

CREATING SEAMLESS TRANSITION POINTS ACROSS DELIVERY AND ENGAGEMENT

By this point in the book, readers should have a good understanding about what business analysis is, the tasks that are required to support the objectives of the role, and how to establish a solid management model that elevates the station of a business analyst from an order taker to a champion for the business.

This book is not just about defining the specific tasks that are completed and how those tasks support the business by enabling strategy and protecting their interests; it is also about ensuring that service delivery is a fluid process that ensures that the services you offer are indeed the same services that are obtained by the business.

We have to take the services designed so far and determine how we will manage them across service delivery, and how clients can be positioned to accept them in a way that actually benefits and supports their overall objectives. Business analysis can only accomplish its goals and objectives if it is delivered and received in such a way that it is utilized to its full potential. In essence, we have to ensure that the business gets the full benefit of Business Analysis Stewardship and business analysis services through the way in which we deliver them, and the way in which the business engages us.

When we build services, we have to think of them in terms of the delivery of those exact services to the client. In fact, unless you are running a garage sale where things are sold "as is," we have to consider how that product will be delivered to the customer.

We design the product for the benefit of the client. But that effort assumes that the product has the same value and potency once the customer has it in their possession.

Say, for example, that you hire a caterer to deliver good hot food to guests for an event. You, the client, tell the caterer what time the guests will be sitting down to eat and to plan accordingly. However, activities at the event last longer than planned, and the guests sit down to eat later than scheduled. This possibility would need to be considered by the caterer despite the client's role in the matter, and have the good hot food available for delivery when the guests actually sit down to enjoy it.

So, even though we can create a service model for business analysis, we have to consider the delivery mechanisms as well as the need for the client and preparedness of the client to receive those services in such a way so they are still effective deliverables. To that end, business analysis has to be managed across delivery, and it must be planned and coordinated regardless of who claims accountability for the results that the assigned resources are producing.

Ultimately, if you are in consulting, it is your company's name and reputation on the line. If you are building an internal service for business analysis, you are going to be accountable and responsible for the bottom line. With a properly defined business analysis service model, you could effectively reposition your services group to directly impact both the top and the bottom lines.

You impact the bottom line when you employ sustainable methods as described under the business analysis model that supports Business Analysis Stewardship. It is these methods that enable you to reduce your costs and create that sustainable practice. However, when you utilize methods that create higher quality products, and you can reduce the time to market of those products, you effectively impact the top line.

It is the combination of the well-defined services, as well as the delivery of those services, and the engagement by the business that make this happen. This next section outlines all of the factors that you will need to consider in order to make key decisions around service delivery and services engagement. These considerations will also provide you with the information that you require in order to develop effective models for each.

The information provided goes beyond the basic types of models that you can have for service delivery, and outlines some important considerations. Whereas the information that you are likely to find in other sources may be limited, the following chapters fully describe the types of models that you have available in each area and how individual companies have defined their own models. Business analyst managers will deepen their understanding of how their clients are going to benefit from their services.

8

SERVICE DELIVERY

Another key element of a solid business analysis services organization concerns service delivery. Service delivery is made up of elements that dictate how delivery will be managed, and where it will be delivered. The complement to the service delivery model is the engagement model, which encompasses how the service will be delivered in partnership with the client organization.

Service delivery is the process by which a defined set of services are delivered to the client (either internal or external). In essence, it is the sales and delivery process of the services that the group provides. Service delivery is a critical part of the technology industry. It is not enough to say that you got the "product" into the hands of the customer, especially when you are in a service based industry. The real money is made in having repeat customers and a positive image.

Every consultant that you put into a client site, or every person that you put in front of a stakeholder, is a representative and a reflection of your organization as a whole. They have to provide the levels of service delivery and customer satisfaction that the organization dictates, but you also need to understand the delivery process and what that process entails. It is never a pleasant experience when you have to pull resources from client sites because they just were not meeting these expectations.

Each element of service delivery contains key components to ensure that a full and complete service delivery model is established, and that all services are delivered in accordance with this model. How delivery is managed includes components for:

- Charge backs—How to bill projects and departments for the services provided;
- Service expectations—Quality levels, project specific tasks and activities, and the anticipated deliverables to be generated;
- Defined services—The exact services that will be done by the group or team.

Where services will be delivered includes delivery of micro-models for onshore, near-shore, and offshore delivery. Service delivery management may look different across each of these micro-models because within each, many factors will change.

As with any other business, you cannot simply say, "We can do anything you want." You have to prescribe a specific and quantifiable set of services that you will provide to your customer base. Anyone that cannot adequately define *what* they deliver will be hard pressed to also define a solid and comprehensive strategy for how it will be delivered, and how it will be managed throughout delivery. This is equally true of business analysis, especially when there is a tendency to overlap and combine the roles of the analyst with other roles.

Having a detailed set of service definitions will enable your group to set realistic boundaries, and also provide clear expectations for quality, enabling more accurate project forecasting, estimating, and planning. In addition to this, having a clearly defined set of services means that your group is responsible and accountable for a specific set of tasks on the project. This clarity greatly contributes to the overall sense of confidence that the analyst needs in order to be successful.

A lack of clarity, or feeling like they have to be at the beck-and-call of the business, stakeholders, and the project manager, decreases the analyst's ability to focus on and be assertive about the requirements. In other words, lack of clarity can lead to scope creep! Service delivery in business analysis should still look like, well, service delivery. As with any other service, it should add value to the customer (even if that customer is internal), and demonstrate both return on investment and fiscal responsibility.

BILLING FOR SERVICES

Every well-organized and managed operational model includes a process and work-flow for billing customers for the services provided by the group, even when that group is internal to the same company.

Do not think for a second that just because you pay the individual salaries for some or all of the resources (i.e., they are your own employees), that there should be no detailed financial accounting and mutual internal billing. If you do not have mutual billing, you cannot get an accurate picture of real project spending, no matter how hard you try. In addition, employees who do not have to account for their time in great detail tend to take longer to complete the work. Why? No one is really accountable in this type of model. Without an accurate picture of the spending, you cannot start any type of lean management and you certainly cannot pinpoint any problem areas.

While many companies utilize a cost-center approach, I suggest that you blend that approach with revenue generation for allocating and delivering business analysis services. What do I mean? Well, in the cost-center model, the manager and employees are responsible for its costs, but they are not responsible for revenues or investment decisions associated with that center. Nevertheless, what if they were responsible for costs and they could be a revenue generator as well? In essence, they could be responsible for both costs and revenues.

By applying specific techniques for business analysis, the team could measure their own productivity and revenues generated. In addition, they could account for additional revenues generated by products that decrease overhead project costs, and because of higher quality and shorter production times, they could also account for additional revenues created by getting the products into the hands of the internal or external customer faster.

SERVICE EXPECTATIONS

Anyone who pays for a service must also have a corresponding set of service expectations to manage how the services will be delivered, what the end product must meet, and how the project team will interact with the business, even when the services are internal. These expectations are most often written into the agreements and contracts (or the project charter) between the business and the service provider, and can include expectations for:

- On-time service delivery
- Minimum qualifications for allocated resources
- Dress and deportment of allocated resources
- Accountability for tasks
- Responsibility for certain areas or features
- Escalation procedures
- Communication plans and matrices
- Team and client reporting structure
- Types of deliverables produced
- Key performance indicators (KPIs) used to measure performance
- Productivity metrics
- Service delivery locations (onshore, near-shore, or offshore)
- How and what is to be reported on progress
- Billing for allocated resources and services performed

These delivery expectations will govern and guide the project teams at the tactical level to ensure that the end product aligns to business needs and is mutually beneficial. It is imperative that all of the expectations are discussed, documented, and agreed to, so that there is no miscommunication later on. One of the advantages is that these expectations can also cement the relationship between the teams.

Quite often, client-facing business analysts are not privy to the negotiation of service delivery expectations. This can be either good or bad because they are going to be accountable for them, but will need to ensure that their performance aligns to those expectations in order to meet them. However, that means there must be some way to bridge this gap without overburdening the business analyst.

A good way to accomplish this bridge is to build in the most common service delivery expectations into the business analysis KPIs, as discussed in Chapter 7. One of the important things to keep in mind is that the perception of an individual resource's performance, competency, and capability are often biased by their ability to meet service expectations, and differences in measures between clients and the services organization can confuse this evaluation process and its results.

Adding Value to a Business Relationship

Did you know that buffet style restaurants typically do not have a very profitable business? This is because consumers will actually eat almost three times the normal amount at this type of restaurant. The reason for this is simple: people are trying to get the most value for their dollar.

However, value is in the eye of the beholder, and is only partially due to the amount spent. Value has as much to do with our sense of personal satisfaction that we get from earning the money that we are spending, as it does with getting the largest amount of tangible goods.

In a buffet style restaurant, the value that we get is purely in the amount of food we can shovel onto a plate, as many times as we can manage, and eat ourselves into gluttony. In a typical restaurant, we get as much value from the food as we do from the serving staff. We demonstrate this by offering gratuities to the staff to show appreciation for good service.

In business, we measure value by the quality of our product, our employees, our corporate image, and our ability to win. Our perception is that the ability to win is about having the most money and controlling the most resources.

Having the most leads us to manipulate and maneuver clients and sales around our own perception of influence. It is a contentious environment where *the* ability to win at the expense of all else is key. Contracts are routinely written and negotiated based on this idea of influence.

I recall a major consulting company that prepared two sets of billing sheets for their clients: one set, which detailed the actual costs over the last period, and the other set, to show the client how much money they had "saved" by contracting their company. Typically, this second set of numbers was grossly exaggerated. The attempt was to show the value the client was receiving for their investment. However, it actually had the opposite effect, and left the client feeling disempowered and cheated.

To add value in a business relationship, we need to examine two factors that influence the perception of value: product quality and employee quality. In addition, we also know that loyalty to a particular vendor, based on these two factors, plays a large part in the request for proposal and request for qualification selection processes. In the submissions for each of these processes, there is a balance between product and employee quality as a means of representing what the organization brings to the table.

It can be said that quality employees generate quality products. The problem is that not enough attention is paid to the development of quality employees. In fact, many companies have great employees who are often stifled by a lack of autonomy, recognition, and empowerment.

Because product quality is dependent on employee quality, it stands to reason that we add value to business relationships most effectively through our employees on a daily basis, through every interaction. The determination of "adding value" is dependent on the client and the unique situation. Therefore, if we foster loyalty and quality among employees, we ultimately add value to our clients.

We have the tools to help advance almost all of our employees to greatness through training, recognition, and building an internal infrastructure that fosters and encourages personal ownership, responsibility, job satisfaction, personal effectiveness, and empowerment.

How do we translate quality employees into quality products? Simple: *Listen*! Listen to employees and clients. Go in and listen to what they are trying to accomplish, not just in a single project or program, but overall. Ask the question, where do you see yourself in five years? Then sit back, listen, and take notes before offering any advice. Encourage the employee or client to take the steps necessary to reach their goals. After all, the role of information technology is to *support* business function and goals for the future success and sustainability of the company.

DEFINED SERVICES

The service delivery model has to include a detailed set of *defined* services. What are you selling? What will you do, or not do? This is extremely important to define so that, as discussed in regard to defined roles in Chapter 6, the segregation of duties is maintained.

It is easier to charge for defined services, and easier to set and manage expectations on both sides. By defining the services that your business analyst group will provide, you are accomplishing two things: establishing the parameters for customers and providing a specific target for the analysts to work towards.

In addition, defined services have other intrinsic benefits. The analysts gain confidence in what they are doing and can feel a sense of ownership toward it, as well as a sense of empowerment from knowing that there are boundaries for the type of work that they will be called upon to perform. After all, as discussed in Chapters 2 and 3, business analysts are not order takers, they are partners that enable the strategic goals and objectives of the organization through the development of products and solutions that align to those goals.

Impacts on Business Design

Traditionally, the laws of supply and demand continue to drive the life cycle of a business. If a consumer needs something, businesses compete to supply it. Major recessions come along less frequently than the minor ones that occur every decade or so, but they are still part of a cycle, and most economies have thus far recovered from them. If history is any example, economies recover and even improve the quality of life as a result. After the last big recession of the early 1980s, we saw business soar and shift into a more global economic model.

From one perspective, recessions weed out the unstable businesses and enable the more secure and well-designed ones to thrive and expand. Opportunistic and well-designed businesses can take over the gaps left by those that flounder and eventually succumb to downturns as economic roadkill.

This is because recessions force businesses to react and reduce expenses where and when they can. As a result of the current recession, organizations are striving to improve the effectiveness of their core business engines. They are reacting by furiously undertaking value-stream mapping activities for their services and core business processes, scaling back activities in efforts to apply lean management, reducing roles from their workforce in an attempt to flatten the organization, and in a way "bootstrapping" by extending the life and uses of existing tools (in the same way that many consumers have decided they do not need the new car in spite of the poor condition of the old one).

The best approach to business management in this economic climate is to stop merely reacting and become proactive—take the time to reassess the situation, transforming the overall business design and management techniques (both of which are beyond value-stream mapping, lean management, mass layoffs, and increasing the demand on existing tools).

To be clear, the goal is to become both proactive and optimized, not simply to write-off current solutions or cling to them because of the investment in a given solution. Unfortunately, this can be difficult to consider and achieve because of the escalating level of commitment needed to implement the chosen solutions and the immense pressure created by the economic climate.

To facilitate a proactive approach, organizations must define robust business designs and mature the methods and modes of delivery. This means that intelligent business design must include elements of all of the individual solutions in order to find the most well-rounded foundation. A proactive approach must include a blending of multiple solutions because the impacts to the supply and demand ratio affect every aspect of the organization. For example, it could be about defining business life cycle models that incorporate elements of strategic scenario planning, value-stream mapping, lean management, and collaboration into the overall business model and corporate culture. By defining specific services and roles to deliver those services, as well as all of the other elements needed to manage and deliver them effectively, you are creating an environment that is both reactive *and* proactive. This is the type of environment that will foster success.

It is important to make sure that business analysts within the organization know exactly what their job is, and that the client and everyone else does too (including the project managers). You do this by defining specific parameters for what the job looks like, how the tasks will be delivered, how this aligns to their competencies, and how performance will be measured. These are then married with the client's expectations and engagement model. This is extremely important because not only will you avoid miscommunication between your business analysts and your clients, it will also ensure that you are paid appropriately for the jobs that are being done, and that the analyst has performance evaluations that are in line with what they do.

The defined services should have a detailed description of the specific services and tasks that business analysts will be expected to perform and deliver to the client. These should also be aligned to the services expected from the various career levels because the specific responsibilities are different for each level.

Clearly, it is not enough to say that you offer and provide "business analysis services." You have to educate your client a bit, and tell them what it is and how they can expect to benefit from the services when done right. Having this level of detail gives everyone the ammunition and empowerment to make that happen because the participants have a clear expectation of the work to be accomplished.

The basic services outlined in your service definitions will include the various elements from the business analysis model described. It is imperative that you identify the tasks that make up each of the elements, what those tasks look like while being performed, and identify the inputs and outputs along with the expectations for the deliverables. This gives everyone enough information about what is going to be done from a business analysis perspective to set expectations for service and engagement planning.

It is imperative that you look at the service delivery model from the business analysis services perspective because it is an area where not enough is done consistently to ensure that valuable services are actually being delivered. Let's look at it this way. As we discovered in our decomposition of the current state of the allocation and management of business analysts in Chapter 1, analysts are typically allocated from one of three primary sources: the internal talent pool or bench, the consulting firm that we have engaged, or recruiters contracted to locate and secure one-off resources.

The internal resources are the most obligated to perform at the levels that are expected by the business, and so perception is that they will end up performing the greatest level of service delivery expected. Consultants are managed in some form or another by their parent companies, and so they will have some form of service delivery expectations. That does not mean that they are managed well or appropriately, so be wary of making that assumption.

Contracted one-off resources will deliver what you ask and generally no more, unless there is something in it for them. They are not typically contractually obligated to any degree of service delivery, and they are not managed in any real sense of the word.

Overall, organizations have to consider that the resource's time and work may only be managed to a small degree, but more often than not resources are dropped onto a project with the expectation that the project manager will know what to do with them and how to manage them. That is not service delivery.

Unfortunately, if we take an honest look at the current state of business analysis as a whole, delivering great service through business analysis to projects is generally the exception and not the rule. Furthermore, business analysis is not being utilized to its full potential or as the business tool that it could be. Business analysis could do much more for both the client and the parent company. It could be a vehicle and mechanism for creating opportunities for the future.

ELEMENTS OF AN EFFECTIVE SERVICE DELIVERY MODEL

Where a management model effectively manages and coordinates the resources and tools for capacity, as well as the capability of the resources, the service delivery model coordinates and manages the services provided. These include how those services are designed (to meet the objectives), delivered (channels), monitored and measured (for ongoing continuous improvement), service strategies (that align the services to the delivering organizations objectives and goals), and transition points (coordination between where services start and end). The operations of individual services in order to effectively "deliver" the services to the customers in an efficient and effective manner are also included. The elements of an effective service delivery model are:

- Service strategy
- Service design
- Service operations
- Service transitions
- Continuous improvement of services
- Delivery mechanisms

In the service delivery model, as shown in Figure 8.1, the individual elements that form the framework and infrastructure for service delivery also intersect with points across the functional management model. This reduces conflict between policies and procedures, and ensures that the individual service delivery elements and attributes align with the overall business vision, mission, and objectives, so that the functional management elements can be managed at a strategic level, and the services delivery model can focus on the how to accomplish the strategic objectives through service delivery.

Service Delivery Strategy

Part of the planning that prevents runaway projects is planning the details of how you are going to deliver the best solution for the problem. For many companies, this means alignment to strategic goals, deciding how to resolve a problem or evolve their business, making the build or buy decision, and determining high-level resourcing decisions for the project. However, strategy is really about figuring out how you are going to connect all of the impacted systems and components, tools, and resources in a dynamic way to achieve your goals. At the same time, it is about determining what will make those parts move in unison toward the same goals.

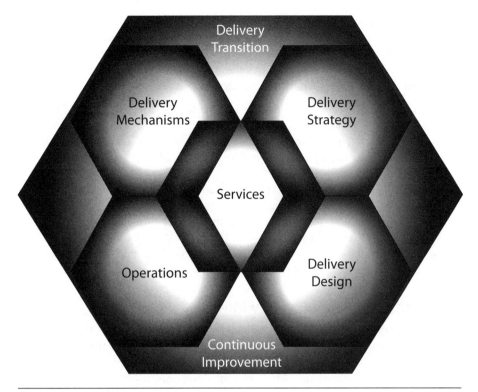

Figure 8.1 Service delivery model

Service strategy provides the guidance by which individual and service groups are defined, delivered, and managed across the life cycle in order to meet the overall business objectives. In other words, service strategies are subsets of the business strategies at a micro-level, and determine how individual services will be delivered in order to meet the overall objectives.

For business analysis, the problems that arise in requirements are deterministic when there is no service strategy in place. This is quite simply because the connections between all of the moving parts within the service, its practitioners, and its subsequent delivery, have not been mapped out.

Service Design

Service design provides a clear set of parameters for the design and creation of services and related service delivery models. It does this as a means of ensuring adequate ROI is received from the service, but also to ensure that a clear and specific service is defined and delivered, instead of the typical hodgepodge of uncoordinated tasks and services being performed on an *ad hoc* basis for the customer.

To design effective services, you must consider key attributes that lend to the efficiency of individual services. It is important to note that these attributes are a high-level view of the elements of a service delivery model. This is because in designing a given service, there are critical attributes from each of the elements that must be considered within the design itself. These attributes are:

- Specific—The service itself is specific, performs specific tasks, and achieves specific outcomes.
- Consistent—The service provides consistent services, delivery mechanisms, and frameworks that are aligned to the overall business frameworks and infrastructure.
- Scalable—The services must be individually scalable to accommodate fluctuations and attrition within the need and resource pool.
- Sustainable—The services and the delivery mechanisms must be sustainable for the lifespan of the service so that the full ROI can be achieved.
- Maintainable—The services and the operations of the individual services must be maintainable without causing any undue burden on the business.

Specificity in Service Delivery Models

A solid delivery model is a detailed and specific model that describes the who, what, where, and when of the elements of service delivery, and forms an intrinsic part of the foundation for the delivery strategy, which in turn, describes how service delivery will occur under specific conditions. Much like the development of a business, you must consider factors such as how to meet existing needs, what the goals and targets are, what others in the industry are doing, what results (or standards) do clients expect, and what results (or standards) you will expect.

Each of these factors must be developed and defined to a granular level of detail in order for you to have an accurate picture to compare against. This creates a benchmark. Without this benchmark, you cannot accurately monitor and measure performance, or determine when things are not functioning and why.

Meeting Existing Client Needs

As with building any other business, when you are determining specific services and how they will be delivered to the customer, you must also consider how the service meets the customer's needs. Observing and measuring trends in the immediate needs of your existing customers, as well as on an on-going basis enables your organization to keep abreast of customer needs and to proactively prepare to meet them, as well as to track the success of delivery against those needs benchmarks.

In business analysis, this is important not only to you give a picture of the individual analysis services, but also to give you an indication of the health of your overall project capabilities and the health of your services delivery mechanisms. In this way, you do not just ask the question, "Will it meet the needs of existing customers, and how?", but also ask, "How can you meet additional needs of existing customers, and how well?"

Goals, Objectives, and Targets

A key question in making the determinations of "what else" and "how well," is to understand the goals, objectives, and targets of the client as if they were your own. This again lends to the strategic alignment of not only the services you offer, but also to the projects that you run and the products that you build with those projects.

Without a clear understanding of all of the factors and elements that will either contribute to or detract from this alignment, projects will continue to be managed using the hit or miss "shotgun approach" instead of being managed like precisely measured and calculated intricate works of art (as they should be), where every detail has a place in contributing to the overall masterpiece. It is then that you will begin to see significant improvements in the alignment of projects and results, as well as decreases in defects and unused features.

One of the key areas that many service companies fail to plan is the establishment of clear terms for internal, client-specific, and industry standards. Quite often, these companies are really good at defining what their own standards will be, but fall down when it comes to communicating and then enforcing them. They leave a big, unspoken gap in terms of what client standards are and how those standards relate to industry standards, and then defining a plan for how they will manage and meet all of these standards. Their expectation, it would seem, is that they do not want to presume and attempt to control the client, and they want to be unique within the industry, so they may not even consider the clients' standards as relevant.

Internal Standards

Naturally, a company's own internal standards are easier to define and manage because they can exercise greater control over those standards. Whatever those standards may look like does not matter nearly as much as having them in place. For the most part, resources will follow the standards, but that does not mean that you do not need governance in place to ensure consistent compliance. However, this does not always happen, and frequently there is a lack of compliance governance because it is often overlooked until significant issues arise and they hit the top or bottom lines.

But here is where quality starts to decline. In addition, there are increases in poor productivity, high attrition rates, low employee satisfaction, and high conflict rates, all because people know there are no real consequences for their actions. The result is that the questionable resources get away with doing half of the job, showing up late, or bullying, and then the sense of unfairness kicks in for the good resources, becoming unhappy and unmotivated to contribute in any significant way other than showing up.

Client Standards

Again, when it comes to building a relationship with a client, many service organizations often only consider their standards for the particular project to which resources are assigned. They tend not to ask or detail in formal agreements what their overall standards are, what success and failure looks like to them, or how this is enforced and encouraged for their resources, whether internal or contracted. This is a huge mistake, and I will tell you why.

So many relationships rely on the results and how each party feels within the relationship, and this includes business dealings. In this relationship, if one party glosses over and minimizes the needs or standards of the other, at some point the relationship breaks down. So why would a company seemingly ignore the needs and standards of its clients? Well, I have been in the business long enough to observe some common behaviors. When selling a product or service, it is only natural to think that what you offer is better than what others have, or you would not be in business for very long. However, some become so involved in what they have to offer or even so engrossed in meeting the client's immediate needs, that they end up ignoring the overall needs and standards of their clients. Others believe so much in what they offer to the point of becoming arrogant about it and their actions are more deliberate. They project an attitude of how they are going to save the client from themselves (even if they do not verbalize and share it).

In either case, they are shutting down or limiting communication and putting the relationship in jeopardy. When conflicting standards become apparent, they attempt to push their own standards onto the client because they assume that they are correct, and often they have successful case studies to "prove it."

Still others believe that relationships should be more fluid and have room to grow organically, so they do not talk about how the standards will work together with the client's standards, or which ones compete or conflict, or how that will be managed. When this situation arises, either they end up in conflict with the client or bend to whatever the client wants instead of finding the best techniques and strategies for meeting both sets of needs.

Industry Norms

Finally, when it comes to industry norms, many service organizations often forge ahead into client relationships with some knowledge of industry norms, but often do not really consider how they will impact the standards on both sides of the relationship. They only consider how they will impact the services that they deliver and the resources that they bring on, and some companies do not even do that.

Unfortunately, when you do not consider the norms of the industry, it is much harder for you to compete for both talent and clients. You have to ensure that your services delivery aligns to the standards set by the industry, simply because the customer has most likely come to expect a certain level of service and you have to know what that is in order to meet it. You cannot expect your clients, even if they are internal, to accept less in terms of services.

Consistency in Service Delivery

Once you have defined the specifics of your service delivery systems, you need to determine and plan for how the services will be delivered consistently. One of the key areas of concern with business analysis today is that there is little consistency from project to project, or resource to resource. While that stems from a lack of governing systems and protocols to follow, the service delivery frameworks also contribute to this, simply because of the way in which business analysis services are delivered. The need for improvement is demonstrated very clearly with this overall lack of consistency.

Resources can vary so dramatically between each other in terms of knowledge, techniques, experiences, and education, that you cannot anticipate finding two candidates who are exactly alike, even if they are both at the same level and on the same career path within the same domain.

Furthermore, individual resources themselves tend not to perform consistently from project to project or from one client to another. This is due in part to the overall lack of formalization and standardization that I have been preaching about in this book, but it is also due in part to our inability to clearly define effective service delivery models, and then to enforce the guidelines that those models impose.

In order to create consistency, there are several key things that you must do:

- Define what you are going to do (the objective or in this case, the services)
- Define how you are going to deliver or meet the objective (the method or service delivery)
- Record what you do step by step (governance)
- Describe how you measure it (benchmarking)
- Detail what you observe (issues and lessons learned logs)
- Describe your conclusions (what will you do to improve it)

While this is not "rocket science," the folks over at NASA utilized this same technique (the scientific method) repeatedly, and without it they might not have even made it to the moon, let alone sent a land rover to Mars. Why? Because without these kinds of steps, you cannot problem solve or tweak the design until it works. There is no trial and error.

Consistency is borne out of repetition, and that includes consistency of results in business analysis. People may say that "insanity is doing the same thing over and over again, and expecting different results," but I would also say that insanity is doing different things every time and expecting the results to be consistent. Business analysis and business analysis service delivery are certainly evidence of this.

Many analysts perform a smattering of tasks here and there on projects, and then wonder why their results are so different. But the problem is that they are doing this every time they do a project, and since it is never the same set of tasks performed every time, they are a bit guilty of being insane on both counts. That is, they are repeatedly doing the shotgun approach to requirements and expecting the same patterns to appear, but they are continually surprised when they do not.

However, the fact remains that requirements and project issues are, for the most part, deterministic because of incomplete service delivery strategies and models. Unless organizations start planning and managing the delivery process through execution, there will be no significant leaps in results.

Developing Consistency Through Capability Models

As we just discussed, consistency in service delivery is the ability to effectively and repeatedly provide the same quality and types of services. In order to accomplish this level of consistency, organizations must be able to measure, manage, and maintain a specific level of abilities within a given practice area (such as development or project management) and business analysis service delivery is no different.

As discussed in Chapter 6, where *competence* is the ability to perform a specific set of services with a degree of proficiency, *capability* is the ability to access and deploy the competencies effectively in order to achieve what needs to be done. To this end, a capability model tells us the specific competencies that we have on the team and in the arsenal as far as tools and techniques, and also describes a plan for how these will be applied and employed to accomplish the work to be done.

The elements of a capability model include summaries of our role-based standards, competencies, performance management, deliverable standards, and infrastructure. The model itself describes how each of these elements will be applied and utilized towards the achievement of our service goals and in the delivery of our services, but it is the service delivery strategy that will enable us to utilize the capability of our team to our advantage in the actual delivery of the services.

Using the Capacity Model to Deliver Consistent Services

Once we have a detailed understanding and plan for our capabilities, we need to understand and determine our capacity model. While competence tells us "who" and capability tells "how we need to get the work done" by utilizing the competencies that we have, *capacity* tells us how many resources (people, tools, and techniques) we have in place to achieve the work. By developing and incorporating a capacity model, we are outlining the plan that will enable us to forecast future areas where resources will be needed and deployed, and also to deliver those services consistently.

In terms of business analysis, this not only tells us how many we will need, but also supports succession planning for future expansions or contractions in the demand for services and ensures that services are delivered consistently across these fluctuations. This, in and of itself, supports cross-training as well as the ongoing fluctuations (scalability) that naturally occur in staffing and other resource usages.

Creating Realistic and Consistent Staffing Models

In order to ensure that we meet our obligations to our clients through fully defined competency, capability, and capacity models, we need to ensure that we are also creating *staffing models* that support the successful ongoing delivery of our services to clients. We have to consider all of the factors in successful implementation of these models, and they must collectively and independently account for each of the following areas:

- Resource transition
- Ongoing mentoring
- Performance management
- Deliverable quality

One of the key issues identified by clients that utilize consulting firms is the negative feeling of "bait and switch." While many outsourcing firms will deny that this is occurring, the fact is that when the outsourcing firm "wows" them with an expert resource and then pulls that resource once they have won the bid, and then fails to manage performance and quality as though the expert was still in the background overseeing the entire delivery, it is truly a bait and switch situation. Worse, they have set the unrealistic expectation with the client that this expert is representative of their entire team.

That being said, we also have to consider that two other things could be going on: the client's expectations and work environment may differ dramatically from what was presented and they are not bringing out the best in the resources that are allocated; or, the services delivery model has holes big enough to drive trucks through it, and again the resources are becoming complacent in their performance because there is little incentive or motivation to deliver better services.

Managing Resources to Achieve Consistent Service Delivery

If you have one hour before you have to be at the airport, but you still need to pack and it takes you one hour to get there when there is no traffic, what are you going to do? No, it is not a math problem; it is a management problem. Why, you ask? Because not only do you have to manage your time and other resources effectively to get out the door as quickly as possible, you also have to consider traffic, routes, and speed limits as well as the car's capabilities. Does the car have gas? Do the brakes work, or are there other issues with the car? Are you driving, or is someone picking you up? If someone else is picking you up, are they going to be on time? Can that person help you to finish packing and get you out the door faster?

While technology service delivery might be a slightly different situation, there are very similar considerations to make in order to coordinate the delivery of services as expected, on time, and for the agreed price and quality. You have to manage every aspect of service delivery as a unit unto itself, and ensure that you plan for every aspect of it, in order to be successful and keep clients.

Monitoring Service Delivery to Ensure Consistency

You also have to closely monitor how you are doing service delivery, even if the client will never know that you made a misstep, in order to ensure that you are delivering consistently. That means that you have to be proactive and incorporate checks and balances for monitoring the progress and health of your service delivery system.

How does this relate to business analysis? For one thing, it will enable your clients to provide consistent and accurate evaluations of your business analysts while they are working. If something is not working, you can rectify the situation before damaging the relationship with the client. This information can be applied to business analysis KPIs and performance evaluation criteria, as a means of ensuring that a full 360° view of their capability and performance is measured.

Measuring Service Delivery Elements for Consistency

Utilizing the measurements that come out of managing and monitoring progress is an important factor in the overall success of a given service delivery channel because this information can enable you to deliver services that are increasingly more effective and cost-efficient, as well as consistent. Measuring, in turn, can lead to more refined strategies for the delivery of services as well as your business analysis services as an entire entity.

You could say that there is a codependent relationship between the service delivery model and the services that you are providing because one cannot exist without the other, and each relies on the other for information to refine themselves. It is only by measuring delivery factors and elements that the entire relationship can be a success.

Scalability of Service Delivery

The competency, capability, and capacity models will each contribute to our understanding of how scalable our individual services are. We have to ensure that we have mechanisms, plans, and procedures in place to accommodate the scalability of resources. That means that we have to account for the likelihood that resources may often be let go through no real fault of their own, as is often the case in the consulting world.

I do not recommend keeping resources for the sake of it or because of personal attachment to them unless you can provide cross-training and optional roles for these resources. Three things happen if you do: you end up with a bunch of resources that no one wants to work with, the resources are not productive and do not actually perform any significant work while you are continuing to pay them, or you end up pushing resources into inappropriate roles that they are neither trained for nor capable of doing. The problem is that these organizations generally do not support the resources while they are on the job, and then the organization is at a loss to explain why they have no control over the quality of services being provided to clients.

Ability to Increase or Decrease on Demand

Scalability is the ability to either increase or decrease resourcing levels as needed. In order to scale resources effectively, you need to have two things in place: well-written escape clauses in employment agreements and cross-training programs that can identify candidates who may be worth hanging onto, so that you can shift them as needs change in different service areas.

For business analysis, you need to be careful about where you place resources and how you cross-train because you want the resources themselves to continue to be successful as business analysts, but you also want to be able to shift resources around as needed. That means that you have to consider the career goals and objectives of the individual analyst themselves, as well as how and where they are willing to shift in order to accomplish their own professional objectives, as well as the objectives of the company.

Scalability When Creating a Need

One of the areas where scalability becomes necessary is when you have identified and created a need with individual clients, sold them on it, and now have to deliver on it. Business analysts are in a prime position to be identifying new opportunities and needs simply because of the nature of their work.

In conducting a gap analysis for individual projects, business analysts often encounter areas of need that will not be addressed by the project, and while they are bound to document it, the client is not bound to act on it or to incorporate it into the current project because it does not always make sense. The analyst can identify future needs and set the stage for capacity planning, as well as scalability, through capability planning.

Sustainability in Service Delivery

Sustainability is one of those areas where people in general rarely think about the long term when there are such great short-term benefits. You see, just because the customers are knocking down your door and money is pouring in does not mean that you can keep doing what you are doing over the long haul and remain profitable or even in business. To determine sustainability, you need to compile data, set a benchmark and then start forecasting how you will sustain service delivery across all of the changing factors. In essence, sustainability is really having the ability to keep something going at a consistent pace, at a consistent quality level, over either a specific period of time or indefinitely.

The necessary data includes all of the models we have created thus far, including capacity planning (how many people do we need to staff it over that period), and succession planning (how will we replace and move people around during that time). One of the factors that organizations must consider is the specific needs that will change over time, how those needs will change, and how to anticipate the changes in order to plan accordingly. Once you understand all of this, you can start to fully comprehend sustainability.

Unfortunately, not every company considers sustainability. In fact, many are actually not running sustainable consulting firms or business analysis services. They rely purely and solely on the fuel provided by the client. When that fuel burns out, they drop their resources, move onto another client, and find more resources. Firms would be better off using the principles of Business Analysis Stewardship to plan and manage business analysis services so that they can deliver long-term solutions. This would enable sustainability so that in the event that a single project or client dried up, they could move on without sinking the entire ship.

Maintainability Across Service Delivery

The next issue to contend with in business analysis services is *maintainability*. Any time you build something, you have to address the question of maintainability. Even if a service or product is fairly disposable, there are always questions surrounding the need to maintain it to some degree for its lifespan. In the case of a product, it must survive long enough to get into the hands of the consumer and long enough for them to use it.

When it comes to business analysis services, you need to consider the big question "How easy is it to maintain the service delivery model?" To make that determination you need to look at the adoption of policies and processes (rates and challenges), how service delivery is governed, and organizational change management. Each of these will weigh into the formula for how easy it is to maintain the service over dropping it altogether.

Maintainability, Sustainability and Delivery

A number of years ago, a small local company was bought out by a multinational corporation. At first, it was "business as usual," but over time the corporation realized that they could not sustain all of the small companies that it had purchased without centralizing and capitalizing on its size to get discounts with suppliers. So, after ten years of business as usual, this small company was informed (as were all of the other small subsidiary companies) about the move towards centralizing and creating a more stable base for the overall corporation by streamlining and managing processes and resources on a global scale. The small company did not buy into this idea and resisted it every step of the way. They wanted to continue running as a "Mom and Pop" style of operation instead of a corporation. After two years of rejecting new policies and procedures, it was announced that staff was going to be let go because operations could not be maintained as they were.

People who had been with the company since day one were leaving, and only about 80 employees out of a few hundred were retained. Those remaining employees could see the writing on the wall, but they continued to push back and reject the governance initiatives, policies, and processes.

In the end, only a handful of people were given offers to transfer to other locations when the corporation finally shut down the office. Because the people of the small company refused to buy into and adopt the direction of the corporation, the small company lost its maintainability, and it had to be cut so that the corporation as a whole would not suffer. While the smaller company had played a huge role in their own demise, so did the corporation when it determined how to run its businesses and sent out the edicts for everyone to jump on board.

You see, it wasn't just push back from the small company and delivering an edict from the corporation that made this a deterministic outcome, it was not answering questions about service delivery and maintaining that service delivery model upfront that also contributed. If we think about the question that I asked right before diving into this story ("How easy is it to maintain the service delivery model?"), it was a question that was only asked in reference to cost and the bottom line. It was never asked in reference to practicality, governance and the people that would be accountable for implementing it.

Maintainability is about setting something up properly from the start, and managing it from implementation to decommission, and that includes new organizational structures and systems. In fact, if this simple question had been asked initially, there would have been a lot less push back from the employees of the small company because they would have been able to see that business as usual was not only limiting, but also not maintainable indefinitely.

The actions taken by the multinational corporation in our example are not unique. Many companies do this same thing with business analysis, and analysts can sometimes be the first group dumped when a company feels that the service does not add value and is not worth maintaining over the long haul. However, if you add proper service delivery strategies and Business Analysis Stewardship, the tables will turn and business analysis as a service will become not only a maintainable part of the overall strategy, but a critical service that enables the continuity of the business as a whole. The key, as with anything else in business, is to set it up correctly and to manage it effectively, so that it can contribute appropriately and is not just optional overhead.

You do not want business analysis to be perceived as just a part of the cost of doing business when it can become a key success factor in the business, sustaining and maintaining itself over the long haul. But you cannot implement a half-baked solution either. Successful business analysis is not like a Frisbee or anything else that you throw at clients, and then they throw it back once they are done with it. It takes careful planning, monitoring, and benchmarking across the delivery cycle to ensure that it is going to remain stable and consistent across delivery. Once this is achieved you can scale up that delivery to multiple clients and industries, and really start to build a business with it.

Service Operations

Service operations are the effective management and coordination of the service itself in order to meet business objectives and identify customer needs. To a large extent, this includes the governance that is in place to ensure that the specific services are delivered in a manner that is consistent with business policy and that those services are managed to meet the strategies they were designed to execute.

While management should provide a basic framework for what is to be done, by whom, where, and how it will be governed and improved over time, service delivery should provide a basic framework for who does what, where, when, and how often. Where management is tasked with managing sets of services and the resources that perform those services, service delivery is tasked with the delivery of those services to customers by specific allocated resources.

Service Transition

Service transition considers how services will be consistently delivered across multiple projects within the same customer, and when we are transitioning to or away from delivery of a given service. In other words, transition occurs when there is a change in the level of service delivery provided by the business, but is intended to ensure that the consistency and the quality of service are maintained. This ensures that the customer is never dropped and there are no lags in service delivery when key elements change.

To that end, the ability to transition between levels of service as well as individual services is largely impacted by the scalability of the service itself. While this is primarily developed and built-in during design of the service itself, it must meet the business ability to transition services in multiple ways.

One of the most common problems with service delivery and transition planning is the lack of exit planning. At some point in every business, you will make significant changes to a critical system, or the project or the relationship with the services team will break down. This means risk to your organization's ability to deliver on some aspect of its obligations to customers, suppliers, employees, and financial institutions. Many project planners do not even want to plan for disaster by having an exit strategy. When they are set to implement, they do not always think about what happens in the event that the existing systems or infrastructure crashes and project teams have to undo the changes made to implement the new product. Every organization wants their projects to be successful so they hope for the best, but they have to be realistic and plan for the worst.

Continuous Service Improvement

Continuous improvement is the ability to measure and monitor progress of a given service as it is delivered, and then work toward improving that service through ongoing improvement initiatives. A key objective behind continuous improvement is to ensure the sustainability of the service over the long term. A business can effectively continue to deliver the same set of services as long as there is a market need and the business remains responsive to that need by constantly improving the services according to the evolving needs and expectations of the customers.

Unfortunately, the way that business analysis is currently being "delivered" for the most part is not sustainable. This is due in part to the lack of ongoing management, but also to the fact that improvements cannot be quantified, and the costs of running the services as they are, are too prohibitive.

DEVELOPING EFFECTIVE SERVICE DELIVERY MODELS

In order to develop an effective service delivery model, you not only have to answer the questions about how you will manage services across delivery so that they meet your requirements for specificity, consistency, scalability, maintainability, and sustainability, but also questions about how each of these factors are determined across each of the delivery micro-models. In other words, you have to organize resources in specific ways in order to accommodate and engage the customers that the model will serve. You must utilize all of the smaller elements of the service based on not just *what* you are selling to your customers (in this case, business analysis as a service), but also *how* you are going to deliver it to them.

In the service industry, we have to remember that our service essentially *is* our people. Therefore, in establishing service and engagement models, we need to understand exactly how we are going to engage clients, and how this will feed back into the service delivery mechanisms and achieve the specific results that each service provides.

In order to be successful in developing effective service delivery models, organizations have to understand that the primary difference in each of the delivery micro-models is the level of face time that the resources have with the clients. In addition, while many believe that this should and does impact the type of work done by the resources from various locations, it is the career level and competency of the individual resources that should dictate the type of work done by business analysts at the varying locations. Any system, no matter how diverse and geographically disseminated, can be sustained and maintained effectively if it is well managed by a consistent support structure.

In this case, the support structure includes consistent definitions, stewardship, and governance initiatives so there is little room for disconnect in interpretation between the proverbial left and right hands, so that when issues arise, there is a system in place to catch, mitigate, and remediate them as quickly as possible.

The Onshore Model

The *onshore model* represents the placement of resources into a client site face-to-face with the business. The bulk of the work is conducted at a single location (usually the client site).

This is the most traditional and widespread model for business analysis because the profession started out as a role to work with stakeholders and user groups within the business to collect and specify business requirements. However, as the role has evolved into more of a bridge between the business and technology, so too has the idea of business analysis and requirements.

Requirements are no longer considered to be the documented wish list of the stakeholders and user groups, but the definition of the results and the business objectives that are required to make the business more efficient, gain leverage, and correct any impediments to business. Requirements and business analysis in general, have gone from being very user-centric and requiring heavy interactions with the business on a daily basis, to more research and analysis-oriented, which has reduced a lot of the need for daily interactions with the business.

That is not to say that the onshore model no longer has its place. In fact, this model is still critical in the delivery of effective business analysis services in that some face-to-face business interaction is required to create a personal connection between the analyst and the business. In the long run, even in near-shore or offshore engagement models, face-to-face interaction upfront is critical to creating that bond between the analyst and the business as a means of enabling and supporting a greater sense of understanding, and enhancing the lines of communication in ways that are simply impossible through telecommuting.

The onshore model can have a negative impact on requirements for two reasons: a) The constant bustle of the onshore client site creates a more social atmosphere and can actually reduce the productivity of resources and b) the resources are more likely to seek inputs from sources that may or may not positively affect the outcome of the requirements. In other words, more people are likely to want to put their two cents into the requirements simply because the business analyst is around and easily tracked down.

Don't get me wrong, being onshore can also be good. The important thing to remember is that no matter where the business analyst sits, the results and deliverables should still be the same. The business analysts should outline the requirements to create the specific results needed by the business to develop the situation that they want; those results should align back to the overall strategic objectives.

The Near-shore Model

The *near-shore* model utilizes resources that are geographically located in similar regions, but who are not necessarily reporting to the client site every day in the same way as the onshore model. In this case, the resources tend to have some onshore (i.e., on-site) presence in order to get that face time with clients, which is critical to the relationship.

The benefits of the near-shore model are quite simple: lower costs that are passed onto the customer due to the analyst's reduced travel or relocation expenses and not having to provide facilities for the resource. A larger talent pool is available to draw from without having to force candidates to uproot and relocate for projects. There is an increased sense of empowerment for the resource, who generally contributes higher quality work products and works longer hours, without feeling the need to be compensated for every minute because they become focused on delivering results for the client instead of merely putting in time.

In addition to these benefits, the outsourcing company that employs the near-shore model generally enjoys an increased loyalty from the resource as well as the ability to have the resource multitask during nonpeak times when things are slow with a single customer. That means that resources can also be tasked with additional internal duties on top of any tasks and activities that they are performing for clients.

The near-shore model does not imply that there will be more quality issues or lower productivity rates. It can be quite the opposite when the right governance, service delivery, and engagement mechanisms are put into place to support the model. With the right communication channels, escalation procedures, and change management strategies in place, this model can actually boost the levels of productivity on the team and produce high-quality results and deliverables.

Two primary factors that determine the success of this model are: a) the ability to change the perception of the requirements document from a user wish list to a results-driven deliverable and b) conducting a proof of concept project. The utilization of the proof of concept (or pilot) project will dramatically enhance the team's ability to embrace this model.

The near-shore model also does not mean that the business analyst team works in a different region or office than the client; it means that the client is engaged in a way that is conducive to creating a stable long-term partnership by the shared management and utilization of the resources assigned to a specific client. It also means that the resource must take time initially to meet with the client face-to-face in order to create and solidify the relationship. This ensures that the work completed is more strongly aligned to the client's needs without the excessive back-and-forth that may occur where the lines of communication are limited to telecommuting channels such as web meetings, telephone, or VOIP sessions.

The Offshore Model

The *offshore model* locates resources in a completely different geographical region, who rarely, if ever, have any face time with clients. While the onshore delivery model puts business analysts in front of the client on a daily basis, and the near-shore on a semi-regular basis, resources in the offshore model are located somewhere else entirely. The only interactions that they typically have with clients are through telecommuting connections and channels, such as VOIP and web meetings.

This can be an important engagement model for clients who may already have a strong offshore development presence, need to reduce overhead, or assign the task of creating results to the outsourcing firm without demanding onshore engagement.

From a business analysis perspective, the offshore model may be limited to the types of tasks that can be performed when an onshore presence cannot be established or maintained with any consistency. By limiting the scope of activities conducted by the offshore team, they are merely there to augment the onshore team and to provide services that make sense for them to offer. These might include research-based tasks and activities, document preparation and censoring, reverse engineering to uncover or discover processes and rules that may be embedded within code, or analysis of elements compiled by the onshore team and completion of the documentation. Other tasks may involve the onshore team acting as a facilitator of the offshore team by providing them with meeting notes, research, and access to documentation gathered to conduct analysis and to prepare and validate requirements.

Building an Effective Offshore Delivery Model

Delivery means resources, talent, opportunity, allocation, management, scaling up and down with client needs, anticipating needs, delivering value, and ensuring the ongoing success and business continuity of clients. Delivery is a symbiotic relationship between the client and the vendor that assures the ongoing and mutual benefit of both. Defects and other issues in the delivery of products and services are deterministic. That means that issues actually start at the beginning of the sale and as delivery of services to the client is planned. How? Quite simply, our attitudes and ability to plan and prepare for the end-to-end delivery of services ensure that resources performing the tasks and activities are well qualified and prepared. Planning ensures that resources do not become complacent or disenfranchised during the delivery cycle, which can contribute to or compound increasing levels of quality issues and defects.

One of the biggest opportunities for the future of business analysis lies within the development of a successful offshore delivery model and a tight-knit relationship with onshore clients. While the role of the business analyst is still evolving and standards are inconsistent, there is tremendous opportunity for the establishment of a client delivery model that includes an offshore component. In order to be successful, the delivery model must include clearly defined standards, delivery methods, and communication channels. Each of these will contribute to the establishment of a seamless onshore-offshore model.

This section highlights the areas where the typical delivery model breaks down (understanding what will and will not work), what the offshore business analysis service delivery model looks like, how we can build an effective onshore-offshore delivery model for business analysis (building and customizing your own model) by selling it to traditional face-to-face clients and then transitioning those clients to the new model (implementing it).

Any and all of these models can be successful if there are adequate means in place to manage the relationship and to translate the interactions between the onshore presence and the offshore teams. This is especially effective when the outsourcing company provides for an onshore presence to establish and maintain the client relationship, and communicate the culture, environment, and expectations to the near-shore and offshore teams.

In the end, business analysis is about creating results for the client business. Provided that the business analysis service provider can ensure that this happens, it should not matter where the business analyst is physically located.

ADDRESSING COMMON SERVICE DELIVERY PROBLEMS

Not Establishing an Environment for Success Early

Management has the opportunity to create a complacent, toxic, or a dynamic working environment for success. It does not matter what management has written on the wall for everyone to see, behavior speaks louder than words. It is important to ensure that you have a positive and empowering team in place to manage your service delivery, so that it enables your resources to successfully carry forward a positive message about your organization through their work.

Managing Expectations

Far too often, I deal with people that do not set and manage realistic expectations with customers. It surprises me how many of them are afraid to tell the customer bad news. Unfortunately, this can lead to disjointed teams moving in different directions and making uncoordinated attempts to complete the project in isolated parts. You would have a better shot of winning a three-legged race with a goat! The worst expectation management dysfunction in service delivery is when they push the responsibility onto other team members and even the stakeholder. So who is footing the bill while this dance is going on? The client organization is, of course.

I once knew of a project manager who was fully aware that he was not going to deliver what was expected on time. He told the client one thing and the team another, and left both feeling dissatisfied. The best way to prevent chaos later on is to manage the delivery throughout, telling the client exactly what stakeholders can expect and when to expect it. If that changes for any reason, the service delivery provider needs to sit down with the client organization to help them understand the reasons behind the changes, explore the best options from a risk perspective, and reset the expectations to fit the new plan.

Transparency

One of the biggest concerns that I have heard over the years is the lack of transparency in service delivery. All too often, account managers do not want to give bad news or escalate when things first start to go wrong because they want to attempt to manage the issues and keep them contained. Unfortunately, this leads to a lack of transparency in service delivery and engagement, and contributes to the business' inability to maintain service delivery standards because they have to take drastic measures in order to keep the business on track.

Now, usually when I hear that there is a lack of transparency with outsourcing, my "spidey" senses start to tingle and I want to know more. Because when you think about it, a client that expresses concerns over transparency could actually either be expressing concern over feelings of a loss of control, or they could genuinely be expressing concerns over transparency.

The difference is that someone with control issues is more likely to be a micro-manager and not necessarily concerned about loss of transparency as much as about the not knowing and having a hand in every step and detail of the project. Loss of transparency occurs when the resources do not live up to their end of the service level agreement, and end up impeding the success of service delivery because they are not communicating.

Communication is the most critical aspect of a relationship. Without it, there is no relationship. From a service delivery perspective, we cannot jointly monitor progress and mitigate failure; we cannot deliver a product that will meet client needs, and both of us become helpless in preventing the situation from turning into utter chaos.

Lack of Crisis Communication Planning

Planning for communication in a crisis is one of the least developed and detailed activities. In fact, I would consider it to be one of the most underutilized plans within technology because many within the industry seem to confuse an accountability matrix and an escalation plan for a crisis communication plan. They seem to think that those pieces are the only ones that are needed in order to deal with a crisis. That could not be farther from the truth.

Planning how you will communicate, and what policies and procedures will be enacted in a crisis, are absolutely critical to the success of service delivery, especially when you consider the delivery micro-models and then factor in the engagement models. In technology there is often a mixture of resources that belong to parent companies other than the client organization, and they need to have clear directions and guidelines as well as procedures to follow in any kind of crisis. I am not just talking about breaking something during implementation and having to back out your changes to some server somewhere; I am also talking about actual crises such as bomb threats, earthquakes, and other disasters as well as catastrophic business events that can occur. To develop a crisis communication plan, you will have to be able to answer these questions to be effectively prepared for any kind of crisis that can occur:

- Do you have a key person assigned to talk to the media?
- Does the key person know how to handle calls from the media?
- Do you have a central location for all of your employees to report to during business hours, so that they can be accounted for?
- Is the location accessible?
- Does the location have its own source of electric power?

- Are there phones and other equipment to manage or maintain the services that you need to continue to supply in a crisis?
- Can the location be utilized as a central command center for your business?
- What kind of data, call, and server traffic volumes can the location handle?
- What is the chain of command during a crisis, and who is in charge?
- Does it differ for each location?
- How will issues be escalated, managed, and prioritized?
- How will issues be communicated to your staff and other resources?
- Who is responsible and accountable for communicating information and updating it?

A strategy and well-thought-out plan for managing communication in a crisis is an essential.

Escalating Levels of Commitment

Too often, the more we spend on something the less likely we are to throw it away. Imagine that you have just spent $2 million on a project and it is only a quarter of the way through its five-year timeline. Now, imagine something happens and the business changes its strategic plan, making this project unnecessary, or that the project falls substantially short of your governance criteria. Are you going to continue spending the remainder of the $8 million dollar price tag that in reality will end up being a lot more like $16 to $32 million by the time you are done, or do you stop now?

Shockingly, many companies would continue. Why? Because the level of commitment to the project escalated by spending a large amount of money on it. These companies need to stop throwing good money at bad projects and work to ensure that their services delivery model contains a solid plan, follow through, and activities that prevent projects from running away like a team of horses.

Not Adapting Activities

Junior business analysts and most intermediate analysts lack the knowledge and experience to understand the context or value of the tasks and tools. Without this understanding, they are not able to tell you which tasks, or which part of those tasks, and tools can be adapted to get the most amount of value from the work that they are doing.

A highly skilled senior business analyst will use best practices and processes that have been refined over the years to be able to pick up a project, rescue it from disaster, and give the business the highest degree of needs coverage that they can. These processes provide the luxury of choosing how much to apply in any given situation. This means the skilled senior business analysts can apply customized tools and tasks "on the fly" to meet evaporating budgets and shrinking timelines due to underestimation or lack of early planning. If they cannot meet all deadlines in a shrinking timeline, they will outline a strategy and road map for getting the rest of the way there and a team that will be happy to stay on until it is all done.

Having the ability to identify risks, impacts, and critical failure points early and then to manage them throughout the process, enables the highly skilled analyst to prevent, mitigate, and drag your projects back into alignment while the cost is low. The way you do that is by implementing ongoing monitoring strategies throughout the service delivery process for addressing problems in real-time, so you get them back on track in real-time. Most companies do not do enough of this. They let the alignment slip continually and then wonder why they are so far off course when they did nothing to prevent it.

Building Unrealistic Estimates

How often have you heard that deadlines are slipping and there is a need to extend a project? Underestimating the length of time and ultimately, the cost, based on the way that work is performed is all too common on projects.

Sure, things happen; after all, no one can plan for everything even though organizations generally try to plan for at least the most critical risks. However, part of the service delivery process is building the right team of people that will get the job done well and on time. In the end, that saves money, yet what tends to happen is that the service organization builds an estimate, and then conservatively builds in an extra 15 to 20%, just in case. Then they go and staff the project based on who they have available, not based on the skills and roles that they really need to fulfill to be successful in the project under the terms and conditions that they described in the estimate.

Frequently, if outsourcing a business analysis service, the provider will be happy because they have won the work and now they can place the lowest cost resources that they can find to complete the job in order to increase their profit margin. Unfortunately for the client organization, this means that quality, time, and the budget suffer. So if you were the client organization, would you rather spend $85/hr for six months and get 90 to 100% of the features you need, or $45/hr for one year and get only 20% of the features you need? Getting what you want and need to be successful in your business should not be rocket science, and you should not have to settle for hit and miss success rates around 32%.

It is important to conduct an audit that will describe exactly where you can improve service delivery and stop the leaks of both the time and money that do not give you something real in return. Ideally, one senior solution consultant can perform this activity from a role on a project that does not add bulk and actually gets the inside scoop on what is really going on and why your project may be struggling. The added bonus is that if this is done well, you can place the person *incognito* on a struggling project, and they can help bring it back on track, so that you can accomplish two things at once.

SUMMARY

This chapter provided an overview of how to establish an effective service delivery model for business analysis. It highlighted issues within traditional consulting delivery models and drew a connection to the impacts of those issues on the quality and integrity of the outcomes. In addition, key elements for you to consider were outlined in order to create a complete, end-to-end service delivery model. Again, service delivery is about more than just getting products into the hands of customers, and it is more than just dropping off allocated resources to the client site to deliver the requisite services.

Typically, when organizations hear the term "service delivery" in connection with consulting, they think of the three main delivery vehicles for the services (onshore, near-shore, and offshore). They do not consider the components and other factors that will either contribute to or detract from the quality of the services being provided. Further, they assume that the resource is well versed in service delivery expectations and will not forget the little details that can interrupt service quality along the way.

Consider services in the same way that you would a satellite or network connection. Just because you are sending a "signal" does not mean that there will not be other factors that contribute to the loss of integrity. When the signal gets to the other end (the client side), there could well be losses in strength due to various conditions on the line or distribution system.

Within consulting, one needs to understand that resources and their effectiveness, productivity, and motivation are each subject to the conditions under which you expect them to deliver the services. That means it is just as important to plan, measure, monitor, and control all aspects of the delivery. This is the only way that you can ensure that the services are provided (in this case delivered) at the same rate in which they are expected, and that resources have the ability to perform at their potential.

This information will help you to establish a well-planned and controlled services delivery model that delivers effective services at the rate that they are promoted to the client and are expected by stakeholders. It is imperative to understand the gaps and issues that arise in the traditional delivery model, so that you can mitigate risks, close the gaps, and remove the impediments to successful service delivery.

Services are not delivered in a vacuum. You must recognize that service, in and of itself, is neither complete nor valuable without a solid and pragmatic plan for the delivery process. This includes factoring in the mechanisms for feedback and quality control across that process. It is factoring that allows for the services to be delivered with the good faith and integrity with which they were intended, based on the proficiency of the team.

9

ENGAGEMENT MODELS

In order to firmly establish a solid, end-to-end business analysis services model, we need to consider how services will be received by the client and what must be done to ensure that the client is well-prepared to receive the full value and benefit of these services. To accomplish this, we need to gain an understanding of the client side of the equation and what must be in place in order for them to fully and successfully engage business analysis services to reap the return on investment and full potential benefit. Not to do so would be like building a bridge and not considering how to connect it from the other side.

To provide a complete view, this chapter discusses engagement models. It illustrates how to build an effective engagement model and what the major elements are. Issues that occur during engagement are used as a means of exposing potential loss of integrity and quality that will directly affect the overall effectiveness of the services that are to be provided.

Engagement models are used to depict the ways in which the services and the service delivery models connect with the client organization to create a seamless bond for the duration of the relationship of the two entities. They represent the relationship from the client organization in the same way that customer relationship management represents the vendor organization.

Again, engagement models are both strategic and tactical. Every service delivery organization should have a generic engagement model that outlines the relationship as a whole at the strategic level and accounts for all of the smaller tactical engagements in general terms. The tactical engagement models are specific to individual projects and resource allocations, but utilize the same techniques with key considerations to differentiate them. Typically, the strategic and tactical considerations for engagement models include two primary elements that can be found across all types of engagement models: engagement strategy and vendor management (see Figure 9.1).

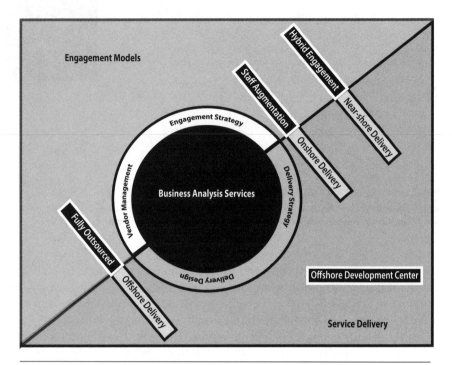

Figure 9.1 Engagement and service delivery model

The most common types of engagement models include staff augmentation, full outsourcing, hybrid coordination between staff augmentation and full outsourcing, an offshore development center (ODC), and build-operate-transfer (BOT). Each of these intersects with one or more of the service delivery channels (offshore, near-shore, and onshore) to create a full engagement or bond between the two organizations in order to accomplish the goals of the client organization.

ELEMENTS OF THE ENGAGEMENT MODEL

Again, the primary elements of the business analysis engagement model are the engagement strategy and vendor management. Where the strategy dictates the focus and direction of successful business analysis engagements, vendor management ensures that the appropriate vendors are selected and managed to deliver on those results that are indicated by the strategy.

Engagement Strategy

The creation of an engagement strategy is critical to the success in the development and management of engagement models because it determines the course of the individual elements and factors that will contribute to the success of the engagement. For business analysis, we have to develop strategies that take the services, management of those services, and the corresponding service delivery models into consideration. In essence, the engagement strategy will tie these elements together so that engagements can be effectively and efficiently managed from start to finish.

Vendor Management

Vendor management is the control and governance of the vendor relationship (often under the auspices of supplier performance management or supply chain management), that is applied to measure, analyze, and manage the performance of a vendor in an effort to reduce costs, alleviate risks, and to drive continuous improvement. The overall intention is to identify potential opportunities, as well as issues and their root causes, so that they can be resolved to the benefit of both organizations.

Considerations that we have to make in vendor management are to define and understand how the vendor will be held accountable and responsible for the delivery and performance of the expected services. To effectively manage the relationship with the vendor, we have to outline key strategies for the appropriate utilization of vendors (whether internal or external), the governance of the services provided by the vendor, the channels utilized by the vendor to engage the client organization at all appropriate levels and to improve the quality of relationships that the client organization has with all of its vendor organizations.

Remember the insurance company discussed in chapter 2 with the bad program that it paid the vendor to develop? In that case, the director who was responsible for vendor management did not have any type of service level agreements in place to ensure that the vendor was actually accountable for providing a minimum level of service to the broker portal. Unfortunately, the only thing being measured and monitored was the overall percentage of time that the portal was functional, and the director did not look at any other type of data that could be used to conduct a root-cause analysis or identify trends in the problems that might pinpoint a solution.

Vendor Selection

Vendor selection can create quite a buzz in developing engagement models, especially when the criteria for the types of vendors, the request for proposals, and the request for queries can seem like exhaustive lists that build massive hurdles for the vendor organization to meet before they can even be considered a viable option. The selection criteria does not always matter if the vendor is an internal or external organization because the client organization is still accountable for costs and return on investment for whatever the vendor produces, and however they are engaged.

It is important to generate selection criteria that includes accountability for the elements of the business analysis service model (the performance indicators and the governance of the business analysis processes) that will be utilized to meet your specific needs and to achieve the results that you require, as this will enable you to make a more informed vendor selection and translate into a better engagement down the road.

Other selection criteria for an individual business analysis vendor might include the types of services that they offer under the guise of business analysis, their track record for service delivery, and the types of deliverables that they can create, as well as the results that they can achieve based on their resources. To this end, many client organizations not only include the typical proposal for specific services, but also request testimonials (references), practical examples of past work, past client lists, past project lists, and proposed resource profiles.

Unfortunately, this may not be all that is necessary in the selection of an appropriate business analysis vendor because it assumes a basic commonality of services and understanding of the role. We have already seen throughout this book that "understanding" can vary dramatically from resource to resource, and project to project. Vendor selection has to set the expectations for the services to be performed, the quality levels and measures that will be employed, and the vendor stability and viability of the proposed solution.

Many organizations, however, put a lot of effort into the front end of vendor selection and forget that, once they have made selections, they still have to manage the relationship. This goes right back to the concept of Business Analysis Stewardship, in that it is necessary to remain financially responsible and accountable for the effective management of all resources, even when those resources are allocated through a vendor organization.

Governing Vendor Relationships

The key to any successful relationship is communication. You have to establish both incoming and outgoing communication channels. These channels have to be fostered and nurtured under all conditions and circumstances, so that when things do go wrong, you can work collectively and collaboratively to rectify the situation.

Having a sound set of channels creates a foundation of trust that removes some of the issues, as discussed above, specifically the issues surrounding transparency. *Transparency* is the perception of openness and honesty that exists only when communication is fostered and strong between any two parties.

Again, according to Business Analysis Stewardship, organizations have to ensure that we are managing all of the resources, and ensure financial responsibility and accountability. This cannot happen if we fail to govern the relationships with business analysis vendors as a part of our overall engagement strategy.

Vendor Accountability

All planning activities build a foundation for the client relationship and planning sets you up for either success or failure. Unfortunately, there is a miscommunication about who is responsible for ensuring that all the foundational pieces are included in planning and initiating your engagement. Typically, vendor organizations are brought in to do the planning work because the client organization needs it to be done and wants their advice on how to do it.

There is an expectation that, because the vendor organization often has more diverse clients and more consistent exposure to a broader business community, this exposure represents a more well-established ability to make decisions that come from a more rich set of experiences. The knowledge gained is no longer a single perspective, but factual observations over a larger set of projects and companies.

To be done thoroughly, planning for individual engagements, vendors, and projects must include a needs analysis, identification of your goals and objectives, a strategic plan, risk and impact assessment including mitigation strategies, a communication plan, and a change management plan. It is having each of these components firmly in place that will enable and support vendor accountability across the engagement, as well as create alignment to the original engagement strategies.

Monitoring Vendor Performance

In order to be successful in managing your business analysis vendor organizations for more productive, effective, and efficient engagements, it is imperative that vendor performance is measured and monitored. Unfortunately, many client organizations do not measure the vendors' performance to the degree that is necessary to identify and mitigate issues in service delivery and service quality. The costs of vendor quality to the client organization are enormous when you consider that individual projects are constantly derailed and run over budgets and timelines. Individual performance indicators for business analysis vendors include:

- Scrap, rework, ramp-up, and losses in productivity across processes that are utilized by the vendor organization.
- Warranty expenses due to the poor quality.
- Increased operating expenses due to the poor quality of products.

Conducting Vendor Audits to Ensure Alignment to Service Level Agreements

In general, audits are one of the most effective means of ensuring that vendors are following the processes and procedures that were outlined in the service level agreement and dictated during the selection processes. The audit identifies any issues with noncompliance in business analysis, service delivery, change management, and quality processes. After the audit, the vendor and client organizations collaborate to identify remediation that must be adopted by the vendor within a specific timeframe.

Future audits can ensure that the remedies have been successfully adopted and implemented. The client organization ensures that the audit process itself is efficient and effective, and allows for the systematic audit of all vendors in order to ensure alignment to the strategies and objectives of the organization.

Improving Vendor Management

As with other aspects of business, you have to constantly focus on reviewing and improving the processes and services that are being utilized. This is the only way that your organization can work toward sustainability and maintainability. Consistent improvement to your engagement model, as well as to your vendor management element, is a key way in which to accomplish sustainability and maintainability. However, there are other considerations that are unique to vendor management that you will want to have in place. These include cost recovery and closed loop corrective action.

Cost Recovery

Client organizations should proactively work with vendors to constantly improve their deliverable quality. A cost recovery system, in which vendors are penalized for providing poor deliverable quality, is an effective way to enforce discipline and accountability into the vendor organization. When companies implement vendor quality management systems that aggregate costs, and then use it for charge-backs, they would be able to recover the costs of poor quality and adopt disciplines that enforces rapid improvements to the quality of deliverables.

Closed Loop Corrective Action

Systematic reductions in the costs attributed to quality issues with deliverables can be achieved by adopting a vendor quality management system that includes a closed loop corrective action process. In a business analysis organization, when process deviations, service level agreement noncompliance, undefined requirements, scrap and rework, or stakeholder complaints occur, remedial actions have to be started to correct the issues.

Once issues are identified, the first step is to conduct a *root cause analysis*. After the root cause is identified, remedial action items are created and escalated for necessary approvals. Once they are approved, the appropriate changes are adopted. These changes may include corrections to procedures and improving the competency and performance of individual resources. In addition, the details associated with compliance issues could be used to start and run cost recovery processes.

It is imperative that business analysis engagement models utilize closed-loop processes. This process ensures that the necessary information flows through the corrective action process quickly and accurately, so that nothing is lost and the integrity of business analysis services and stewardship is maintained. In addition, it ensures that the entire change control and governance processes are auditable from end-to-end. In this way, audits become a core driver into the service delivery process and a key tool for continuous improvement.

Appropriate vendor management affects business analysis and business analysis services in three ways. First, vendor management impacts business analysis in that the type of engagement model, coupled with the strategies and vendor management model, will ultimately determine the services provided and the measures for quality and performance, as well as the deliverable types and quality expectations. Second, it enables the vendor organization to increase their capability in this area. Third, the increased capability enables the vendor to provide higher quality services and deliver higher quality results, ultimately enabling the client organization to achieve its own goals and objectives.

TYPES OF ENGAGEMENT MODELS

Engagement models can impact the organizational structure as well as the services provided because in some instances (like staff augmentation and hybrid models), the resources are placed with the client organization and it is not just about delivering the results that are necessary for success, but also about delivering results by utilizing the client's service, service delivery expectations, and infrastructure. Sounds complicated, right?

To reiterate, the engagement model affects business analysis based on the business analysis model that will be applied. Each engagement model will imply that resources are managed by differing groups, and therefore, it will be the understanding and model for business analysis that is utilized by the group that will determine the deliverables, outcomes, and tasks of the business analysis role.

This can be good or bad, depending on whose idea of business analysis is followed and the results from the business analysts that come from that idea. In fact, some organizations limit the success of business analysis tasks when their understanding and application of the business analyst role is vastly different from that of the vendor organization.

Typically, when vendors are engaged to accomplish business analysis, business analysts come into the organization with an understanding of how to get things done. They must have some time to ramp-up when the expectations of the client differs. In other words, they have routines and roles that they are accustomed to performing. It will take time and understanding, as well as some coaching, to level-set expectations and ensure that everyone is on the same page. This time will also save some frustration later on. Of course, this really does depend on the engagement model and the level of management over the resources that are negotiated with vendors.

To the business analysts, the engagement model is more than just "where do I show up for work." It is about the reporting structure that is in place to accomplish the work, the communication forums within that structure and the accountability for the work that they need to accomplish during the project. However, it is also about where they can quickly find the information about the client organization that they will need to be successful, and what the deliverables will look like once they are completed.

They will adopt those things that have been accounted for within the engagement model, but they will also improvise if things like deliverable templates and processes do not exist for the client organization. Finally, it is important to note that each of these situations with the business analyst resources will also vary, depending on the engagement model applied.

Staff Augmentation

Staff augmentation is where the client organization contracts resources to extend their own team by contributing to ongoing technology work. Typically, these are long-term engagements where individual resources could spend years working with a single client organization. These resources report directly to the client organization and that organization determines the business analysis model that will be utilized to perform and deliver business analysis services within the organization. They manage all aspects of the services and the service delivery within the client organization, and merely approach vendors to bring on new resources.

From Chapter 8, remember how the primary difference between the onshore, near-shore, and offshore service delivery micro-models was facetime with clients? Well, in this case, the most common and preferred service delivery models to be coupled with this engagement model are onshore and near-shore. This comes down to the level of control that the client organization has over the resources when they are face-to-face, as opposed to completely offshore (remote).

Full Outsourcing

Full outsourcing is where the client organization brings on a vendor to provide the end-to-end solution development, including the required services, and relies solely on the vendor organization to manage all aspects of services and service delivery. It is the vendor organization that determines the best use of resources, budgets, and services to achieve the results required by the client organization.

This enables the vendor organization to make its own determination for the applicability of the service delivery model to meet the needs and achieve the results. In business analysis, this can mean that there is any one of a number of scenarios that occur. For example, you can find business analysts working onsite and working face-to-face with the client organization and relaying information to an offshore team, or all business analysts could be working offshore and getting information directly from the client organization stakeholders through virtual means.

Hybrid Model

The hybrid model is a combination of various engagement models as a means of offering more options and a customizable experience to the client organization. This model generally impacts the billing models used by the organizations for service delivery and engagement as a means of controlling costs at various points in the performance of the contracted services. An engagement can start as a fixed bid to initiate the project and then move to a time and materials engagement in order to allow greater control over the project expenditures, where the work being performed is more predictable and limited to a smaller set of deliverables.

It impacts business analysis in that utilizing a fixed bid can often limit the scope of the deliverables and the tasks being performed under the business analysis services umbrella. Unfortunately, it also has some significant issues related to its application and inconsistent approaches. These are outlined later in this chapter. It is important to note the issues and build an engagement model that will account for mitigation strategies to offset these issues.

Offshore Development Center

In an offshore development center, the vendor organization provides both the facility and the resources with a bare skeleton of management services to manage the resources and the facility. The client organization (essentially) "rents" or contracts the facility and the resources from the vendor, and they are essentially on a staff augmentation engagement, but happen to be on the premises and under the management of the vendor organization. In essence, the vendor contracts out the resources on the staff augmentation, and then also agrees to manage the staff as if they were a part of the client organization. They follow the standards, guidelines, and processes for all services and deliveries as prescribed by the vendor organization as if they were in a regular staff augmentation engagement onshore.

One key way that an ODC can influence business analysis is that the resources feel as though they are actually immersed in the client organization and working onsite, so the psychological barriers of reporting structure conflicts are reduced. It is also a way in which clients can feel as though they have greater control over the resources and the work being done. While the resources are purely offshore, they have a *feeling* of being onshore.

Build-Operate-Transfer

The build-operate-transfer model is not very common in business analysis. However, it does happen. In this case, the engagement model begins by utilizing any of the above models and at some point the ownership is then transferred over to the client organization. It tends to be most common with an offshore development center, or where the client organization has some vested interest in maintaining the existing staffing and other resources as a means of continuing the work being carried out by the vendor team under their own business.

In some cases, a BOT engagement is written into the vendor and service level agreements to accommodate a risk mitigation strategy for the client organization (e.g., the risks associated with the failure of the vendor organization).

ISSUES ENCOUNTERED DURING ENGAGEMENT

Up to this point, the main issues that impact business analysis as a direct result of problems within the existing model for the management and deployment of business analysis resources have been discussed. We also detailed how it really is not a model at all but an *ad hoc* conglomerate of poor management practices that can end up coming out in the products and services provided by the business analysts themselves. Now, we really have to look at the current engagement models and expose some of the issues that arise in requirements, project success, and even business analysis itself as a result of some minor missteps throughout client engagement.

Discovery and Planning Stage Issues

Typically, when we talk about engaging particular services to support a project, one of the first people that the client or business will meet with is a senior consultant—the so-called "guru." This consultant is basically a functional or technical resource that has moved up through the ranks, and probably has a great deal of knowledge about what you are trying to accomplish. He or she may even have a perfect fit solution in mind.

Unfortunately, the expert who wows you is not usually the expert that will be on the project team. In fact, they may not even be around when you get the project off the ground. The consultant is not even likely to end up mentoring or supporting the team once the project gets going. You may not see that person again unless you start another project.

So, what is the senior consultant actually an expert in? Are they an architect, a business analyst, project manager, or a senior developer in disguise? Chances are that he or she is actually one of these four roles, but the problem is that you need at least two of these roles in order to define a solid solution. The reason to involve multiple roles is simple: one person defines the results that the business needs to see, and the other person has the expertise in designing those results. If you think that this means that I am recommending a senior business analyst and an architect team over any other combination (including a project manager), you have got it right.

Realistically, a project manager can only tell you when it can happen and how long the whole thing should take, based on the input provided by these two others. Unless they have filled both the analyst and architect roles expertly in the past, the project manager has no real bearing on the solution definition or how to achieve the necessary results required by the business. The business will be responsible for identifying the problem, defining the solution, and then dictating that solution to the project manager and the team.

So, how can they come up with a solution that looks and seems well-rounded on the surface? Most likely, the expert is taking a lot of notes and relaying information to a team of intermediate resources somewhere else to help create the solution.

Let's face it: senior resources are expensive. The more senior resources they have on site figuring out a solution to your business situation, the more they are spending to try to win your business. Most service providers and consulting firms hope that companies are going to pay them to come in and tell you how to solve your issue, and what they would do to make that happen. The reality is that this is a service, not a bargaining chip. It is a service because they are there to provide you with an answer and an initiation package to start your project. You need that initiation done right because there is so much at stake.

Inadequate Project Planning

One issue related to engagement models and planning for both delivery and engagement is that there is often a disconnect between the vendor and the client organizations about who is responsible for what tasks during discovery. Typically, discovery includes the bare minimum number of senior resources from the vendor talent pool who will provide the bare minimum amount of project planning tasks and deliverables.

These vendor resources will outline the goals and objectives, identify the problem that the business is trying to resolve, generate a "10,000 foot high" view of the solution, a rough project plan, a "10,000 foot high" view of the solution architecture, an estimated timeline with how much it will cost, and finally, kick-off meetings. At best, the senior vendor resources hope for participation from executive sponsors, working sponsors, or technical sponsors, and usually get the bare minimum amount of participation from the bare minimum number of resources that the client organization can spare for the time that they are there.

One of the key issues is that if the senior vendor is a project manager with no other background, they will not have enough detailed and in-depth knowledge of the processes utilized by the business analysis teams. They will only be able to provide a high-level estimate for a generic set of tasks that may or may not be in line with what is really needed to develop the requirements for the overall solution. This is going to lead straight down the miscalculated budget and schedule path, which will be difficult, if not impossible to recover from later on in the project.

Inadequate Staffing for Discovery and Planning Activities

As mentioned, most discovery and planning phases are completed by a bare number of assigned resources. The work must be done by resources who wear multiple hats. For a smaller project, this may not be an issue, but for larger projects, this can spell disaster before the project even gets out of the gate.

Unfortunately, when multitasking occurs, the client organization is in danger of getting incomplete work that is not thorough enough to set a solid foundation for the project. Unless this is known up front and mitigated, many clients will not find out until much farther down the road when you start running into issues with requirements, and even then, you may not recognize the real root cause.

The work in discovery must be done by a minimum number of resources with differing responsibilities that match their skill set. I recommend two to four senior resources with differing expertise, and establishing a core team of mixed intermediate to senior resources for follow through and completion of the project. This leverages their skill sets and talents to maximize results of the project.

Issue #1: Lack of Mentoring Junior Resources

Naturally, everyone wants to put their best foot forward, and it is good business practice to put seniors where they will earn the most revenue and provide the most value back into the provider's own company. Honestly, I am a big proponent of a team structure that includes a mix of resources from all career levels. I do not agree with pulling seniors, and leaving the less qualified resources to fulfill the work that has been promised to the business, because this only exacerbates preexisting issues and introduces new ones.

All lesser-qualified resources must have mentoring and their work performance managed so that they can deliver results and not have to pay for the "rocket scientists" for the full project. In essence, the juniors need business analysis subject matter experts that they can connect with for ongoing project support to ensure that this is a win-win for everyone.

One of the key benefits of utilizing a mixed team and/or business analysis mentors is that it increases your ability to conduct succession planning and to manage ongoing attrition rates within your own talent pool. You are not going to be forced to outside vendor organizations that will serve to increase the overall costs of the projects or introduce an added layer of complexity from having to negotiate services, delivery, and engagement terms.

Issue #2: Incomplete Engagement and Collaboration

Something that I could not figure out early in my career was why change management is not viewed as inherent to the process of any new IT project. I now see it as people wanting advanced warning to know what to plan for. I have seen the most well-educated, onboard people balk at change when they were not kept in the loop. Keeping people informed can break down resistance to change.

Lack of Inherent User-Community Informational Activities

Change is a part of life, and no business is exempt. Nevertheless, we all want to feel like we matter. That means our job and how we do it becomes part of our identity. When something threatens our identity, we want to be able to have input, and have our concerns heard and questions answered. Projects and service delivery mechanisms that do not do that (or do it well enough) are doomed because the user community will revolt against them.

Typical projects must start with a high-level set of activities that informs the executives and begins to get them involved. Once they have begun getting involved, information must be dispersed to the employee and customer communities. This need not be a heavy or intensive process, but simply a forewarning that change is coming.

This forewarning must also come with messages about what to expect; who the change will impact; what the benefits of the changes are; the participation that is needed; how to find more information; and how to connect with the project team with any questions, comments, or feedback.

Lack of User-Community Input Funnels

A well-designed engagement plan contains elements that include combinations of informational and input activities, and on-demand input funnels, for directing user input throughout the engagement life cycle. Many businesses seem to think they can cut costs by not building an engagement-centric informational site (either internal or external), but both change and service delivery can actually take so much longer when you are constantly having to sell it to the community. It could potentially consume the time of at least one dedicated point of contact resource to respond to common queries repeatedly when there is no website to provide FAQ's, scheduling, or other updates to the information that people need to stay in the loop and maintain delivery standards.

Lack of Inherent User-Community Input Activities

Many businesses also seem less concerned about the ability for employee-users to contribute to the overall service delivery process. Part of where this thinking comes from is the attitude that since you pay them to do a job, they must do it and are not allowed to question or resist. This is a big mistake! They will rebel or become totally disengaged if you do not provide adequate input channels and actively involve them where and when it is appropriate to do so.

Part of the richness that your business brings to its customers and business community is built and based on the employees and vendors that they interact with. After all, not every customer deals directly with the vendor. It is important to keep in mind that all resources bring forward their own skills, talents, passions, and personalities, and will know empty rhetoric when they hear it. I once worked for a bank as a teller, and I cannot tell you how many speeches we got from the executives about how we were the front lines and the most important members of the branch team. The speeches were actually de-motivating because the words and their ultimate actions were totally in conflict.

We previously discussed in Chapter 8 the ways in which the lack of crisis communication planning can impact service delivery and why establishing an environment for success early is so important. These issues should be considered in the development of effective engagement models as well. Understanding all of the factors (no matter how small) will contribute to setting up an environment that supports full engagement as well as individual and team success. An environment that supports the team is informed, involved, motivated, empowered, and on the same page. Each employee, manager, team member, and customer believes that they personally contributed to the project's success.

DEVELOPING EFFECTIVE ENGAGEMENT MODELS

In order to develop an effective engagement model, you must determine the best and most effective means of achieving your goals. You will need to understand and factor in the service delivery model options of vendors that are available to you, with the vendors that you have selected, and you will have to determine the best vendor management and engagement strategies across the specific model that you are going to utilize.

As with service delivery on the vendor side, you can employ a variety of models if you have an adequate capability of managing each model individually and collectively for a successful outcome. Selection of the basic model is much more than determining that you want to utilize something like staff augmentation; you will also have to determine the kinds of vendors that you will look for, and then where the services will be delivered. If they are delivered on your premises, you will need to consider facilities for the individual resources such as desks, lighting, computers, and so on. Some of the questions that you might ask yourself in establishing the engagement model are:

- How will we manage the resources?
- How will we manage the projects under this engagement?
- How will this engagement meet our needs?
- How will this engagement deliver the outcomes and results that we require?
- What are the financial obligations of this engagement?
- What are the service delivery models available to us by the vendor organizations?
- How can we capitalize on these delivery models to meet our needs more efficiently and cost effectively?
- Can we utilize an option that will reduce our costs for this engagement?
- How will we manage the vendors under this engagement?
- How will we keep them accountable?
- How will we utilize this engagement to achieve our business objectives and goals?
- What are the primary drivers behind developing this engagement?
- How will we communicate with the vendor at various levels of their authority?
- How will we engage the vendor?
- Do we have the capability to accomplish this engagement with existing vendor organizations?
- What are the risks associated with this vendor?
- What is their reputation?
- How will we protect ourselves in the event that the vendor fails?

By answering those questions, you can start to understand the details that should be included in your engagement model, and how it should be put together. Engagement models are more than just brief depictions of where we want the services delivered and who will manage the resources; it is about how you will achieve your objectives for the business by utilizing this engagement.

SUMMARY

This chapter effectively closes the loop on the provision of end-to-end business analysis services through the use of engagement models. It walked us through the different types of engagement models, and illustrated how those align to the complementary service delivery models in order to create a closed system. As with service delivery, there are hosts of factors that will contribute to the quality of services that are received. Many of those were identified as the issues that can occur within engagement models. In closing, several questions to ponder were listed in order to develop an effective engagement model. Again, it is important to note that services are not delivered in a vacuum. They are provided to a customer that has a specific set of expectations, and in order for the business analysis team to be able to meet those expectations, highly effective *service delivery* is a must. The client must be fully prepared to accept the services in order to receive the benefits from them.

CONCLUSIONS ABOUT SERVICE DELIVERY AND ENGAGEMENT MODELS

In this section, we covered two essential models and frameworks of a well-developed business analysis services organization. These are service delivery and engagement. We talked about how imperative it is that we both empower and position BAs to help the business achieve its goals and objectives through the creation of processes and products that do just that. We reinforced the need for Business Analysis Stewardship which focuses on the results and safeguards the business by employing sustainable methods.

Service delivery is made up of elements that dictate how delivery will be managed and where services will be delivered. We looked at issues within current delivery models and further drew a connection to the impacts of those issues on the quality and integrity of the outcomes. We then discussed how to establish a more effective service delivery model. We covered the elements of this new effective service delivery model: service delivery strategy, design, operations, transition, continuous improvement, and delivery mechanisms.

Strategy means alignment to strategic goals, deciding how to resolve problems or to evolve the business, making build or buy decisions, and determining high-level resourcing decisions for projects. A subset is service strategy, which is about figuring out how to connect all of the impacted systems and components, tools, and resources in a dynamic way. Service strategy provides the guidance by which individual services and service groups are defined, delivered, and managed across the life cycle in order to meet overall business objectives. It is the planning that prevents runaway projects.

For business analysis, the problems that arise in requirements are deterministic when there is no service strategy in place.

We also explored the design of an effective services model from a high-level view by looking at some of the key attributes that must be considered: specificity, consistency, scalability, sustainability, and maintainability. We discussed the three main delivery vehicles for services: onshore, near-shore, and offshore, as well as how important it is to plan, measure, monitor, and control all aspects of the delivery.

We defined some key components of each delivery model element that are needed to ensure that a full and complete service delivery model is established and that all services are delivered in accordance with this model. How delivery is managed should include components for service expectations, defined services, and charge backs or billings.

Next we discussed the complement to the service delivery model, which is the engagement model. It encompasses how the service will be delivered in partnership with the client organization. We began by covering strategy and vendor management, then continued by reviewing various problems in many existing models and provided tips on how to avoid or prevent them. Naturally, there are positives and negatives to every model. The key is to be consistent and to establish the framework for continuous improvement of those models.

Finally, we discussed how to develop effective types of engagement models: staff augmentation, full outsourcing, hybrid models, offshore development centers and build-operate-transfer.

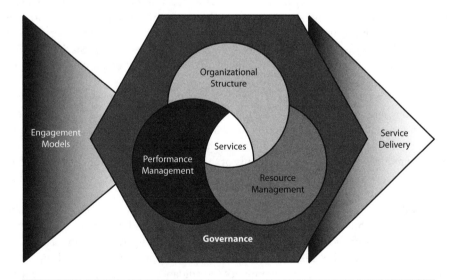

Figure S3.1 Managed services model

This information will help you to establish a well-planned and controlled services delivery model that delivers effective services at the rate that they are promoted to the client and are expected by stakeholders. The most important aspects of creating an effective and managed model for business analysis have now been covered (see Figure S3.1). In addition, how to develop the means for delivering and receiving business analysis services were discussed in order to reap the full benefits of those services. In the end, the effective and efficient delivery of services can mean the difference between success and failure.

TRANSITIONING TO A MANAGED BUSINESS ANALYSIS AS A SERVICE MODEL

The last major question in this book is how we are going to transition to a managed business analysis as a service model? What we have discussed to this point is a fundamentally different view of business analysis. That means that we cannot simply build the model, drop it into place, and then expect that everyone will adopt it and abide by the precepts. To transition to the new model, we have to define how this model will impact projects and how it will fit into the existing structure. In addition, there is the need to plan and schedule the implementation across projects that are in various stages of progress. You are going to have to package the model and sell it to the business analysts, the business, and to information technology.

In the early stages of transition and implementation, you have the opportunity to do two things: finalize the services design and showcase it to everyone. To this end, you will focus on developing a common vision, tying the model to the existing infrastructure, identifying leaders, and running quick-win pilot projects.

Building a new service or department shares some similarities with building an addition to a home. Imagine the construction of a new addition to your home was just completed. Now, fast forward a few months to a particularly cold winter where the ground beneath the house has shifted as a result. All of a sudden, when a ball is dropped on the floor in the kitchen, it rolls towards the outside wall. This did not happen when the addition was first completed. So you take a level and check the floor at various points, discovering that the house has sunk on one side. This is nuts! It is a new addition on which a lot of money was spent. Plus, it was a big inconvenience to be out of the house for those months while it was being built. So you call an engineer to come and have a look.

The engineer tells you that the contractor did not extend the joists under the floor back into the house and connect them to the existing joists the way it should have been done. Instead, the contractor bolted a ledger board onto the outside of the house, and attached the addition to it. The engineer further explains that by attaching the addition joists to the existing ones, the stability of the addition can be assured. By using ledger boards, a segmented component results that is not really an extension of the house, and therefore not stable. At this point, you learn that it is going to cost thousands of dollars to fix. However, you don't have much of a choice because the walls have started to crack and moisture is seeping in, causing a lot of damage.

When building a new service or department, it must be strongly tied to the existing organizational structure for stability, or eventually the whole thing breaks down and damages both structures, even if the first one was very stable. This section takes what we have learned and shows how to develop and incubate the new business analysis services model within the organization so that it takes root and becomes a part of the existing information technology division, fostering exponential growth.

10

DETERMINING YOUR
TRANSITION STRATEGY

Before you can successfully transition to a new managed business analysis services model, you must do two important things:

1. Define the target. In other words, know what you are building.
2. Determine your transition strategy. Services and service delivery is merely a part of this strategy.

In order to define the target, you need to do more than just understand the services that you have outlined—you also need to create a vision for the new model by defining the mission, how it will be managed, and its success and failure criteria. These will provide focus for the analyst team as they move forward toward the goal and for the business and other groups as they work to interact with and navigate the new structure for getting resources allocated, managing them on projects, and releasing them back into the talent pool.

To determine the transition strategy, you will have to understand how the model will fit within the existing infrastructure, as well as how you will foster empowerment and obtain buy-in from everyone involved with the business analysis organization, technology group, and the business community.

In some cases, the strategy may pull authority away from other external groups such as project managers and resource management groups. In the past, some of these groups had complete authority and autonomy to locate and hire/contract business analysis resources for their specific projects.

In this model, project managers and resource management may continue to locate and ultimately hire/contract the business analysis resources to meet these projects. However, they must ensure that the candidates are screened and assessed by the business analysis manager or group in order to ensure compliance to the new standards. A benefit to this step is that the resource(s) coming on board will be made aware of the expectations for business analysis within your organization, and will be more likely to live up to them.

Remember, in the long run, as business analysis develops and is empowered within your organization, other groups will accept it and may even welcome it once they understand the benefits of the new protocol.

VISION

The vision for your business analysis services group is a summary of what the group will achieve over the long run. It provides motivation for resources to collaborate and to make the vision a reality, but also enables them to participate and align their contributions toward the overall long-term goal, instead of only the most immediate project, where they might be tempted to cut corners.

The group's vision statement should describe the overall purpose for why this group exists, and how it will benefit the business and technology projects. The vision statement should outline specific results that the group will generate for the business community, project stakeholders and sponsors, project teams, and individual projects themselves. This vision should also detail specific results that the group will achieve in terms of revenue, benefits realization, operating costs, sales profits (internal and external), and growth.

As a general rule, the group's vision statement should also define the target market for the services, the products and services that are going to be sold, revenue, profit and growth goals, group size in location, project type and domain expertise, an organizational chart, as well as a unique selling proposition and timeline for hitting critical benchmarks. Other considerations that you will need to make in creating a common vision are:

1. Who are the personalities you have within the analyst team?
2. What are the team members' skill levels right now?
3. What types of domain knowledge currently reside within the group?
4. Who will act as a champion for your group?
5. How will services be delivered—onshore, near-shore or offshore?
6. What types of services can you offer today?
7. What are the current operating costs of the business analyst team(s)?
8. What are the current revenue potentials for the group?
9. What is the current revenue?
10. What percentage is profit?
11. How much money is the company willing to invest in this group?
12. What type of support will it need?
13. What type of support will it have from other groups?

14. What type of service can you offer that makes your group a clear choice over other service providers?
15. How are you going to qualify opportunities that arise?
16. How will you allocate resources to opportunities?
17. How are you going to attract customers (even from within)?
18. What is the strategy for enhancing and deepening customer relationships?
19. What is the date that the group's vision will be completed?

MISSION

The mission statement for the group is a shortened version of the vision that must be shared with other groups, the business, and outsourcing partners.

SUCCESS AND FAILURE CRITERIA

Another critical factor in establishing a new group is developing a common understanding of what success and failure looks like for the group. It needs to grasp the concept that when the time comes for a project to no longer be funded, the plug needs to be pulled. While you cannot dig yourself out of the hole, at least you won't make it any bigger.

Have you ever known a gambler who sits at the same slot machine for hours while dumping in good money after bad because they are certain that it will pay off if they are patient enough? Well, the truth can be harder to accept. We have to predetermine when we will pull the plug on projects, resources, and the group or services if they are not working. Quite often, we do not cease or recommend a work stoppage because there are major events along the way that escalated our own level of commitment to the idea, and we cannot accept reality.

Escalating the Level of Commitment

As a case in point, I once worked on a project where I replaced another team lead. During the hand-over meetings, the team lead asked for my plans for how to complete the work that was left. During these discussions, I often heard from her, "That's not the way things are done here." If I only had a dollar for every time I heard that statement during my career!

Finally at a closed meeting for the ending of her assignment, I told her that I had been brought in and been given specific instructions to challenge the way that things were done, to bring in new ideas and fresh techniques, so that the business could grow from my experience at larger corporations. She seemed shocked, and never mentioned it again. The point is: just because we can, does not mean we should; just because we always have, does not mean we have to now.

In this case, the project and requirements activities continued in spite of some glaring flaws since no one wanted to stop the workflow. This was clearly a case of an escalated level of commitment and an inability to accept what was really going on within the project.

PLANNING MANAGEMENT AND FIT WITHIN THE ORGANIZATION

With any implementation, planning the tasks, resources, budget, and timeline for the transition is a crucial key to success. That does not mean just scheduling it and letting the implementation run its course. It means actively managing the implementation and the resistance that may go along with it. You have to ensure that other groups impacted by this new group are informed and that the processes between them align.

Understanding the Far-Reaching Impacts of Process Changes

As a case in point, when I began rolling out new business analysis processes while helping a Fortune 500 company build a Business Analysis Center of Excellence, it was not only processes for conducting business analysis and performing the tasks that were being changed. What also changed was how resources were screened, hired, and allocated; how performance was managed and measured; who was accountable on the project for managing business analysis outcomes; how services were delivered and managed; how business analysis services were engaged by clients; and who was involved in all of the processes. Deliverables for each group also changed.

All of this change meant that I had to work closely with the resource management group to ensure that the new screening, hiring, and allocation processes were followed, and that people stopped randomly hiring or placing unqualified business analysts in projects (and putting the organization at risk). It meant that I had to work closely with the project management office to ensure that the project managers knew how to assess performance using the new tools and key performance indicators. In addition, it meant that I had to work with developers, architects, and testers to ensure that new deliverable templates would enhance their understanding of the requirements and improve the end product as a result.

During planning, you will need to set criteria for implementing the model across resources who are engaged in projects. It is not going to be practical, feasible, or cost effective to simply conduct a mass rollout to all resources. All you will do is create headaches, fear, and frustration, and get people to dump the idea of change before it is fully adopted and they can see the benefits of the new model. Any time that there are new processes and techniques, you want to consider your options for a timed and staged implementation.

It is important to select the right projects based on a variety of factors, including the stages of the projects that you have in mind, allocated resources, type of project, and project objectives. You cannot simply change over all of your resources in one fell swoop because this will cause issues during individual projects and could result in higher than normal defect rates. You would actually lose credibility in doing this, and ultimately you will lose buy-in to the new model, ending up back at the start. Unfortunately, I have seen many companies fall into this trap. Instead, you need to set criteria for each project type so you can really show how the new model works.

There are three types of projects, based on stage of life, which you need to be concerned with when beginning to plan a transition to the new model. These are projects at the planning stage and not yet started; projects at the early initiating stage before the requirements phase has started; and projects at a later stage that are well underway and at least in the midst of the requirements phase.

Pilot projects are optional projects that can be transitioned over to the new model while you are still determining the schedule or fate of the remaining projects. You would typically start with a pilot project as a proof of concept. Do not worry about making mistakes in the implementation at this point. A pilot is understood to be a learning exercise and an opportunity to fine tune the model based on the practical application. Remember that what is good in theory is not always good in practice, and utilizing a pilot project will allow you to work out the kinks as you determine the fate of the other projects.

Even under the umbrella of each project type, you will need to consider team size, openness of the team, health of the team dynamics, and state of the project (red, green or yellow) as a part of establishing criteria to implement or not. Each of these factors will play a vital role in the overall success of the implementation and could ultimately determine the fate of the project. The goal is to implement new processes without "breaking" any of the projects, causing them to be overrun, or starting a mutiny. Future projects do not need a lot of criteria, because once you have worked out the kinks using a pilot, you can start using the new model from day 1 to refine any of the remaining issues.

The same goes for initiating projects, in that they do not have to have a lot of criteria except to be at a point in which the team can rapidly adopt and ramp-up new processes. However, you have to be careful! You want to consider the type in terms of domain and complexity, as well as exactly how far along the projects are, including the individual resources who were allocated to it. Remember that it can be very hard for people to change course, even in early stages of a project, because they are accustomed to doing things in a certain way and you are disturbing that former sense of balance.

The projects that you want to consider carefully and weigh out specific criteria for are those projects that are well underway. You not only have to consider domain and complexity, team and size, but you also have to consider the status of the project (red, green, or yellow). My preference would be to strongly advise against pushing for unnecessary work on projects that are either solidly green or teetering into yellow, and potentially even those flirting with red status. Consider the old adage, "If it ain't broke, don't fix it."

The primary reason that you want to reconsider which projects to tackle is because changing the processes and protocol will change the deliverables and expectations for the deliverables. You could end up with a disconnect in the deliverables, as well as a huge waste of time and money when the team makes efforts to flip deliverables into the new format, as this could result in heavy amounts of rework on deliverables that already suffice based on the criteria that was set at initiation.

That being said, if you have a project that is phased, you may definitely consider the implementation at a later stage so that the final deliverables do align to the new standards. In addition, you want to give some thought to utilizing your new approaches, processes, and techniques to save any of those projects that are well underway and are not flirting with the red status, or which are firmly entrenched and in danger of complete failure. At this point, what do you have to lose?

Again, team dynamics and openness are factors that you want to consider, but you also have to be sure that you use the situation to your advantage. You want to be certain, for projects that will migrate to the new processes, that everyone is informed upfront. This includes the business analyst team and all other teams within the technology organization because they can either be a strong source of support for the changes or undermine them.

Change Management—Bracing for Impact

Change management is designed to address the specific issue of how major changes will affect the employees of the business and obtain a degree of buy-in from them. Change management uses specific communication tools to reach broad audiences and address the issues and feelings of uncertainty that could sabotage any project when all else is progressing smoothly. It is important to have a number of strategies and protocols in place to address the needs and styles of the target audience.

Four basic strategies include normative, coercive, adaptive, and rational (Bennis).[1] These strategies are geared to meet the various behavioral styles of employees. Where *normative* seeks to reeducate, *coercive* utilizes the balance of power, *adaptive* proposes that people will gradually adapt to new circumstances, and *rational* appeals to self-interest.

However, before you can begin to implement strategies and protocols, you need to identify key individuals who can give you an idea of what to expect within a given

[1]Bennis, W., Benne, K. & Chin, R. Editors. (1969). *The Planning of Change* (2nd Edition). Holt, Rinehart and Winston, New York.

department or section. These individuals will be able to provide insight into which tools will be most useful in their area, and you will be able to formulate an action plan to follow. They may also be able to identify specific individuals who require personal attention, and the specific strategy that will help ease them into the idea of change and change processes.

Based on the strategies and protocols in place, communication tools may include an informational Intranet site, joint application development sessions, random individual contacts, specific contacts with various departments or sections, and follow-up protocols such as random contacts, an online troubleshooting guide, and post-change meetings.

It is imperative to address the needs and styles of the individuals within the organization, as well as the overall business need in the plan, because final implementation and integration is an employee responsibility. While a team of managers and subject matter experts initially rolls out the change itself, it is the front line employees that will become responsible for maintenance of the new system. By addressing their needs for security, consistency, and confidence in their ongoing role within the corporation, the overall transition will be a smoother process with low amounts of resistance.

Corporations, like individuals, have momentum. Change, managed properly can enhance that momentum and increase efficiency. After all, no organization is greater than the sum of the people whose daily dedication and performance maintains its health and vitality.

COMMUNICATION

Every successful transition and implementation has a solid foundation of technical and people aspects in place to support it. Planning the transition determines how you will conduct the rollout, and may include aspects of change management to determine the best route and the path of least resistance. That means that you have to establish and maintain an environment where communication is a two-way street, and no one is afraid to communicate.

Open communication requires that you establish and develop a solid communication plan, and that you plan stages and levels of communication and involvement by the teams. No one wants to feel like they have just been hit by a steamroller, but without communication channels and routine communiqués going out, that is exactly how people will feel. Their disempowerment will become a lack of trust, and a lack of trust can become subversive actions to sabotage the project or the roll out at every chance.

Here you really want to communicate the plan to the teams and establish both incoming and outgoing communication channels, using them even if people are not using the incoming channels. They will become engaged in what is going on and what is happening if you bring them into the loop often enough. During the communication stage, it is very important to ensure that you take time to reach out and connect with *every* business analyst resource on the team or that will be on the team. Remember, this is as much a marketing campaign and sales job as it is an implementation.

LEADER SELECTION

The difference between leaders and managers is that leaders will adopt the new processes and support the initiative, even if they do not fully believe in it, and encourage everyone else to do the same. Why? Because leaders recognize that the way to fix something or to change a process is to work from within; opposing a fix or change only keeps leaders on the outside, where they have little or no influence on the results. Managers direct people to follow. Unless managers are also leaders, that is all that they will do, unless it is to penalize someone for not following suit.

That is exactly why the next two things you want to do are to pick your champions or leaders from the team, and then give them control *where you can*. It is an important distinction to remember that people resist change when they feel as though they have no control. Sometimes, they cannot have control over what is being done, but they can have control over how and how well it is done. So when you give leaders and managers that control, they will embrace the change and still feel satisfied.

When you select champions/leaders from the team, make sure you select them based on the natural leaders in the group already, as this will be an advantage. I tend to find the loudest opponent of what is happening and work with them, so that they can become the biggest advocate for the program. Sure, some people also have a history

A Sense of Control Changes Everything

To illustrate this point, I would like to share this personal story with you. As a young mother in my twenties, I had to work outside of the home, and that meant taking my son to daycare. Almost every day, he would cry and want to stay at home with me. It was very hard until I figured out how to handle the situation so that we both felt better about it.

I explained to him that I had to work so that we could have a nice home, good food, and the toys that he liked so much. That meant that he had to go to daycare because he could not come to work with me. And, I told him that he could control how much fun he had. Of course, he was just three or four and would not have gotten that part, so I added that he *had* to go, but that he was not allowed to have any fun without me (a little reverse psychology).

Then, after saying he wanted to have fun, I "reluctantly" agreed. When I picked him up after that conversation, he would tell me how much fun he had all day. After that, he agreed that it was okay for me to work because he was having fun with his friends. Once I gave him some control over the situation, even though it was not going the way he had originally wanted, he was happy to exercise the control.

This story demonstrates a simple scenario about giving some power and control to a small child. You might think that it has no bearing on what we do in technology because we are dealing with well-educated adults. However, I want you to think back to Rita's story in micromanagement from Chapter 4. Rita was a well-educated adult, but education doesn't always alleviate fear, in fact sometimes it can compound it. The one thing that does alleviate fear is a sense of ownership and control. Fear (of anything) is really the fear of a loss of control or the ability to control what happens to us. Giving people control where they can have it helps to alleviate that fear of uncertainty.

of not playing well with others because what they are really good at (other than their particular job) is letting everyone know if they are or are not happy. Most other people will keep this to themselves, so this person can be intimidating if they are not happy. But if they are happy? Wow! They can be the best mentors and champions for what you are trying to implement. Remember that the single biggest weapon that you have in your arsenal to help you win over reluctant champions and leaders is *listening*. Do a lot of listening and people will follow and become the leaders and champions that you know they can be.

Another thing to keep in mind when you are doling out choice assignments (*aka* control) to key contributors, is that people support what they help build. You are not giving them complete control *over* the situation, and not just handing them an undefined piece of work they can do at will with no parameters or expectations attached to it. You are giving them very specific *input* into what is happening around them so that they are engaged and gain a sense of ownership and control over the new model. A good example might be to elicit suggestions and tips for best practices that they currently use, and give them a specific timeframe and format to provide them in.

I have seen numerous instances where people felt a total lack of control over the implementation of new processes. These people basically took control where they felt they could. They ultimately resorted to passive-aggressive means of getting their needs met. This is the key reason for giving leaders and team members *specific* control over a limited set of inputs.

Do not kid yourself: disengaged or disempowered people can hold up your implementation and actively work against you, or try to rally the team against the new model. Engagement and empowerment is critical even in the most politically charged situation. Even when the management and stakeholders have little or no trust in the people you want to empower, your careful and precise distribution of control is exactly that—empowerment. Again, you have to take slow and deliberate steps to get there. Listen to the team members, give them an excuse to find you, and then start the conversation.

There is a lot of energy and excitement in starting a new project. The best way to convert people is by getting them excited and involved, and showing them how to carry it forward. When we inform people that change is coming, it is new and exciting, yet scary. We need to overcome people's fear of being replaced, phased out, or being incompetent, by training and listening to them. My advice is to find the person who asks the most questions or seems the most opposed to the changes, and win them over. You win them over by understanding their basic personal and emotional needs.

Do they need more information? Do they need to feel a sense of control? Select the person that still objects when you answer all of their questions and yet comes up with more questions that do not make sense. That person needs to feel in control. Give that person a "special" job on the project. This job could include mentoring and communicating with others about the change, which means one-on-one training to do the job, and recognition at the end if they do a good job.

The formerly resistant person has just become your ambassador, and will turn all of that negative energy into positive energy. He or she will create a grassroots, peer-to-peer movement to adopt the changes. If you do this and learn to do it well, you will never need to add another change management team to your projects again. Your employees will become self-motivated and will adopt the changes faster than using a traditional training model.

SELECTING QUICK WINS AND UNITING THE TEAM

Once project leaders are in place and starting to interact with the team, you will need to select your quick-win projects and pilot them. Setting criteria for pilots under the three types of projects and setting up the schedule for implementing the new processes and management across the technology organization were discussed previously within this chapter, but here we need to review that list before we start considering how easy it will be to "win" this project within a short timeframe.

You want to have some small early successes to help motivate people within the business analysis team, but also within the rest of the project team, including stakeholders, project managers, developers, and testers. Having these kinds of small early wins does not only help to fine-tune the processes being implemented, but also demonstrates for people that it can be done, and how easy it is to apply the new techniques. This creates a feeling of being competent, and increases people buy-in simply because they have the feeling that they know what is going on and that it will work.

Now, do not be surprised if the Number 1 thing you hear is, "That's not how we do it," or "We've always done it this way." Remember that people are generally hesitant to adopt new ways of doing things. After years of doing things in a certain way, they become accustomed to it and even if it is broken and they know it, they would prefer to keep going than to start something new that they are unsure of: "The devil you know is better than the devil you don't."

Remember that change is hard and scary, especially when people feel they have no control over it. Again, give them control and empower them where and when you can. So, for example, I would set clear criteria for the types of projects that best suit being a pilot or quick-win project, and then let the teams choose or opt in themselves if their project meets the criteria.

Another thing you may want to do even before the new processes are rolled out and pilots are going is to get the business analyst team members talking and interacting in team-building events, lunch-and-learns, or other types of regular knowledge sharing sessions. You can do this even before you get full service definition. Get the business analysis team together and create collaborative camaraderie among them to help create solid bonds between the team members, especially where there has been a cross-functional model in place. Bringing this group together cuts through some of the forming processes and struggles that the team is going to face as people adapt to the new social and organizational structure.

It is important to recognize how people generally react to new teams and new team members, especially if you bring in an "outsider" to manage the new group. When we come together, the team goes through the stages of forming, storming, norming and performing (Findlay).[2] That means you will have people competing for the roles and pecking order on the team before they start functioning as a cohesive unit. In fact, you might notice a definite difference in team dynamics as soon as you start the communication process.

Many companies actually hold off communicating for this reason. But the reality is that the employees' behavior is perfectly normal. By not providing support for change early enough in the process of transition, you can actually amplify team conflict. But, by bringing people together early in the process, you can help move them through the rough stages, and they can be ready to hit the ground running right after the transition is complete.

Change Management—Hitting the Wall

A fundamental premise behind change management is that it represents the organization's understanding and recognition of the value of individual employees, regardless of their role or seniority. It involves responding to the relationship that exists between the organization and its employees.

Change management can be approached from two different directions: top-down or bottom-up. The top-down approach seeks to utilize the legitimate power base of the organizational structure to reduce the resistance and gain compliance during the process of corporate change. The bottom-up approach tries to gain a degree of buy-in from the employee base during this process.

Both of the approaches, the top-down and bottom-up, are associated with main components of an organization: culture and structure. In order to develop a strategic plan for change management, we must first understand the corporate culture or how people relate to each other within it ("the way we do business"). This insight is important, as it illustrates how employees navigate the system of corporate policies and procedures to accomplish their main responsibilities, often superseding their own levels of authority. It is this knowledge of corporate culture that may be used in the development and implementation of normative, adaptive, and rational strategies in a bottom-up approach to change management.

In addition, understanding the organizational structure or the formal chain of command will help the change management team navigate through the barriers

---

[2]Findlay, L. (1993). *Groupwork in Occupational Therapy*. Nelson Thornes, Cheltenham, UK.

presented at the employee level. The chain of command regulates the impact of change through the development of coercive and normative strategies by taking a top-down approach to change management.

Something to keep in mind is that "The power that individuals use is the power they respect," which means that while overall strategies serve as a baseline for how the company wants to deal with the resistance that it will receive when attempting to implement large-scale change, we can tailor these strategies to the individual situation. Remember, change management strategies are designed to mitigate the impact of change on both the individual employee and the corporate environment.

In the wake of an announcement of impending change, people will quickly identify themselves according to the strategy that will best suit their needs. Bear in mind, that 80% of the people will use 20% of your time, and conversely 20% of the people will use 80% of your time. The language, image, or overall "look and feel" of both the announcement and the foundation of the corporate change itself, whether it is a deployment, new policies, or a merger, should be consistent with the existing culture. In this situation, the adaptive and normative strategy would account for 80% of the employees. However, the remaining 20% will require the implementation of coercive and rational strategies, such as working closely with their supervisor and demonstrating that the majority of employees have already integrated the change into their workday.

What If?

Scenario: As a member of a software deployment team, you have identified that many people in the corporation are happy with the way their computers currently operate. In order to prepare for absolute resistance (the employees who will respond with flat refusals and hostility toward the software change), you devise a strategy for contacting the next higher-up in the chain of command, and utilizing the credibility of his/her position to sway the employees towards integration. Acceptance and buy-in will come later, so there is no reason to worry about that now.

Developing and implementing a rational strategy will be reliant on your knowledge of the corporate culture. However, these employees also tend to separate themselves into the 20% of employees who will be resistant to change. The important difference to recognize is that these employees are more likely to ask for additional information before they agree to integrate the change. By providing information, you can quickly assimilate them back into the 80% who will use only 20% of your time. The types of rational statements that you can use should be based on the type of concerns that they express in an initial interview with them. A sample conversation might look like this:

Argument from an employee: "We're moving to an inferior product. I won't be able to do the same kinds and quality of work anymore."

Your possible response: "Actually, both products are comparable. Many people often express a personal preference for one or the other, but the company has decided to standardize its software base, and after careful review of all of the factors, the company determined that this one would become that new standard."

Developing a strategy for facing resistance is going to be critical to your success in this scenario, but you are also going to need to execute that strategy and support those who are doing so.

The importance of generating an overall strategy that uses *both* top-down and bottom-up approaches cannot be underestimated. It is the combination of normative, adaptive, rational, and coercive strategies that will be the most effective in addressing the needs of the entire employee base. Change management is about managing the relationship and fostering goodwill with employees. It is about making the effort to get a degree of buy-in from the majority of employees and compliance from the remainder. We need to recognize that people have an intrinsic need for control over their own circumstances. In times of change, this control is threatened, and people will react simply as a means of regaining that control.

To this point, a roadmap for the business analysis services model was created that defines the core services and plans how the new services will fit within the organization. Leaders are selected, as well as pilot projects for quick wins, and people are engaged in conversation about the project. Each of these elements will support and enable a rapid adoption and ramp-up of a new services model.

Core services will provide us with a clear image of what we are trying to accomplish in that it includes the vision and mission statements, and defines the success and failure criteria. We can use this information to keep the teams and the business focused on what we are trying to achieve, and how this will benefit them. In addition, we utilize this information to educate the business analysts so that they are able to report on issues or other factors that create disconnects in where we want to be and where we are actually going.

By planning the fit within the greater organization, we are able to align the new processes that are being implemented with those of other groups that are external to the business analysis group. This alignment will not only ensure stability, but will also ensure that other groups respect the new protocol, and either comply or enforce on our behalf (where appropriate).

In selecting leaders, we identified people that will best act as champions for the new processes, as this will ensure a more rapid and widespread adoption. In addition, an external consulting firm can help to establish and implement your business analysis services model, decreasing the reliance on a consulting firm after implementation has been completed.

By now, we have a clear understanding of the projects that can be used to test and showcase the new model and techniques. This will serve to identify and isolate any problems that will arise once you get to the practical application of the techniques and processes that you are implementing, so that they may be changed efficiently, before they are set in stone. Moreover, it will help you to show the business analysts, the business, and the technology organization how the new processes will benefit their work.

The next chapter will close the loop on the information developed to this point, and explore the implementation of your new business analysis services model. Whereas this chapter helped to identify the individual pieces of implementation that you will need to manage, the next chapter explores the application of the pieces, turning them into a well-defined implementation plan.

11

IMPLEMENTATION

The final stage of transition, and the finalization of your business analysis services model, is the implementation of the model into mainstream operations. The goal is to institutionalize and internalize the new model, so that your business customers utilize the services and they become a part of the overall technology suite.

Implementation is the careful step-by-step, monitored, and measured process of putting the new components and techniques into place. Implementation also sets and manages project expectations so that the overall transition is smooth and that the adoption of the new processes is fairly seamless. Implementation is not as simple as installing something, or a case of "build it and they will come."

Eighty percent of implementation in technology is convincing people to use it. Convincing people is the art of selling them on the new model, and then working with them through change management to adopt and internalize it.

By the time you get to the implementation (or roll out) stage, what you have is the start of a grassroots movement. You should be on your way to a well-orchestrated transition to the new processes and organizational structure. The transition should be grassroots because you have opened the lines of communication and brought people on board, turning them into champions for the new services and processes. You should be on your way to an orchestrated transition because you have started your marketing and pilots, and have leaders in place to help you to define the transition and move it forward.

Everyone should be well-engaged, on board, and feel a sense of ownership over what is being implemented. They should also feel a sense of control and empowerment over the implementation process. However, that does not mean that your job is done and that you can sit back and watch it unfold.

Next, focus your attention on the entire organization and its adoption of the new processes. You will need to determine how to promote and market the new services (even if internally), and you will have to continue your efforts to provide training where needed.

In order to market your new services properly, you will need to clearly understand the elements of change management discussed in Chapter 10 and build on that. Use your group's vision and mission statements as discussed to inform others about the services, and to demonstrate how others will benefit from using them. Remember that just because people may work for the company does not mean that they may not need a sales pitch.

By this point, your business analysts should be starting to follow the new processes while undergoing training for each of the new tasks, activities, and processes that you have defined as part of your new services model. You should determine who, among your leaders, will carry forward training through the process. By having chosen your own leaders, you are already in good shape because you have people on board that will be able and available to support others through the transition process.

The team should also be taking advantage of the communications channels, and adding issues and suggestions to the issues and lessons learned logs. In addition, they should also be working closely with the leaders and managers to ensure that they understand the new processes, and are starting to report into the management and governance frameworks on the established metrics and benchmarks that will lay the foundation for consistent improvement. Finally, those who are actively working on pilot projects or have begun using the new techniques are beginning to apply those techniques as appropriate.

During this period, there are two critical things that you need to ensure will happen in order to maintain your success and continue with implementation (other than reporting into management and governance): ensure that people remain engaged and determine the schedule for making future improvements to the processes. You ensure that people remain engaged in the transition by keeping the lines of communication open and by establishing a marketing and training plan.

It is imperative that you continue to keep the momentum going with the team and support the team dynamics by continuing the regular team activities. Doing so encourages people to continue to interact, break their old habits, and begin to rely on the new team. It also ensures that they accept the new team and the roles within the team. Remember that win or lose, sports teams continue to practice and meet even in the middle of the game when there is a break. They are planning to win, and sometimes that means reworking the game plan at half time, so that the team keeps heading toward the same objective.

At some point, you have to stop fine-tuning the new processes, and set the new processes in stone. From here, you must take time to ensure that they are adopted as-is. Then, you must determine a schedule for how often the processes will change. Once you have done that, you will need to determine the process for actually changing the business analysis processes (change control or governance processes).

A cut-off point is created to ensure that you can actually move into the performing stages, and that you have enough active data from using the techniques across multiple pilot projects to ensure that you really are improving them when you do make changes. A cut-off point leads the way into controlled change instead of chaos or *ad hoc* changes that occur on the fly. Moreover, a cut-off point creates an opportunity for people to stop focusing on how to do things, and simply get them done.

All of the pieces of implementation have to be defined or you will end up with issues. If you think of implementation like being at a construction site where all of the heavy stone blocks and other building materials are being assembled to create a building, recognize that every little aspect has to be in place for the building to remain standing. You cannot put blocks in place without mortar; you cannot build frames without hammers and nails. Every detail has to be accounted for and monitored so that the building goes up, and stays up.

Building and implementing a new group within an organization is like constructing a new building. When the build is a part of an existing complex, you have to consider how you will tie the new structures into the existing ones aesthetically and structurally, so that it looks like it was always there, and so that you do not damage the structural integrity of either the new or the old structures. Essentially, the first structure evolves into the new one.

Again, you will have to account for change management and how people will react in the midst of change. We have discussed how people will usually react to the news of pending changes, and how you can start off right by establishing clear communication channels and strategies to ensure that people get used to the new idea. Next, strategies that you can do while the changes are actually happening, to ensure that people remain engaged throughout the implementation process, are detailed.

CHANGE MANAGEMENT—IN THE AFTERMATH

By and large, a common platform for the implementation of large scale corporate change is a project. The intrinsic nature of a project is to accomplish change in as little time and with the least amount of money possible. This alone can leave team members and employees feeling as though they are being swept up in a whirlwind. In like fashion, projects have their own momentum, which is more often than not a world apart from the corporation itself.

With this in mind, it would be easy to understand why change management teams have their work cut out for them. Strong, overall strategies and effective consistent communication throughout the process of implementation can result in minimal impact on the corporate culture and employees. Nonetheless, there will be some degree of fallout.

For instance, when the coercive strategy is utilized and compliance is the only available option, politeness and courtesy are of the utmost importance, so that in time, as the employees become more comfortable and versed with the new policies, they will feel that they have regained control and not lost any dignity during the change experience. They may even become the champions of future changes. However, in order for future changes to be considered, you have to review the most recently adopted changes, and learn how you can improve on the process to ensure that new changes are implemented as seamlessly as possible.

During the process of change, you have the opportunity to learn more about the employee base from their perspective, as well as the technical side of the project (the tools and approaches that worked best). From the employee perspective, the change management team needs to assess the level of empowerment and buy-in, overall comprehension of the change itself, how their roles and duties were affected, and moreover, what was the level of individual participation in the process? Technically speaking, the team needs to assess the tools that they used both to communicate with the employees and to implement the change.

Part of the assessment of the implementation tools is documentation throughout the process. The other part is to review that documentation afterward to find what worked best. For example, how often and what kinds of information was accessed from the project website?

In order to fully review the project from the employee perspective, the change management team can use tools such as follow-up meetings, online surveys, data mining from the project website, and other information tracked during the process. The most comprehensive project review will utilize a combination of these tools in order to reach as many employees, and obtain the most feedback, as possible.

Change, in one form or another, is an inescapable part of corporate life as it represents the organization's ability to advance with social and economic change, and its ability to respond to the needs of its employees and customers. To better understand the implications for future changes to the organization, you need to understand the changes made to date, how the changes affected things like employee and customer loyalty, and what the long-term ROI will be. This understanding is not possible without two-way communication.

KEYS TO SUCCESS

Ultimately, your ability to be successful in developing and implementing an end-to-end business analysis service model will depend on your ability to tie all of the pieces together into a single, coherent model. That ability is contingent on your ability, commitment, and dedication to create a great model and deliver business analysis services that maximize technology by enabling strategy through employing sustainable methods.

Again, the real keys to success in implementing new business analysis processes are:

- Planning the process of change and ensuring that you have established metrics to monitor and measure the changeover, as well as the future progression of improvements.
- Appropriate communication that goes out to all members of the business and technology organizations, and provides incoming channels for feedback.

- Selecting appropriate quick wins to pilot where you establish the projects that will both test and showcase your new business analysis services.
- Engaging the business analysts in meaningful discussions and learning events, so that they are well prepared to buy-in and adopt the new processes and feel empowered throughout the implementation
- Careful, staged implementation that includes a cut-off point and benchmarks to measure and monitor progress as the new processes are both adopted and controlled.

As long as you have these fundamental elements in place, you can make mistakes and learn from them without losing the credibility of the business analysis team. Without them, it will not matter how detailed or perfect your model is—you will have an uphill battle in selling and implementing it, not to mention maintaining and sustaining it, over the long term.

Remember that implementation is more than just a delivery. It is about ensuring that people use the tools provided to them. You have to understand why and how they buy, and what will keep them using the product. You also have to sell the product and the benefits by showing them what to realistically expect. You have to make sure that they have the support and encouragement, after they have made a change, to keep using it. That means that implementation of a change is all about the marketing, change management, pilot projects, and training that you provide as you bring them new products and processes. Successful implementation is about not overlooking the critical details discussed throughout this book that could ultimately lead to missing the mark.

CONCLUSIONS ABOUT TRANSITIONING TO A MANAGED BUSINESS ANALYSIS AS A SERVICE MODEL

In this final section, we discussed the two main tasks that are needed to take the models that you have created and implement them into the overall organizational structure and processes. In this discussion, the nuances and change management strategies were covered that will enable you to fully implement the model in a way that it becomes adopted and socialized by the organization as a whole. Implementation is critical to the success of building the model, as is having it utilized by the organization in a transformational way that allows it to reach its full potential. Implementation is not only a matter of dropping off the new model, but carefully and deliberately placing it into the organization so that it will be utilized and useful as a tool for maximizing the potential ROI that is latent within technology.

Most people tend to forget about details like establishing a vision, success criteria, or ensuring that they know exactly how the new model is going to fit within the organization, and assume that the details will get covered when they create the services and define the delivery model. I cannot overemphasize the importance of the many details discussed in this section and throughout the book. Do not assume anything. Proper attention to the details at the appropriate point in the process, including those that on the surface may seem of minor importance, can mean the difference between success and failure. Let's say that you are putting in a new tile floor in the kitchen. The prep work that the contractor has to do is to rip out the existing flooring, level the subfloor, clean any debris that remains from the old flooring adhesive, and sweep the entire area. Once that is done, the contractor can start to apply the thin set that will secure the new tiles.

Before starting to lay the tiles, however, the contractor has to have a clear picture of the pattern that the tiles will make, and understand the other flooring heights and materials that the tiles will butt up against at doorways and cabinets. He will have to plan how the final floor will look at each of these points. If all of the planning was done up front, the contractor can be certain that he won't be short by one tile on one side of a doorway, or make tile cutting mistakes that would lead to wasted time and materials.

As for the development of a managed business analysis services model, it is much the same. While there are still many details to consider after the new business analysis services model is developed, the bulk of the work and attention to detail is performed on the front end.

In this section, the details that you will need to manage and complete a business analysis services model were presented in order to ensure that you will have a seamless implementation and subsequent operation. Some of this information will help you to implement the new model, and the rest of it will help you to socialize it. Socialization and internalization of the model, the new processes and roles, are key to the overall adoption both inside and outside of the technology organization. Therefore, this section was heavily loaded with marketing and change management elements that will help you to bring everyone on board.

The key pieces of information that you have acquired will help you to develop and utilize a solid and cohesive implementation plan. In addition, this information will enable you to market the new services and to control the implementation through a step-by-step, regulated process.

EPILOGUE

Business analysis as we know it today is an *ad hoc* practice with inconsistent standards and processes, coupled with an overall lack of management, governance, and sustainability. It is this *ad hoc* approach that has generated the appalling results that we see each year in The Standish Group's *Chaos Report*. Yet, every year, many analysts sit by and wait for the report to be released as if it is going to be dramatically different than it was last year or the year before. To be honest, there are those analysts that decry its authenticity and legitimacy, but in truth, those of us who anxiously await it look forward to saying "I told you so" to everyone else in technology. Individually, there are pockets of people trying to make a difference and to change success rates for the better. However, it will not be until we all unite that we will start to see a major shift in the results.

Business analysis has to start focusing on the big picture. The big picture is to enable strategy by creating tangible solutions, while utilizing financially sustainable methods to ensure the overall continuity of the business. That means that we are safeguarding the interests and the financial resources of the business, and that we are carefully planning and managing business analysis methods and resources to achieve this.

Clearly, the quality of business analysis deliverables and outcomes is the bi-product of many seemingly small yet unrelated factors. We should all understand that quality is not merely the product of how something is done (methods). Quality is also the product of who does it (resources), the environment (delivery and engagement), and finally, how all of the moving parts are managed.

When we bring all of these elements of business analysis management into alignment, we will assuredly start to have a level of quality that permeates everything that we create. We will also have something more important: A road forward toward leaner and more cost-effective ways of doing things.

However, in order to get there, we need to understand, define, and combine all of the factors presented in this book. We can no longer take the "half-baked" approach to business analysis, and expect to see quality at the end, any more than we should be complacent and give up on trying to make things better.

This book was intended to bring the issues to you, so that they are as plain as day, presented as cold, hard facts of business analysis and the current state of IT, not only so that you could see where we are going wrong, but also to see tremendous opportunities. This book was intended to illustrate that business analysis services are not only a crucial part of business continuity, but that they are a deterministic factor in the success or failure of a business. This presentation attempted to make it clear that we can no longer pretend that problems do not exist, or that problems are not as bad as they seem. They really are that bad. Not only are the results that we are achieving for the business poor, but so is the quality of work-life and job satisfaction for business analysts. Worse, we have a choice every day to make it better simply by changing our attitudes, and then changing our management, methods, and delivery of business analysis services.

We should have the knowledge and wherewithal to recognize that the current state of affairs in technology is not something that we just have to learn to accept. We should also recognize that it is a product of our own mismanagement of both the resources and the processes that are consistently found to be the source of project challenges and outright failures.

Every day that goes by where we do not take up change, or challenge ourselves to do better, is another day that is wasted. It is another challenged project and another software application that does not do what it promised, or another over-budget disaster that will never deliver positive return on investment to the business. Worse still, it is another day where the business may have to make tough choices because we have failed to help them to remain competitive and sustainable.

From reading this book, you should have a really good idea of the crisis in business analysis, and of the opportunities to make it better and improve business continuity and technology as a whole, simply by building a functional management model for business analysis. We began an exploration of the crisis by uncovering the strengths, weaknesses, opportunities, and threats in a SWOT analysis, and then expounded on a new model for business analysis that essentially repositions the business analyst as a champion for business interests and an enabler of business strategy.

Throughout this journey of exploring and expanding the true role of business analysis in business continuity, we defined the specific tasks that business analysts should be doing, as well as some general terms for conducting each of those tasks. We explored and provided insight into each of the elements of appropriate operational infrastructure and functional management.

We defined the station and purpose of Business Analysis Stewardship in safeguarding the interests of the business by employing sustainable methods across business analysis, and then explored how each element of the end-to-end services model supports the objectives of business analysis. Moreover, we explored service and engagement models, and advantages of a business analysis functional management model for business analysis, before discussing how to build and implement a functional management model into an existing technology organization.

For chief information officers (CIOs) and business analysis managers who utilize business analysis and are considering ways to maximize technology investments through streamlined and coherent business analysis practices and methods, this book should be a valuable resource. It lays out the practical elements of business analysis and how to make better overall decisions to create win-win partnerships between the business and technology organizations.

Some of the glaring issues that business analysts face every day on the job were highlighted to expose some of the problems that exist outside of the role, yet have significant and detrimental impacts on the resulting outcomes. This information can be utilized to evaluate your own current situation and to help you to secure and establish a revolutionary new approach to business analysis—managed business analysis services and the Business Analysis Stewardship approach.

Based on over a decade of working with business analysts, project managers, CIOs, stakeholders, and many other people in technology organizations and projects, I have heard many reasons for project challenges, why a particular industry is "unique," and how a company will "do things differently." But in reality, we are all struggling with business analysis methods and outcomes. We are all claiming uniqueness in order to defend the fact that we do not always know how to make a situation better. However, accepting the situation as-is is not an option. We need to stop hiding behind "unique" or "not how we do it," and stop convincing ourselves that our company is immune from the systemic problems that are associated with a lack of business analysis standards, formal methods, or end-to-end management. Once we do that, we can grow, change, and make things better.

Even if we "start the race" at the wrong spot, if we plan and measure the route, monitor progress, and manage the results against what we think we know, we can improve. We will improve faster by following a process than if we continue to utilize inconsistent methods and standards, and never manage the resources.

Index